THE LAWBREAKERS

THE

LAWBREAKERS

*America's Number One
Domestic Problem*

M. STANTON EVANS
and
MARGARET MOORE

Arlington House

New Rochelle   *New York*

Acknowledgments

The authors wish to acknowledge the help of many people in preparing the material for this volume. For various kinds of assistance in the research and execution of the book, we should like to thank Ross Hermann, W. J. Griffith III, Thomas Winter, Allan Ryskind, Mrs. C. B. LaDine, and Miss Jo Mohr; for continued encouragement and great forbearance, Mrs. Sue Ellen Evans; and for writing so much of the story for us, the members of the Indianapolis Anti-Crime Crusade, Chamber of Commerce, Police Department, judiciary, and school administration, and the Indiana State Department of Corrections.

Contents

The barbarian need not appear in bearskins with a club in hand. He may wear a Brooks Brothers suit and carry a ball-point pen with which to write his advertising copy. In fact, even beneath the academic gown there may lurk a child of the wilderness, untutored in the tradition of civility, who goes busily and happily about his work, a domestic and law-abiding man, engaged in the construction of a philosophy to put an end to all philosophy, and thus put an end to the possibility of a vital consensus and to civility itself.

This is perennially the work of the barbarian, to undermine rational standards of judgment, to corrupt the inherited intuitive wisdom by which people have always lived, and to do this not by spreading new belief but by creating a climate of doubt and bewilderment in which clarity about the large aims of life is dimmed and the self-confidence of the people is destroyed, so that finally what you have is the impotent nihilism of the 'generation of the third eye' now presently appearing on our university campuses.

—John Courtney Murray

INTRODUCTION

Crime and Consensus

Crime, like pain, has some unpleasant but necessary uses. It is a warning signal which tells us that the organism is diseased or wounded, and that its existence is in some way placed in danger. Physical pain intensifies when the individual life is threatened. Crime intensifies when the community is threatened. In either case, we ignore the symptoms at our peril.

Every community operates in terms of a consensus about the way its members are supposed to act—an agreed-upon set of rules revered as custom or formalized as law. If and when this social framework ceases to exist, the community will, in the real meaning of the word, also cease to exist. Released from the bonds of mutual assumption, its members no longer enjoy communal identity, have no common ground on which to meet or common values to harmonize their wants.

Crime is a social convention by which a community defines and judges itself. It is the maximum deviation from the formal system of social value. Its incidence therefore measures the gap between what the society says it wants to do and what it is actually capable of doing. Human nature being what it is, there is always some such gap. But, depending on the quality of the law and the size of the disparity, it is a good deal more serious in some cases than in others. In America, with our special view of things, a burgeoning list of violated laws is about as serious as a problem can get.

In the traditional American approach, positive law is supposed to promote the well-being of the individual citizen. The purpose of our legal system, set forward in all the familiar documents, is to maximize the life and liberty of the person, to insure that he may go peacefully about his business without coercive interference. When an American thinks about "crime" in its proper sense, he thinks of violence or fraud by which one citizen intrudes upon the life and liberty of another. American law is intended to prevent such things from happening.

This conception is to be applauded by everyone who cherishes individual freedom. But it is, all too obviously, a view which provides us with very little margin for error. Having at least in theory reduced the question of law to its bare essentials, we are in no position to have those essentials neglected. Failure to enforce sumptuary laws means one thing; failure to enforce laws against murder or robbery means something altogether different. When crime is defined in terms like these, its continued increase has immediate as well as metaphysical importance.

The problem of crime in America is so complex that the first decision one must make in discussing it is what to leave out. This was a difficulty confronted by President Johnson's commission on crime and law enforcement, which set out to be all-inclusive but ended by acknowledging that certain aspects of the subject would have to be slighted in order to give adequate treatment to others. As it happened, the matters upon which the commission concentrated—organized crime, corrections, use of technical aids by the police—have also been rehearsed at length by other authorities. On such topics we continue to pile up information in generous quantities. But we are still without important data or systematic analysis on other matters which may, in the long run, be considerably more crucial. It is in an effort to get at some of these that the present volume has been written.

Our discussion begins where the official version leaves off—with a paradox. The past 30 years and more have been a time of continual change in the application of the criminal law. Reforming zeal intended to reduce the crime rate has touched nearly everything: the law itself, the way it is construed, the activities of the police, the conduct of the courts, the nature of the corrections system, parole practices, treatment of juveniles, attacks on the "conditions" which assertedly breed crime. The list is long and, if the recommendations of the President's commission are acted on, promises to get longer.

On the projections of the reformers, we should by now be witnessing some kind of decrease in the crime statistics. But, unfortunately, it hasn't worked out that way. We find instead that the crime rate and the reform rate have expanded with equal vigor. With every improvement marked in the protection of criminal civil liberties, and every advance made in the field of humane penology, we have added another notch on the upward movement of the crime graph. Our streets and parks have become jungles where brave men fear to go abroad. The criminals have more liberty and are better treated, but the rest of us have less liberty and are treated worse. And the point of the system, we recall, was supposed to be the other way around.

Today the movement for "reform" is more powerful than ever. New liberties for criminal defendants are elaborated at every term of the Supreme Court; demands are heard for repeal of capital punishment; campaigns are afoot to broaden or abolish statutes concerning abortion, homosexuality, narcotics, pornography, alcoholism. New scope is given to the legal meaning of "insanity," by which criminals are excused from responsibility for their acts. And, as these demands are pressed, the crime rate continues its upward movement. Whatever else might be said of it, the reform campaign has not achieved its predicted goal of diminished criminality.

The issue before us is not whether we should revert to inhumane practice as a method of combatting crime. The goal of maximizing life and liberty cannot be advanced by gratuitous appeals to legal cruelty. The law should in fact be humane, should attempt to redeem the criminal from his crime, should make allowance for extenuating circumstance. Nor do we deny the need for protecting the proper rights of criminal suspects, for treating youthful offenders with due regard for their special status, or helping people achieve an appropriate stake in the benefits of society. We favor such things because they are right *per se* and because, in some cases, they can and do result in a reduction of criminal behavior. In the second half of this book, we discuss some instances in which precisely such a reduction has occurred.

The evidence before us suggests, however, that humanitarian justice and salvationist penology *alone* cannot and do not head off criminal behavior; on the contrary, when applied with sentimental disregard of other factors in the law-enforcement equation, they make things considerably better for the criminal but considerably worse for everybody else. An allegedly benevolent system thus becomes a gruesome caricature, spreading more misery than it forestalls.

The pressing question is whether the reform movement can be adjusted to serve rather than to disserve the original purpose of our legal system—to prevent crime instead of promoting it. It is a question which obviously cannot be answered if, as is often the case in official discussion, it is never seriously raised. The unwholesome results that have emerged from the existing formula, and the unwillingness of its sponsors to acknowledge what has happened, suggest the reformers have omitted some crucial element from their reasoning.

The authors of this book have tried to isolate certain themes which, in the current controversy over crime, tend to get neglected. Foremost among these is the proposition with which we launched our discussion: The inverse ratio between crime and consensus. Positive law is but the outer rim of the consensus, at the heart of which stand religious faith, tradition, custom. For the vast majority of people these internal restraints do more to guide behavior than the coercive power of the state. We refrain from fulfilling impulse at our neighbors' expense, not because we fear legal penalties, but because we believe such things as murder and theft are, quite simply, wrong.

The priority of consensus to positive law suggests it is impossible to halt a mounting "crime wave" merely by tinkering with the laws or material conditions. A continual upsurge of crime means an increasing number of people, for one reason or another, reject the terms of social obligation. Even where failure to enforce the positive law is involved (and there are many such examples), the ultimate cause may be traced to failure at the level of value. The default of authority suggests the majority itself, or its chosen representatives, do not feel deeply enough or think clearly enough about the issues at stake to insure that the law is honored.

This fact, of course, greatly magnifies the problem. It is a relatively easy matter to manipulate words on a statute book, to add or subtract coercions, to legislate subsidies. It is much more difficult to fathom the ways in which people think, the reasons for alteration in their thought, and the methods for correcting thinking which has gone awry. The creation of a value consensus in the first place is a complicated and mysterious business; what can or should be done when it starts getting uncreated is more complicated still.

In setting out to examine such matters, we have had to omit treatment of some other facets of our subject—particularly those which have been fully treated elsewhere. We have, for example, attempted no discussion of organized crime, which has been extensively covered in congressional hearings and in books by Senators Estes Kefauver, John McClellan, and Robert Kennedy. We have mentioned the problems of narcotics and vice, corrections and rehabilitation, only in passing. We have said nothing about wiretapping, and relatively little about the use of computers and other technical improvements by the police. All such matters have, in our opinion, become subordinate to the issue of finding out some of the root causes which produce the criminals in the first place.

The principal object of our inquiry has been "unorganized" crime—private violence, murder, mugging, rape, robbery, burglary, rioting, vandalism. These are the crimes which most clearly deny the fundamental premise of our system, and most obviously disturb and frighten the average American. In dealing with them, we have sought to focus on the central question: *What are the disintegrative forces in our society that destroy the framework of free and orderly existence?* We believe that only by seeking an answer to this question can we hope to get the national crime wave slowed down and reversed. Without such an answer, we shall be engaged at best in the short-term business of treating externals while ignoring the ultimate sources of our affliction.

The authors additionally believe the regeneration of consensus cannot take place solely through the actions of government, but must proceed instead from the efforts and affirmations of individual citizens. We therefore focus, in the second part of this book, on the question of what these citizens, in their private capacities, can do. We offer what we hope is a practical series of suggestions for action in the local community. Just as it is a mistake to concentrate on symptoms at the expense of causes, so is it a mistake to think only of the long-term and to ignore the needs of the present. While seeking future improvement, we must go on with life as best we can. In this area, too, our discussion traverses an area which has received only passing attention from most authorities: The range of action available to the individual.

The authors wish to stress that they are not setting up shop as experts in the field of criminology. Both are journalists who have approached the problem through the publicly available evidence, the opinions of divers authorities, the historical record, and our own observations in our home community. Acknowledging that the matters set forward here cover only a segment of the vast and controversial subject of crime and its causes, we nevertheless believe it is a segment which deserves more serious examination and reflection than it has yet received.

Indianapolis, Ind.
June 23, 1967

PART ONE

A NATIONAL
PROBLEM

ONE

We Never Had It So Scared

Americans in this second half of the twentieth century have been told, with some justice, that they never had it so good. By every material standard, ours is the richest society on earth. We have higher personal incomes, more consumer goods, less poverty, and more leisure than any other nation known to history. And our government has set about, through a variety of programs in every field of human effort, to supply deficiencies in the web of comfort.

Yet if in that sense we never had it so good, in another sense we never had it so bad. Or so scared. Precisely as we have achieved our present affluence, precisely as our government has proclaimed its readiness to spread the good things more widely still, the nation is clawed by nameless apprehensions. Richer than any other generation of Americans, we are also more frightened. Blessed with better food, finer clothes, and more expensive cars, we are also haunted by the fear that the enjoyment of these things might be taken from us by marauders who stalk our streets and attack our homes.

The paradox is of the sort suggested by the Pennsylvania Dutch saying, "The faster I run, the behinder I get." The faster we multiply our material comforts, the greater seems the likelihood of losing them through hoodlum terror. The more our government suggests we are advancing toward utopia, the more we stumble backward toward the jungle. We are a people for whom anything seems possible—except to defend ourselves against primitive evils which the rudest of societies can control.

The state exists to protect its citizens from foreign and domestic violence. If an American is not free from assault or robbery, the state is not performing its most essential function, and other blessings it may bestow upon him count for little. "Without the reasonably effective performance of the task of preventing private violence and retaliation," says Supreme Court Justice Byron White, "it is idle to talk about human dignity and civilized values."[1] It is indeed. Fine public buildings or government-spawned *kultur* are matters of indifference to the grocer mauled by thugs or the elderly gentleman yoked by a team of brawling punks. Yet the signs abound that this first and crucial role of government has been increasingly defaulted.

The President's Commission on Law Enforcement and Administration of Justice sums up the problem in its 1967 report: "There is much crime in America, more than ever is reported, far more than ever is solved, far too much for the health of the nation . . . Crimes of violence are up in both the biggest and smallest cities, in the suburbs as well as in the rural areas. The same is true for property crimes. Young people are being arrested in ever-increasing numbers. Offense rates for most crimes are rising every year and in every section of the country."[2]

Reported crime, the commission found, is rising rapidly. But there is a great deal more crime which is not reported at all. The commission says "burglaries occur about three times more often than they are reported to police. Aggravated assaults and larcenies over $50 occur twice as often as they are reported. There are 50 per cent more robberies than are reported. In some areas, only one-tenth of the total number of certain kinds of crime are reported to the police."[3]

Estimating the real magnitude of crime in America is obviously a difficult task. We know enough, however, to conclude that the problem is enormous, and that it is daily getting bigger. The reported crime rate itself is immense; extrapolate to the unreported crimes as well and our difficulties are almost unimaginable in scope.

The Crime Commission reviews the sheer dollar size of the problem as expressed in money stolen, embezzled, and defrauded, loss of earnings by productive citizens through arson, vandalism, and homicide, insurance costs, money spent to support police services, the budgets of courts and corrections institutions. It comes up with direct yearly costs for crime on which figures are available of more than $25 billion—but stresses that the real cost, in money and human suffering, is not encompassed by this figure. President Johnson has similarly placed the annual cost of crime at $27 billion, noting that there is a "still more widespread cost" in death, injury, suffering, and all-pervasive fear.[4]

As bad as the present problem is, signs are it is going to get worse. Almost all authorities conclude that the rate of crime is increasing faster than the rate of population growth. And, as Miriam Ottenberg of the *Washington Star* reports: "Unless something is done to reverse the trend, FBI crime-reporting experts agree, the nation faces another 78 per cent increase in serious crime over the next decade."[5]

The texture and quality of the fear which rampant crime imposes on the nation are best suggested, perhaps, by abandoning aggregates and glancing briefly at some individual cases. Such cases are sadly familiar to everyone who reads his daily newspaper or has ever seen a television wrap-up of the nation's nightly quota of calamity:

Item: In Chicago, eight student nurses are systematically slain in a mass murder police officials describe as "the crime of the century."

Item: In Boston, thirteen women are brutally murdered by a demented "strangler." In Cincinnati, a similar series of crimes occurs.

Item: In a small Arizona town, a high school student breaks into a beauty parlor and murders four women and a three-year-old child.

Item: In Austin, Texas, 16 people are killed and 17 others wounded by a sniper atop the bell tower on the University of Texas campus.

Item: In Kew Gardens, New York, a woman is stabbed to death while 38 people listen to her cries for help and some actually witness the stabbing but no one calls the police until it is over.

Item: In Washington, D.C., five blocks from the White House, a woman is knocked down a stairway and molested. Earlier the same day a woman was attacked in a rest room in the same building.

Item: In the quiet town of Boonville, Indiana, an 11-year-old girl is sexually assaulted and murdered, her body dismembered and thrown into the Ohio River.

Item: In a St. Louis parking lot, a 30-year-old telephone operator, mother of two children, is struck on the head with a baseball bat. Her unconscious body is dragged into a yard by two teen-age boys. They rape her and she dies.

Item: In Milwaukee, a 15-year-old girl gets on a bus to go to a youth meeting; the only other passenger is a man, who without warning seizes her from behind and cuts her throat with a razor. She dies.

Such events, routine fare for connoisseurs of the police blotter or casual readers of the evening paper, suggest the people of the United States are fast losing one of their most precious rights —the simple right to move as they please, to go to church meetings at night, to shop where and when they would like, to take walks near their homes.

In a study of depredations committed by sex criminals, Gladys Denny Shultz summarizes the various assaults, rapes, and killings reported in New York newspapers for a few selected months. The exercise, handling the cases in the briefest fashion possible, consumes 18 pages in Miss Shultz's book, *How Many More Victims?* She concludes that "no list of sex offenses can be kept up to date. You will have read in the newspapers of several shocking new sex crimes committed while this chapter was being printed."[6]

Efforts of a terrified citizenry to protect itself are seen in every walk of life. Apartment houses that used to leave their outside doors unlocked now lock them; countless women are taking courses in self-defense; churches and synagogues with evening services have hired private guards; detective agencies, burglar-alarm firms, tear-gas manufacturers, chain and lock salesmen all report a zooming demand for their products and services.

A survey conducted by the Crime Commission found that "one third of a representative sample of all Americans say it is unsafe to walk alone at night in their neighborhoods. Slightly more than one-third say they keep firearms in the house for protection against criminals. Twenty-eight per cent say they keep watchdogs for the same reason."[7]

The report further notes that "43 per cent of the respondents say they stay off the streets at night because of their fear of crime; 35 per cent say they do not speak to strangers any more because of their fear of crime; 21 per cent say they use cars and cabs at night because of their fear of crime; 20 per cent say they would like to move to another neighborhood because of their fear of crime."[8]

A *National Observer* analysis similarly remarks: "One current estimate has it that 50 per cent of the population of the nation's larger cities are afraid to walk the streets at night."[9]

In Washington, according to *Newsweek* magazine, "State Department officials . . . set up a special guard system to protect women employees *within* the granite buildings of Foggy Bottom. In Houston, housewives snapped up some 1,000 tear-gas pens . . . And enrollments in judo classes around the country have climbed to some 200,000."[10] (Italics added.)

In New York, a group of Jewish men, fearing for the safety of their women folk and of their community in general, have formed a private association for self-defense purposes known as the "Maccabees"—named after the Hebrew fighting men of the Old Testament. "This whole thing is crazy," says Rabbi Samuel Schrage, "but it had to be done."[11]

Similar efforts at self-protection have been launched in Detroit, Orlando, Los Angeles, Chicago, Dallas, St. Louis. Says the manager of the gun department of a Dallas sporting goods company who is doing a booming business with people who want hand guns for self-protection: "People have sort of lost confidence in the ability of government to protect them."[12]

People in once-respectable New York neighborhoods barricade themselves behind barred windows, high stone walls with barbed wire and broken glass at the top, to keep the criminals out. "The streets," says a policeman, "belong to the germs."[13]

Former Chicago police official O. W. Wilson describes a residential development, surrounded by a high masonry wall and protected by armed guards, as a "sort of penitentiary in reverse—the good people on the inside and the bad people outside. . . ." Our condition is perilous, Wilson says, when our society reaches the point "where it is necessary for the good people to bar themselves behind locked doors to protect themselves against marauders."[14]

What is true in the cities is even more so in the suburbs. The FBI reports that the upward trend in crime is higher in the supposedly settled "bedroom" communities than it is in the cities themselves. *Look* magazine asserts: "Crime is rising fastest in America's comfortable suburbs." In Nassau County, New York, major crimes jumped from 698 to 854 per 100,000 population in three years' time. The police chief of Evanston, Illinois, says: "It's been a steady increase. That's what's alarming."[15]

Crime committed by two-bit hoodlums, footpads, stickup artists and thrill-seekers is the foremost domestic crisis confronting the United States. And, precisely because it is not organized, does not spring from a single identifiable source, it is difficult to deal with. Between 1958 and 1964, the FBI tells us, American crime increased six times faster than the rate of population growth. Between 1960 and 1966, crime grew at almost seven times the rate of population increase.

Willful killings in 1964 increased eight per cent over 1963, "the sharpest trend for this crime in recent years."[16] During the same period, aggravated assaults rose 17 per cent, making a total increase of 46 per cent since 1958. Forcible rape increased by 21 per cent, 30 per cent since 1958. Robberies increased from 53 per 100,000 of population in 1963 to 58 in 1964—a rise of 23 per cent for the year and a jump of 36 per cent over 1958.

Nineteen-sixty-four saw 24 murders committed daily, or one every hour; 56 cases of forcible rape, or one every 26 minutes; 480 cases of aggravated assault, or one every three minutes; 300

cases of robbery, or one every five minutes; and nearly 3,000 burglaries, or one every 28 seconds. Out of every 1,000 inhabitants
of America—a number which might live in a single block in a
large city—no less than 14 were victims of these or other serious
crimes in 1964.

More than 2,600,000 serious crimes were reported—more than
1,100,000 burglaries. Some 1,265 cars were stolen each day;
nearly $300 million was lost—or gained, depending on the point
of view—through the combined efforts of robbers and burglars;
and, the FBI says, "if the destruction and damage to property
which resulted from burglary were known and could be added to
this amount, the total cost of this crime would be substantially
increased."[17]

Recent years have also seen an upward surge of racial violence
and student forays into "civil disobedience." Bloody race riots
in Harlem, Rochester, Detroit, Los Angeles, Chicago, Cleveland,
a large number of senseless racially motivated crimes in the
South, and uncontrollable outbursts by college students have all
become familiar elements in the American landscape. Equally
important, these years have also seen an enormous upsurge in the
incidence of juvenile delinquency.

Juvenile crime is in fact the nation's number-one law-enforcement problem. The figures for 1964 tell us, for example, that in
cases of aggravated assault, "arrests for persons under 18 years of
age increased 22 per cent, while adult arrests were up 16 per
cent . . ." In cases of forcible rape, "62 per cent of the individuals arrested were under 25 years of age, 40 per cent were
under 21, and 19 per cent were under 18."[18]

In cases of robbery, "one out of five of the solved cases involved persons under 18." In cases of larceny, "slightly more
than one-half of the persons arrested were under 18 years of
age . . . The highest arrest rate for this crime was the 15–19
age group . . ." In some categories, juvenile crime has gone up
and adult crime down, so that the juvenile contribution accounts
for the whole increase in the national crime statistics.* [19]

___

* In the cases of larcency and auto-theft, youngsters under 18 years of age accounted for more than half of the offenses and those under 25 accounted for well
over two-thirds. The report sums the matter up this way: "When viewed nationally, arrests for persons under 18 rose 15 per cent (for all major crimes), while

So alarming has the crime trend become that increasing attention has been accorded it in the arena of national politics. In the 1964 presidential campaign Senator Barry Goldwater made "law and order" one of his chief issues. In 1965, President Johnson formed his national crime commission, enjoining it to search out the reasons behind the nation's surge toward criminality. In 1966, crime became a premier domestic issue of the congressional elections. Congress has, over the past several years, given expanded attention to a number of anti-crime bills.

Surveying all of this, the average citizen would be justified in believing that, if we do not have a crime wave, we have at least got hold of a reasonable facsimile. But, that same citizen might be surprised to discover, this conclusion is not accepted by certain academicians and others who make it their business to expound the causes of crime. A concerted effort has in fact been launched to disprove the existence of the crime wave.

Thus Sidney E. Zion of *The New York Times* says: ". . . there has always been a 'crime wave,' and the apparent recent statistical increases ignore many important considerations—including, most conspicuously, the vast postwar expansion of the age group (15–24) most prone to crime."[20]

Similarly, Professor Yale Kamisar of the University of Michigan says: "There are so many factors which account for an increase in crime statistics, that all one can really talk about is a crime *reporting* wave, not a crime wave."[21]

And Columbia University's Daniel Bell, setting out some years ago to scotch the "crime wave myth," maintained that "a sober look at the problem shows that there is probably less crime today in the United States than existed a hundred, or fifty, or even twenty-five years ago, and that today the United States is a more lawful and safe country than popular opinion imagines."[22]

These comments are premised on asserted inaccuracies in

---

adult arrests were up 9 per cent . . . For the country as a whole, these young people comprised 48 per cent of all police arrests for serious offenses . . . A review of total arrests of persons under the age of 18 reveals a continued upswing in their involvement with police . . . Nationally, the number of arrests for crimes of violence and crimes against property rose 30 per cent 1964 over 1960 . . . The young age group arrests for these crimes increased 49 per cent in volume and persons 18 years of age and older 15 per cent."

crime statistics compiled by local police and the FBI—statistics journalist Zion describes as an "inside joke." Essentially, the argument is that police forces have hitherto minimized crime, and that recent apparent increases are merely the result of correcting the figures. Bell additionally argues that an exaggerated crime ratio is achieved by comparing new crime figures to old population figures.

If we analyze these arguments with any care, it appears that the *parti pris* belongs to the sociologists rather than the police. Zion, for example, offers his no-crime-wave argument in defense of recent rulings of the U.S. Supreme Court. And it seems apparent that academicians in the criminological field also have special interests at stake.

This point was made clear in an article by Miriam Ottenberg of the *Washington Star*. Miss Ottenberg related an interview with a sociologist who "admitted to a reporter why critics are suddenly challenging the FBI's long-accepted crime figures":

"For the past decade, he explained, an increasing number of offenders have been put on probation or sent to psychiatric clinics rather than to jail or released early on parole. And the FBI's index of serious crime has risen 58 per cent since 1958. The rate of crime repeaters has also climbed.

"Fearing that some people may make a connection between more crime and more experimental methods of dealing with criminals, these sociologists have solved the problem by attacking the crime statistics."[23]

It is true, as noted, that crime figures have not fully reflected the amount of crime in the United States, and that sudden leaps in the statistics can often be traced to a change in reporting methods.* But the FBI is aware of this fact, and guards specifically against it. The annual figures for major crime are arrived at by comparing statistics for the same offense, and by adjusting

---

* It is also true, as contended by such people as Bell and Raymond Vernon, that there was a good deal of lawlessness in the 19th century—quite possibly more than there is now—in some areas of American big cities. That fact, however, is not demonstrable by the statistics, and provides little comfort to people who are suffering from advancing criminality now. The relevant figures, from 1933 forward, show crime increasing at an alarming rate in the modern era. The apposite question is why Americans in the 1960s are so much more gravely threatened by crime today than they were 10, 20, and 30 years ago.

for and screening out information which appears to be the result of error or altered reporting techniques.

The Crime Commission report, hardly hostile to the sociologists' point of view, observes that FBI data are meticulously assembled to avoid reporting errors. "Through a careful system of checks," the report notes, "the FBI is able to identify the units that are reporting on a different basis than the previous year. It then restricts its computations of trends from one year to the next to those police agencies that have had comparable records and reporting practices."[24] It is, in fact, the FBI's influence which has helped make reporting procedures uniform and worked to eliminate precisely the statistical loopholes of which the sociologists complain.

That procedural changes have occurred in crime reporting should not, in short, obscure the fact that substantive changes have occurred as well, changes resulting from a provable increase in lawlessness. Indeed, since the chief deficiency alleged against the crime statistics is that they have historically *understated* the problem, this argument provides cold comfort any way you slice it.

The point about population figures is also countered by the FBI's method of accumulating its statistics. Its effort is precisely to get an accurate ratio of crime to population, and it keeps abreast of annual changes in both categories. Thus the 1965 crime report says: "According to figures released by the United States Bureau of the Census, total United States population increased 1.3 per cent in 1965. In that year the national crime index rate was 1,435 offenses per 100,000 of population, representing a 5 per cent increase over 1964."[25]

The argument breaks down, finally, with respect to the 15–24 age bracket as well. According to Bell, Zion, and Talcott Parsons, the notion that we are experiencing an upsurge of youthful crime is an illusion prompted by the post-World War II baby boom, so that the apparent incidence of crime has increased as the statistical rate has remained even. Some theoreticians add the statement that nowadays many things are called "juvenile delinquency" which years ago would merely have been written off as youthful mischief.

It is true that the 15–24 age group is "crime-prone" compared to the overall population, and that the number of people in this group has expanded proportionately in the last 20 years. But it is not true that increased crime among these young people can be traced solely to these factors. As Senator Robert Byrd of West Virginia notes: "While the population in the 10- through 17-year age group was increasing 17 per cent, during the years 1960 through 1965, arrests for serious crimes committed by the same 10- through 17-year age group were increasing 47 per cent."[26]

The National Probation and Parole Association estimates that delinquency is increasing at four times the rate of national population growth and that the number of children haled into juvenile court has increased 100 per cent in 10 years. Between 1940 and 1960, the number of juvenile cases increased 150 per cent while the juvenile population was increasing only 25 per cent.

These statistics do not suggest that the juvenile crime rate is remaining constant while the juvenile population expands. They show instead that the crime rate itself is growing at a pace that has assumed catastrophic dimensions. The juvenile crime rate has increased considerably faster than the rate of juvenile population growth, and faster than the already alarming rate for the nation as a whole.

If one goes back to the 1930s he will find similar laments about juvenile and other crime—rightly enough, if one assumes that any crime is too much. But the fact that our predecessors have complained about crime does not prove our present problem is an illusion, or that it is not worse than what preceded it. It is trite to say we are in crisis; it has also become trite to say we are never in crisis. The problem is an empirical one—collecting the evidence, comparing it with what has gone before, and deciding whether a crisis in fact exists. The evidence suggests it does.

Roul Tunley sums the matter up this way:

"When all the figures and charts are weighed, discounted, corrected, adjusted, and dissected, the fact remains that an extraordinarily large number of adolescent males are arrested,

come before our courts and are labeled juvenile delinquents
. . . it appears that 12 per cent of our children are liable to become delinquents during their teens . . . A recent survey in
Minnesota, for example, revealed that 22 per cent of all boys in
the ninth grade of the Minneapolis schools had appeared before
the court, the police, or both, within a period of two years . . .
close to 20 per cent of all our male adolescents get into trouble
with the law and are haled into court."[27]

The FBI crime figures, in sum, are (1) alarming, (2) as solid
as human ingenuity can make them, and (3) specifically exempt
from the charges thrown at them by the sociological fraternity.
Since these are the figures which show crime increasing seven
times faster than the rate of population growth, Mr. Zion's joke,
all of a sudden, doesn't seem particularly funny.

TWO

The "New Morality"

Scarcely less striking than the crime explosion is the rise of something called "the new morality."

Exactly how the new morality ought to be defined is difficult to say. It is a complex of things which are often mutually contradictory, invoking different kinds of values or non-values as their point and purpose. As phrased by its more genteel academic defenders, the new morality is a sophisticated business, as tentative and fuzzy as the brush of a butterfly's wing. According to Dr. Joseph Fletcher, for example, the new moralist is an advocate of "situation ethics," who finds Judaeo-Christian morals generally useful, but is prepared to "compromise them or set them aside *in the situation* if love seems better served by doing so."[1] (His italics.)

Dr. Fletcher's stance, or something like it, is quite popular among academic spokesmen who have reasoned themselves into an easy tolerance of pre-marital sex, homosexuality, or drug addiction. Such things are not to be frowned upon, we are instructed, if they are aimed at advancing "love." Thus one version of the new morality.

On the tongues of other spokesmen, the matter comes out differently. As profusely recorded in the popular press, the new morality has as its object the pursuit and celebration of unalloyed "kicks." It is the catch-phrase of a fun culture embracing such items as the teeny-bopper, the happening, the love-in, the gross-out, the turn-on, the schlockmeister, and the acid-head; it is a universe of topless dancers, profane preachers, go-go girls, gay boys, pot parties, and pill pushers. In this driven world, ever hungering for new sensation, Dr. Fletcher's "love" seems, on the whole, irrelevant.

As these discordances suggest, the new morality is a chaos of attitudes and gesticulations, fads and fugitive enthusiasms. Its only apparent principle of coherence is the demand that impulse be followed wherever it listeth. As practiced by a good many people, the new morality looks suspiciously like no morality at all—or, more precisely, the old immorality.

It should be emphasized that the reach of the new morality is not limited to the fabled funseekers of Sunset Strip or the teens who shriek their adulation of Supremes or Stones. It is also apparent in a general relaxation of moral sinew, a willingness to drift on the swelling tide of sensation, to enjoy-enjoy and let the morrow take care of itself. It is apparent in the decline of religious conviction and an ascending tolerance for behavior which a generation ago would have excited strenuous protest; in an eagerness to mortgage the future for the present comforts of credit card and installment plan; in the pathetic efforts of many adults to placate and copy the cult-like frenzies of the young. It has worked its way deep into the bones of our society.

Generalizations do not tell the story so well as do specifics, and there are so many specifics around these days it is difficult to decide which ones to use. *Esquire* magazine has made an interesting selection which will serve to illustrate the point. The magazine ran a number of items concerning developments in and around Los Angeles, California, as follows:

From an advertisement in the *Los Angeles Free Press:*

Young Swingers' Paradise for Guys and Dolls. Are you irresponsible, young and lovable? Do you crave for wild all-night parties, loud noise, dancing, playing of instruments, swinging, screaming, madness and all forms of group activities, uninhibited by the presence of your prudish elders? At the Sheri Plaza we rent only to playboys who enjoy living and swinging to the hilt, are tolerant of others, peace loving, non-destructive, and who like community living. We want everybody to know and have fun with all other tenants. SHERI PLAZA APARTMENTS, 2025 N. Argyle, Hollywood.

From the *Saturday Evening Post:*

Inspector Larry Wallace recalls bursting into [a Hell's Angel] pad to rescue a couple of children who had been living with their mother and some Angels on beer and cornflakes in an apartment cluttered with cans of motor oil, sprockets, dirty dishes, garbage . . . Angels [have] earned 'red wings,' red-enameled flight insignia, by committing indecent acts. It was all part of something the Angels called 'showing class.' . . . one of the offers the Angels actually did receive was from a television producer eager to find out when they were making their next run on a small town, so that the TV cameras could be on hand to record the carnage. The Angels are currently weighing that offer and dickering with another show that has offered them $2000 for taped shots of Angels at work and at play.

From *Los Angeles* magazine:

Joe Vina, manager of Ben Frank's, is a philosophic man in striped chef's pants who has seen a lot but can keep smiling. He recently saw a 15-year-old boy, flying on pills, go berserk in the early morning hours and shout thundering obscenities until sheriff's deputies came and hauled him away. He's seen a 14-year-old girl hungrily foraging through the restaurant garbage at five a.m. He found out her name and called her mother, who told him he was a liar; that she was with friends, and hung up on him.

From a press release:

Inspector James Fisk says that the 3073 arrests for homosexual offenses made in Los Angeles last year represent merely a 'token number' of those that should have been made. 'If we had ten times as many officers working in that area we could arrest ten times as many homosexuals.'[2]

And so on.

A catalogue of such events—less flamboyant, perhaps, but similar in tendency—could be compiled for almost any large

American community. Such things are not, to be sure, fully representative of the national culture, either in quantity or quality; the vast majority of Americans are not indulging themselves in behavior of this sort. The fact remains that these things are happening far more frequently than in the past, that many influential people are quite sympathetic to them, and that the public as a whole is far more ready to have them happen than was the case not so many years ago. Even more to the point, general public attitudes on a number of questions are tending to follow—at a sedate distance, of course—the cultural lead established by the swingers and the hippies.

Although the matter cannot be encompassed by arithmetic, we have a few statistics available to tell the story. It is estimated, for example, that a million American women undergo criminal abortion each year, that more than 60,000 drug addicts are supplied narcotics through a criminal black market, and that the nation harbors some five million alcoholics. It is generally acknowledged that homosexuality is on the increase, although the numbers are uncertain. One homosexual group, the Mattachine Society, proudly claims that "in politics, we should become an important factor . . . the Kinsey statistics indicate there may be 20 million practicing homosexuals in this country."[3] Illegitimate births are also increasing rapidly. In 1961, notes U.S. News and World Report, "there were 4,268,000 registered births in the U.S., 240,200 of them illegitimate. By 1964 . . . total births had dropped to 4,054,000 while illegitimate births reached 275,700."[4] These figures are probably understatements. Leontine Young, in her book, Out of Wedlock, notes: "No one knows how many girls, yearly, become illegitimately pregnant, but the number is certainly far higher than is generally assumed by the public."[5] Miriam Ottenberg observes that "the FBI's youth crime figures are paralleled by HEW figures showing that in the past decade, the syphilis rate in the 15–19 age group has doubled and the illegitimacy rate for girls under 20 has increased 47 per cent."[6]

Every cultural movement has its high priest, and many candidates have been set forward as leaders of the contemporary drive toward impulse-release—Hugh Hefner, Timothy Leary,

Murray the K, Mario Savio, Allen Ginsberg, and similar orna-
ments of the West. Our own choice, however, is the late Dr.
Alfred C. Kinsey, who had a double contribution to make, and
made it most impressively. Kinsey tabulated the data confirming
the alteration of American attitudes in matters of sexual behavior, demonstrating the tremendous shift in belief and performance that has come over the nation in recent decades. And
he endorsed, through his stress on physical gratification at the
expense of value and impulse-restraint, the standard intellectual
argument for what had happened.

The proper guidelines for sexual activity, Kinsey said, were
"self-assurance," "social efficiency," and "sexual adjustments in
marriage." Unfortunately, he found, these desirable qualities
were "needlessly damaged . . . by the conflict between . . .
practice and the moral codes." This is a running motive throughout the Kinsey discussion of almost every form of sexual activity,
including homosexuality and marital infidelity. The reports
bristle with a scarcely-concealed hostility to "Talmudic" injunctions against various kinds of sexual behavior, and suggest that
the worst reason in the world for not doing something is a
"moral" reason. The great thing is to achieve release and "adjustment."[7]

Kinsey's message is clear: Hierarchies of value are a nuisance,
to be forgotten as quickly as possible. Subordination of impulse
to "Talmudic" morality is an affront to the natural promptings
of the human animal. Such impediments to the gratification of
the self must be done away with.

What has been happening to us in the Kinsey era may be
seen in the evolution of our popular entertainments, our movies
and our novels. The line between honest literature and outright
pornography becomes increasingly dim as we find ourselves
blessed with "courageous" motion pictures (a picture is "courageous" when it directly challenges the production code) and
literary lions who are self-proclaimed homosexuals, lionizers of
homosexuals, drug addicts, masters of the four-letter word, fan-
tasists of murder, rape, and adultery.

There is, to take but one example, the literary vogue of Jean
Genet, convicted thief and self-proclaimed pederast, whose di-

rect statements the authors do not choose to reproduce but the flavor of whose writings may be captured from the review-blurbs his American publishers employ to promote his books. The reader is invited to speculate on the moral condition of the society which has given birth to the following notices:

"A beautiful book . . . The actual social world of criminals and homosexuals, male whores and pimps."—*New York Review of Books*

"A book about criminality and sexual inversion which turns all morality—not merely bourgeois or Christian morality—absolutely upside down . . . A work of artistic genius, deeply felt, powerfully conceived, and beautifully executed."—*Chicago News*

"A fabulous world of transvestites and thugs."—*Book Week*

"The hallucinations of a sick soul reach heights of veritable beauty . . ."—*Saturday Review*

". . . an impassioned archangel of vice . . ."—*Boston Globe*[8]

The problem here is not simply Genet, whose exercises in perversion might be dismissed as private sickness, but the open reception of his fantasies by so many literary authorities and the eager hawking of his wares by publishers who seem to feel, correctly, that sick-soul hallucinations and upside-down morality are highly marketable items.*

Also suggestive are various "reform" campaigns which rage everywhere about us in contemporary America—many if not most of them spurred by powerful elements in the intellectual community. A concerted drive is under way for legalized abortions as a method of "curing" the problem of abortion; for the rollback of anti-pornography statutes and movie production codes; for rescission of various laws covering juvenile delinquency; for removal of legal restrictions against homosexuality; for legalization of narcotics, etc. The Crime Commission itself offers one example of this tendency in its suggestion, among

---

* The epitome of the Genet Syndrome is the fact that this man, convicted ten different times and at last sentenced to life imprisonment, was freed through the efforts of Sartre, Jean Cocteau, Pablo Picasso and other important figures in the artistic and literary worlds.

other steps for handling the problem of drunkenness, that intoxication no longer be considered a criminal offense.*

Similarly, author Lawrence Lipton, who celebrates "the extent to which the beginnings of a new morality have already made their appearance in our culture," gives these prescriptions for social and legislative change in America: "Repeal all the laws and statutes regarding premarital sex. Make legal marriage optional, as religious marriage is now optional . . . Repeal all laws making homosexuality, male or female, illegal . . . Make all contraceptives and abortions legal everywhere and free to all who are unable to pay . . ."[9]

Such suggestions are often backed by the contention that laws should not be used as a method of imposing one's private moral vision upon society. The argument, so far as it goes, is correct. The purpose of the law, after all, is not to punish "sin," but to maintain the arena of civil peace in which people may go in an orderly fashion about their pursuits. The state should not be in the business of policing private ethics.

Unfortunately, the line between purely private behavior and the general regime of public peace is sometimes difficult to draw; in areas such as censorship, sexual behavior, alcoholism, and narcotics, a given act may be purely private when viewed in one light and a direct contribution to sociopathic behavior when viewed in another. The dissemination of pornography to impressionable young people is one obvious example, the behavior of a drunk who gets into a fight and kills someone is another. (Abortion, which is often placed in the category of "private" action, involves still other moral considerations, which we shall review in a later chapter.)

In the present instance, however, we can by-pass these complexities, since a far more fundamental question is at stake. The root issue involved in the "new morality" is not legal, but *philosophical*. The difficulty is not so much that people are being "allowed" to make decisions for themselves, but that they are

---

* The authors acknowledge, as appears in the second part of this book, that rehabilitationist efforts in some of these categories are urgently needed, and we applaud those agencies—such as the Vera Institute and Alcoholics Anonymous—which have set about to do this work on a realistic basis. Our quarrel is with the tendency to "solve" problems by evading them through altered definitions.

being subjected to a whole gamut of influences which *leads them* to make the immoral decision rather than the moral one. There is considerable evidence that what is portrayed as a strictly permissive campaign is in fact undergirded and propelled by a philosophy which encourages, by tacit suggestion and explicit endorsement, the most abandoned species of liberated impulse.

That impulse-release as such is the object of many of these campaigns can be seen by consulting proper academic authority. Prof. Norman O. Brown, for one, urges "the abolition of repression" on the grounds that "the life instinct, or sexual instinct, demands activity of a kind that, in contrast to our current mode of activity, can only be called play . . ." and that the countervailing "death instinct" can be "reconciled with the life instinct only in a life which is not repressed . . ." Brown concludes that "the abolition of repression would abolish the unnatural concentrations of libido in certain particular organs" and would produce a "consciousness which *does not negate any more.*"[10] (His italics.)

Also concerned to produce a "consciousness which does not negate any more" is another academician, Prof. Howard Becker of Northwestern University. Prof. Becker tells us that "our public morality may have gotten too far out of step. Recent reports on college students indicate that a vast number of college girls, whatever their private beliefs and whatever their practice, simply no longer believe in chastity, virginity, and the sexual double standard that was once the American way . . . In the same way, it seems likely that the general public is now prepared to accept revisions of our extremely punitive laws on homosexuality and [drug] addiction."[11] *

These academic opinions have been powerfully underscored by developments in the field of religion. Keeping pace with the new morality is a "new theology" which says we must abandon traditional ethics and come up with new ones in keeping with the secular revolution. Since the "new morality" will not conform to

---

* Becker concludes that "as the indivisible nature of freedom becomes clear, even those who do not engage in forbidden activities will be drawn into the battle, just as physicians, lawyers and ministers have already been drawn into the fight for more humane and rational treatment of addicts and homosexuals. The seeds of independence planted in 1776 will yet bear some strange fruit."

religious teaching, religious teaching must conform to the new morality. Thus Bishop John A. T. Robinson of Woolwich, England, notes the "revolution in morals" and says: "The fact that the old landmarks are disappearing is not something simply to be deplored. If we have the courage, it is something to be welcomed—as a challenge to Christian ethics to shake itself loose from the supports of supranaturalistic legalism on which it has been content to rest too much."[12]

Pressing the thought still further is the school of theologians who have decided "God Is Dead," and that only the immediate secular world counts for anything. "With the death of the Christian God," writes Thomas J. J. Altizer, "every transcendent ground is removed from all consciousness and experience." Man can survive only "by means of an ultimate Yes-saying, a total affirmation of our actual and immediate existence," evil as well as good, embracing the world's "pain and darkness." The "radical Christian," Altizer concludes, "wagers upon the Christ who is totally profane."[13]

Then there is the Rev. Malcolm Boyd, whose "prayers for sexual freedom" include a number entitled "this is a homosexual bar, Jesus." and another which states: "He is twenty-one, she is nineteen. They have been having sex together two or three times a week for two years. Now he has found that she hasn't been enjoying the sex but has been pretending to . . . Can they make something out of their situation, Lord? They're at least trying to talk to each other . . . Take their mutual honesty, Lord, and work with it."[14]

Where all this may be leading us is suggested by the ministry of San Francisco's Glide Memorial Methodist Church, which holds "soul jigs," or rock and roll festivals, in its sanctuary, sponsors a retreat for homosexuals, and staged a dance for male prostitutes. According to one news report, "Glide permitted the Vanguards, a group of young male prostitutes, to have a dance in the church. Glide also has made office space available to the Vanguards, helped them secure a clubroom, and bought them furniture."[15]

The account adds that "Glide ministers haven't tried to 're-form' the homosexuals," but say "some have responded to the sympathetic treatment they have received." To assertions that the homosexuals are taking advantage of the church, one minister replies this is a "very real possibility," but "we have to put ourselves in a vulnerable position so that we can be used to meet other people's needs."[16]

Developments of this sort go beyond the legalistic grey area where public law invades the territory of private morals. These things represent a kind of oozy and complaisant "understanding" which in effect tells us morality should be adjusted to deviant behavior, rather than the other way around. The effects of this "new" approach to ethics could prove calamitous. When the idea is advanced that standards must unceasingly be changed to accommodate the latest exoticisms, standards become meaningless. An emotional and intellectual atmosphere results in which people are ready to be blandly "tolerant" of virtually anything.

This attitude has obvious implications in the field of criminal behavior, since it makes the boundary between purely "private" actions and those impinging on the public good exceedingly difficult to define. Having started off by "tolerating" private deviance, we become tolerant of public deviance as well. If a homosexual is to be forgiven his perversion, why, then, so is a rapist. If impulse-release is the proper rule for dope addicts, why not for murderers as well? If compassion for the deviate is to be the measure of value, are we really entitled to condemn or punish anyone for anything? By removing standards, the "new morality" also removes the pre-conditions of social order.

The spread of new-moralist thinking among young people is apparent. A *Newsweek* survey finds "tolerant" attitudes toward almost all subjects—encouraged, it appears, by those who counsel the students on American campuses. A sample paragraph tells us:

" 'Premarital sex is accepted,' said Allison Hollander, a graduate history student from Washington, D.C., who is now attending a large Eastern school. 'It's not a mortal sin you'll go to hell for.' Her sentiments reflect the popularity of the 'new morality' as preached by many contemporary chaplains. Recognizing the oral contraceptives make fear of pregnancy a poor substitute for principle, the new moralists emphasize that sex is good, but love is better."[17] And so forth.

In similar vein, a profile of students at Vassar College in the 1950s came to these conclusions about seniors at that institution:

> The senior more often than the freshman justifies the breaking of rules on occasion, including civil disobedience; questions whether "Communism is the most hateful thing in the world today" or whether the American way of life should be preserved unchanged; would prefer to betray country rather than best friend . . .
> The senior goes to church and prays less than the freshman and is less likely to believe in the second coming of Christ, a life hereafter, and even that there is a God . . .
> The senior is more likely than the freshman to admit to conduct and attitudes contrary to conventional moral taboos concerning drinking, telling the truth, sexual propriety, and even theft. She feels people would be happier if sex experience before marriage were taken for granted in both men and women, and that in illegitimate pregnancies abortion is in many cases the most reasonable alternative. She thinks she would probably get into a movie without paying if sure she would not be seen.[18]

How such things translate into everyday behavior is indicated by a young lady at a Southern college who wrote a despairing editorial for her school paper. The girls at her school, this student said, no longer seem to know the difference between right and wrong. "Is it that some do not know that lying and cheating are wrong," she asks, "no matter how great or small the degree? . . . I have always been taught that lying was wrong. For 21 years I have been believing this, but as each day passes I wonder who changed the rules. . . . I know morals and values are changing to harmonize with our sophisticated society . . . but has right and wrong faded so much that stealing from a best friend, slipping out of the dorm to 'sleep out,' drinking in the dormitory and worst of all lying to avoid the consequences have become acceptable? These things go on here. Are they right?"[19]

The low estate of honorable dealing is further indicated by statistics on academic cheating. A survey at one high school found that 25 per cent of the freshmen, 30 per cent of the sophomores, 62 per cent of the juniors, and 70 per cent of the seniors questioned "admitted cheating on tests."[20] A nationwide study of 99 different colleges found readiness to cheat rife among students, with up to 74 per cent in some categories having indulged in cheating. "The guilt associated with cheating," *Newsweek* observes, " is diminishing."[21]

Also prevalent on college campuses is the use of drugs, particularly the hallucinogenic LSD, widely advertised and defended by former Harvard Professor Timothy Leary. Drug-taking is particularly noteworthy, according to a number of reports, at the University of California. An article in the *Washington Post* says official estimates have it that perhaps as many as one in ten among U.C. students are drug users. University officials, said the *Post*, were "deeply worried about the situation. But they, like officials on dozens of other campuses across the nation, are not sure of what to do about it. There is every reason to believe that the drug culture is eating its way into many of the nation's ranking universities."[22]

Drug-taking is perhaps the ultimate refinement of the "new morality," since it not only goes against traditional value patterns but comes equipped with a self-justifying mystique arguing that those patterns ought to be overthrown. LSD cultists self-consciously view themselves as the vanguard of a moral revolution, seeking to "turn the world on." The peculiar significance of drug-taking in the moral and social revolution now gripping America will be touched upon in a later section of this essay.

The farthest reach of the "new morality" in all its modulations has probably been the explosion of impulse that has rocked the Berkeley campus of the University of California. One witness to proceedings there in late 1964 described the ideas and actions which were advanced under the rubric of "free speech." Alexander Greendon, a physicist at Cal, related that: "In a university lecture hall, a self-proclaimed anarchist advises students how to cheat to escape military service; a nationally known Communist uses the university facilities to condemn our government in vicious terms for its action in Viet Nam, while funds to support the Viet Cong are illegally solicited; propaganda for the use of marijuana, with instructions where to buy it, is openly distributed on campus. Even the abstraction 'obscenity' is better understood when one hears a speaker, using the university's amplifying equipment, describe in vulgar words his experiences in group sexual intercourse and homosexuality and recommend these practices, while another suggests students should have the same sexual freedom on campus as dogs."[23]

In all of these things we see the failure of consensus. The moral propositions which have defined and maintained the arena of civil peace are obviously being broken up. Affirmation of Self in all its dimensions, the rejection of restraints, contempt for tradition and for objective criteria of right and wrong—these are the coordinates of the "new morality," or, as Father Murray puts it, the new barbarism. A large fragment of our society—its full dimensions not yet determined—has torn loose from the value structure upon which our civilization is founded.

No society, we have suggested, can function in terms of positive law alone. Arrest and punishment can serve to deter or to remove from the scene a certain number of people who are intent upon robbing or killing their neighbors. But if every member of the society were bent on killing someone, there would be no conceivable method of maintaining the peace. The judgment which holds killing and robbing are *wrong* is higher than positive law, and anterior to it. It is inculcated by religious belief, notions of tradition, obligation and symbol, which are in the long run far more powerful than the efforts of the police. When people become uprooted from tradition, shun obligation, and disparage the symbols of belief, then the maintenance of law becomes increasingly difficult.

In various of our comments, certain connections between the "new morality" and the rise of crime have been apparent. As the President's Crime Commission states, "crime flourishes when standards of morality are changing rapidly."[24] Even more to the point is that a continuing assault on the presuppositions of civilization itself, which is the essential program of the "new morality," is in a larger sense the very definition of crime. That the enterprise is bathed in sentimentality and framed in bohemian jargon does not alter the fact that destruction of the consensual basis of society makes orderly existence based on law impossible. When impulse becomes the rule, law is necessarily overturned.

This broader conception of crime is a subject to which we shall return in a later chapter. For the moment, we realize that the pressing question involves something less philosophical, such as broken heads, muggings, killings, and robberies. At this level, the interconnection of "new morality" and lawlessness, although in some cases obvious and vivid, is no simple matter. The actual translation from one thing to another is not always clear, and although we may rightfully question the logical consistency of those who welcome the overthrow of the old tabus but confess themselves appalled by the advancing tide of crime, we are not yet in a position to demonstrate the stages by which tabu-toppling converts itself into head-breaking. We raise the matter here, as the lawyers say, subject to connection, and because even the barest factual discussion of present-day crime would not be comprehensible without some reference to it. We hope to make the connection plain in the succeeding pages.

THREE

What Doesn't Cause Crime

Before attempting an assessment of the causes of crime in America, it is necessary to do some ground-clearing. Certain ideas about the sources and remedies of crime have so durable a purchase on official thought that they tend to block out other analysis. Until these are dealt with, further progress will be difficult if not impossible.

By and large, the prevailing view among American government officials, youth agencies, and social workers is that crime is a product of environment. Specifically, that it is a product of poverty—poor education, bad housing, "ghetto" conditions. So long as these persist, we are told, it is useless to talk about crime prevention; we are merely battling the heads of the Hydra.

This theme is belabored at length by the President's national crime commission, which tells us, among other things, that crime grows out of "slum" conditions and can be cured by applying the poultice of governmental aid. "Warring on poverty, in-adequate housing, and unemployment," the report says, "is warring on crime. A civil rights law is a law against crime. Money for schools is money against crime. Medical, psychiatric, and family-counseling services are services against crime . . . every effort to improve life in America's 'inner cities' is an effort against crime."[1]

A similar stance is taken by the President's Commission on

Crime in the District of Columbia, which says the "roots of crime" are low incomes, bad schools, unemployment and other stigmata of the underprivileged. The Commission's report urges that crime be attacked by assistance to the unemployed, public housing, urban renewal, loosening of welfare restrictions, and deployment of augmented "poverty" programs.

These conclusions are in keeping with previous statements by President Johnson himself. We must, the President has said, go about "attacking crime at the roots," with renewed efforts "to eliminate the degradation of poverty, the decay of our cities, the disgrace of racial discrimination, the despair of illiteracy . . . Effective law enforcement and social justice must be pursued together, as the foundation of our efforts against crime."[2] Former Attorney General Nicholas deB. Katzenbach, in a 1966 statement, has also elaborated on this notion. Responsibility for riots which have ravaged American cities, said our chief law enforcement official, rested not with individuals, but with "disease and despair, joblessness, rat-infested housing and long-impacted cynicism."[3]

It is in obedience to such theories that, over the past generation, we have created a vast apparatus of welfarism designed to upgrade the economic status of the underprivileged. We have diligently tried to purvey "progress" to the disadvantaged through mass education, public housing projects, urban renewal, unemployment compensation, aid to dependent children, surplus food projects, rent supplements, the Job Corps, the Youth Corps, VISTA, and the rest of the "war on poverty."

The Crime Commission report, unsurprisingly, urges still more of all these things. It proffers a spread-eagled enthusiasm for the "poverty" program as a whole, citing numerous of its offspring as precisely the kind of thing we need to prevent lawlessness. Pour still more money into the Youth Corps and VISTA, it says, and we will make important headway in combatting and controlling crime. But will we?

The evidence suggests that we will not. The "poverty" view that dominates official thought is rejected, amazingly enough, by experience, by careful students of criminology, and even—in certain instances—by some of the officials administering these programs. What the merits of "social justice" as urged by the President may be on other grounds belongs to a different branch of metaphysics; but concerning its merits as a defense against crime, the results are pretty well in. On the data available to us, poverty does not cause crime, and welfarism does not cure it. Indeed, it would be fair to say the opposite of this formulation is a good deal nearer to the truth.

The most obvious indication we have that crime is not a function of poverty and will not yield to anti-poverty efforts is our own day-to-day existence. We are, after all, living in the most prosperous society on earth. A smaller percentage of the total population is poor in America today than in any previous time and place known to history. Yet we are simultaneously beset by a mounting crime wave which alarms even President Johnson and his various crime commissioners.

Consider the simple fact that there was so much *less* crime during the depression. If the poverty argument is correct, the 1930s should have been marked by much more crime per capita than the 1960s. Just the reverse is true.

Granted the inadequacy of some of the figures, it is nonetheless remarkable to note that virtually every type of crime statistic relating to prosperity and depression runs counter to the poverty thesis. For the seven major "index crimes" compiled each year by the FBI, the over-all trends are exactly opposite to the pattern suggested by the poverty analysis. In 1933, total reported crimes against the person stood at about 150 per 100,000 of population. This figure dropped steadily throughout the continuing years of the depression and the enforced scarcity of World War II. As the war came to an end and prosperity returned, the line turned sharply upward and has continued to climb ever since. By 1965, the figure stood at more than 180.

In crimes against property, the movement of crime is even more dramatically opposed to the poverty argument. In 1933, total index crimes against property stood at slightly over 600 per 100,000 of population. Like crime against the person, this species of lawlessness declined steadily as the depression continued and war supervened, reversing itself only as the war drew to a close. From that point on the rate went into a steep climb, until in 1965 it reached well above 1,200—more than double the 1933 rate and triple the rate that prevailed at the low point during World War II.

" . . . during the dark days of the Great Depression in the early 1930s," says Judge David Pine, "there existed all over the land abject poverty, distress, and misery, but I do not recall at that time there was a vast upsurge in crime . . . from 1931 to 1935, while the nation's population grew by better than 3 million persons, the number of robberies and auto thefts decreased 35.2 per cent, burglaries decreased 8.9 per cent, and aggravated assault and larceny remained relatively constant."[4]

Things were hardly better at the end of the '30s. Wages were low and unemployment was high.* Yet there was considerably less crime in America than there is today. In 1938, Attorney General Homer S. Cummings announced that the preceding year had seen "nearly 1,500,000 crimes committed"—a number he felt, quite properly, to be enormous. The population of the United States was then estimated at 130,320,000 people. In 1964, no less than 2,729,659 major crimes were committed—an increase of better than 1.2 million. The population was then around 191,372,000. Crime in the United States between depression year 1938 and boom year 1964 had increased by 80 per cent; population had increased by only 47 per cent.

The poverty analysis is further damaged by a statistical survey of depressions and boom years conducted by Andrew F. Henry and James Short, showing that neither suicide nor homicide is traceable to impoverishment. The authors found that suicide, although it goes up in times of depression, does so for the most part among people in higher-income brackets. And they found that homicide actually goes down in times of depression. "Homicide and aggravated assault," they observe, "are correlated posi-

---

* In 1939, the Gross National Product was $91.1 billion, and average per capita income $695. By 1964, these figures had risen to an estimated $622 billion and $2,449 respectively. Unemployment in 1940, the last calculation before World War II pulled the economy out of the doldrums, was a whopping 14.6 per cent—compared to 5.2 per cent in 1964.

tively with the business cycle."[5] During periods of depression, homicide decreases. During periods of prosperity, it increases. The authors found the incidence of crime decreased during 15 of 18 test years in which the business index was falling.

Similarly for juvenile delinquency. In 1939, the delinquency rate for American children was only 21 per 1,000. By 1957, it had climbed to 33.5 per 1,000—or 70 per cent. More detailed figures for Cuyahoga County, Ohio (Cleveland), likewise show a 70 per cent increase in delinquency between 1939 and 1957. In 1940, 200,000 cases of delinquency (excluding traffic cases) were handled by the courts. By 1960, the number of juvenile cases had skyrocketed to 514,000 (excluding traffic cases)—an increase of more than 150 per cent. A report to Congress on delinquency says: "There is some evidence that rates for juvenile delinquency . . . increased during the 1920s, when some features of our society resembled those of today, and declined again during the depression years of the 1930s."[6]

If those long-term comparisons do not support the poverty analysis, neither do more recent data. The American economy in the years succeeding the 1958 recession enjoyed a sustained burst of prosperity—and of crime. From 1958–1964, the Gross National Product increased from $444 billion to $622 billion. But during this same period crime increased by almost 60 per cent. Nor has augmented welfarism done much to halt the crime explosion. In 1939 total government spending on welfare projects amounted to $9.58 billion; in 1958 it had risen to around $35 billion; and in the six years succeeding it increased another 100 per cent to more than $71 billion. Welfare spending shot upward, and crime moved right along with it.

Principal support for the poverty thesis is the fact that a large percentage of urban crime is found in the slums and ethnic ghettos. Analysis of governmental efforts to cure slum conditions or to upgrade the status of minorities, however, fails to support the poverty argument. Repeated efforts to eliminate slums through public housing projects and various forms of subsidy have been accompanied by increasing rather than decreasing crime rates. The problem of minorities has proved even more refractory, in some instances showing oppressed groups with very low crime rates, in others showing over-all economic increase accompanied by continuing high crime rates.

Some "ghettos," indeed, are *more* law-abiding than the surrounding middle-class society. Researchers have found that both Chinese and Jewish enclaves in our major cities have crime rates lower than the average for society. Lawlessness in San Francisco's Chinatown was found to be less than half that for the community as a whole. Sociologist Lowell Carr says that Jewish groups often show a lower delinquency rate "than white, native-born Protestants of the same economic level." Bernard Lander, studying juvenile delinquency patterns in Baltimore, concludes: "The delinquency rate in a stable community will be low in spite of bad housing, poverty and propinquity to the city center." Lander notes of one census tract that it has the second lowest median rental in the city, but "possesses a much lower rate of juvenile delinquency than one might predict on the basis of its economic characteristics." Housing, education, and physical amenities are of lower quality in this area than virtually anywhere else in the community—"indices which mark it as one of Baltimore's most economically depressed sections. Yet it is not among the ranking juvenile delinquency areas."[7]

Oscar Handlin, commenting on the original ghettos of the 19th century, observes that the residents were subjected to "disorganizing pressure" which led to certain types of deviant behavior, but that "where willful defiance of the law was involved, the immigrants drew back. The rate of crime among the foreign born was lower than among the natives." This despite the fact that the immigrants were much poorer than the surrounding society. The paradox, indeed, extends even further. Ernest van den Haag notes that most of the foreign-born had even fewer physical comforts in their countries of origin, and a lower crime rate still.[8]

Similar results were discovered by the *National Observer* in a survey of crime prevention in Johnstown, Penna. This mining and manufacturing community has, in recent years, occupied two unusual and seemingly contradictory positions in American social life: At one point, in 1962, it had the highest unemployment rate of any metropolitan area in the nation—16.6 per cent.

Yet in 1965, this same community, still suffering from economic difficulties, also enjoyed the nation's lowest crime rate—only 328 major crimes per 100,000 of population.

The *Observer* notes that "the economic position of the Negro in Johnstown is not much improved over other communities. . . . Housing for Negroes also is not good. But this factor, so often believed to be critical in other cities as a provocation for anti-social behavior, is less prominent in Johnstown."[9] Negro crime in the community is not, the report concludes, disproportionate.

Results like these are in keeping with the findings of dispassionate scholars, dating from 19th-century French sociologist Emile Durkheim forward. In his classic study of suicide, Durkheim stated that this manifestation of social disorder is not a function of poverty, but often the reverse. "So far is the increase in poverty from causing the increase in suicide," he said, that even "fortunate crises" are accompanied by the rise of self-inflicted deaths. In some instances "poverty protects against suicide . . ."[10] Durkheim's general thesis has been confirmed by a large body of data in the intervening half-century. As Herbert Hendin writes, "it has long been known that countries with much poverty have low suicide rates."[11] Erich Fromm reaches similar conclusions in tallying up statistics on suicide, homicide, and alcoholism in the Western democracies. "We find," Fromm says, ". . . that the countries in Europe which are among the most democratic, peaceful and prosperous ones, and the United States, the most prosperous country in the world, show the most severe symptoms of mental disturbance. The aim of the whole socioeconomic development of the Western world is that of the materially comfortable life, relatively equal distribution of wealth, stable democracy, and peace, and the very countries which have come closest to this aim show the most severe signs of mental unbalance."[12] Conversely, Prof. van den Haag notes, "the countries with the lowest living standards usually have very low suicide and homicide rates."* [13]

* Henry and Short, as noted, found that suicide tended to go up in times of depression, but did so among higher-income groups. Their explanation is that for these groups, the depression means not impoverishment *per se* but loss of status relative to lower-income groups. The lower-income groups themselves do not show

What has become increasingly true in the United States has long been accepted in other countries of the world. Roul Tunley says: "Progress . . . was recognized as a major factor in delinquency in almost every country I [have] visited . . ."[14] He quotes a government official in India as saying relative poverty and backwardness are deterrents to juvenile crime and relays the comment of a British authority on delinquency who says: "Twenty years ago people in Great Britain said that if you could do away with poverty and slums, it would help do away with delinquency. But we've done away with lots of poverty and we've improved housing, and it's worse than ever."[15]

In Sweden, Tunley notes, every welfare measure conceivable has been employed to alleviate poverty or the fear of it; yet the Swedish crime rate continues to soar: "If the theory of most of our prevailing experts were correct, namely, that juvenile crime springs from an underprivileged status, Sweden should be a country with little or no delinquency. Yet we know it has one of the highest rates, if not *the* highest, in the world."[16]

William S. Schlamm, discussing the rise of juvenile delinquency in Germany, says: ". . . the socioeconomic explanation of the phenomenon—poverty of the parents, slum conditions—must be discarded. In Germany this young generation started its bizarre conduct while all of Germany was going through the greatest economic uplift in its history."[17]

One intensive study of 794 German youngsters arrested for rioting, Schlamm notes, discovered that they were "by no means primarily children of lower-class families or broken-up homes; every element of German society, the whole scale up and down, was represented. Nor are the *Halbstarken* [the "half-strong"— delinquent youth] financially starved: on the average, the investigated *Halbstarken* earn or administer DM 235 a month—more than one half of the adult German's average income."[18]

A 1960 United Nations report similarly concludes:

> The existing data suggest that the improvement of living conditions—what is called a better standard of living—does not neces-

___

such a marked tendency toward suicide in times of depression. This confirms the essential Durkheim theory that the cause of suicide reposes not in objective material conditions but in subjective attitudes.

sarily . . . reduce juvenile delinquency . . . Although statistical data are incomplete, it would seem . . . that juvenile delinquency is not caused by poverty or poor economic conditions alone.[19]

So apparent is the non-correlation between poverty and crime that Mrs. Katherine B. Ottinger of the Children's Bureau has remarked that juvenile delinquency is "more likely to increase in a time of prosperity than in a time of depression."[20] And the Children's Bureau comments that "providing additional recreation facilities in an area usually does not bring about significant changes in the volume of juvenile delinquency."[21] Studies by Eleanor and Sheldon Glueck of children who had received no outside assistance, as against those who had had the benefit of "clinical treatment, friendly supervision, recreational activities, neighborhood meetings, health examinations, counseling and so on," likewise disclosed that such assistance "seemed to make little difference in their delinquency rate compared with those children who didn't get treatment."[22]

Crime in America has, in fact, followed affluence. People who as recently as a decade ago were in lower-income brackets have been absorbed into the middle class and have moved steadily into the suburbs. They have more money to spend on themselves and on their children and increasingly find the amenities of middle-class life available to them. Today's young people spend so much on so many products that manufacturers look to them as style-setters and fashion whole industries to their whim. By 1971, it is estimated there will be 27 million U.S. teenagers disposing of an aggregate $21 billion a year in consumer-good purchases.*

---

* "Teenagers buy $3.6 billion in clothing a year," says a *Time-Life* survey; "teenage girls, only 12 per cent of the total female population, buy 27 per cent of the cosmetics; the number of teenage stockholders has tripled in five years to 500,000 with minors holding 10 per cent of Comsat shares; girls buy 50 per cent of all records; teenagers own a million TV sets, 10 million record players and 20 million radios; they buy 20 per cent of all the cars sold in the U.S." ("The Young Americans," *Time-Life* Special Report, 1966; p. 74.)

In addition, teenagers buy 16 per cent of all cosmetics, 45 per cent of all soft drinks, 24 per cent of all wristwatches, 81 per cent of all phonograph records, 30 per cent of all low-priced cameras. "This generation lives the good life," says *Newsweek*, "likes it, and wants more . . . A majority find life is easier for them than for their parents . . . With a flourishing economy, their nation can afford to

By the logic of the poverty argument, these suburbanites ought not to be afflicted by rising crime rates or juvenile delinquency. Yet it is precisely these suburbs, precisely these children, who are a main source of increasing crime. Car thefts, wild parties, vandalism, and dope addiction are nowadays a common scandal in the "very best" American communities including Westchester County, N.Y., the Philadelphia main line, etc. Most people around the United States today can testify, either from personal experience or from newspaper accounts, to similar developments in the prosperous suburbs or their own communities.

Harrison Salisbury of *The New York Times* lists instance after instance of middle-class, suburban youth crime, concluding that "split-level delinquency in the quiet suburban communities is just as deadly a menace to the younger generation as are the festering conflicts of the housing projects and the old slums."[23]

The nation has repeatedly been stunned by lurid stories involving young people from well-to-do families. Some months ago the scion of a wealthy Philadelphia family was apprehended in the death of a young girl who had been using narcotics. In Tucson, Arizona, the death of three young girls led to the discovery of a teen-age vice ring involving children from prosperous families. In one plush Eastern suburb, a young debutant was killed in an automobile accident after a drinking spree. A survey of the crime problem among young people notes that "in one state—Connecticut—low-income families, which once produced 60 per cent of the narcotics violators, now account for only 28 per cent."[24]

So plain has all this become that James W. Symington, formerly executive director of President Johnson's committee on juvenile delinquency and youth crime, has attacked "the myth that poverty causes most juvenile delinquents." Symington observed that "present figures show that children of the middle class comprise the majority of juvenile offenders."[25]

That some crime stems from economic motives, and that many

---

keep a large part of its potentially productive population inside classrooms through high school, basking in the warmth of a social incubator. And in the citadel of conspicuous consumption there is no consumer group quite so conspicuous as the teenagers . . ." Louis Harris observes that "high-school Americans have never known drastic economic depression or wartime shortages—they're happy now and believe the future can only get better." (*Newsweek*, March 21, 1966.)

personality factors leading to crime can be found in "slum" conditions, are obvious facts of life. The mistake of the "poverty" analysts is to assume these are the only facts, or, in present circumstances, the most important ones. It should be apparent that, whatever the truth for other eras, these can hardly be the major causes of crime in modern America. Crime of this sort is supposed to go *down* in times of prosperity, up in times of need. Rising crime in a period of prosperity cannot be accounted for by poverty, just as the lower crime rates of Jewish or Chinese "ghettos" cannot be traced to affluence.

Acknowledging that economic factors have played a serious role in the causation of crime, Prof. Pitirim Sorokin provides a list of eight cautionary findings based on an encyclopedic survey of the available data:

Several studies . . . have shown that an extraordinary increase of crime in the periods of social upheaval is due to other than purely economic conditions.

Secondly, not everywhere nor always do the poor show a greater proportion of crime.

Third, many poorer countries have had less crime than the richer countries.

Fourth, the improvement in the economic conditions of the population of the Western countries in the second half of the nineteenth century, and at the beginning of the twentieth, has not been followed by a decrease in crime.

Fifth, among those who commit crimes against property there is always a considerable number of well-to-do people and, on the other hand, many of the poorest people do not commit such crimes.

Sixth, it is an ascertained fact that, in the causation of crime and criminals a great many non-economic factors play an important role.

Seventh, practically all correlations between economic conditions and crime are far from being perfect, or even notably high.

Eighth, there is only a relatively low coefficient of correlation found between crime and business conditions . . .[26]

The evidence that poverty does not cause crime is, in short, convincing. It suggests that attempts to trace the present access of criminal behavior to material deprivation will end, necessarily, in failure. If we would fathom the sources of our distress, we must press our inquiry onto other ground.

FOUR

The "Now" People

Just why social disorder should accompany increased prosperity is a matter which has begun to puzzle the general run of social scientists and has long been a topic of speculation among their more discerning colleagues.

It was precisely this seeming paradox which inspired Emile Durkheim's studies in the pathology of suicide. Evidence that cultural disorder increased in time of affluence led Durkheim to focus his concern on interior rather than exterior matters—to examine, not simply the materials through which desires are expressed (although he did examine these), but the desires themselves. His emphasis was the reverse of that insisted upon by our present-day crime analysts.

Durkheim concluded that human appetites, freed from interior restraint, are insatiable. Unless checked by an internalized value structure, desire will absorb and surpass all amenities designed to quiet it. To the Faustian palate, all delicacies grow stale; something more, something different, will always be needed. This condition of unsatisfied and unsatisfiable yearning Durkheim called "anomie."*

The key to anomie is the breakdown of limits—limits dictated

---

* The concept and the word are Greek. The original "anomy" meant, appropriately enough for our discussion, disregard of the divine law.

by social custom and by the individual to himself. When these are abandoned, life becomes an endless plain where gratifications beckon, like mirages, in all directions. And, like mirages, they afford no real enjoyment once attained. We arrive at a condition in which appetites "become disoriented [and] no longer recognize the limits proper to them." Thus:

"At the very moment when traditional rules have lost their authority the richer prize offered these appetites stimulates them and makes them more exigent and impatient of control. The state of de-regulation or anomie is thus further heightened by passions being less disciplined, precisely when they need more discipline. . . .

"From top to bottom of the ladder greed is aroused without knowing where to find ultimate foothold. Nothing can calm it, since its goal is beyond all it can attain . . . A thirst arises for novelties, unfamiliar pleasures, nameless sensations, all of which lose their savor once known."[1]

If the Durkheim view is correct, it follows that the modern breakdown stems not from a lack of material goods but the reverse—from the doctrines and practices of a rampant materialism. It is idle to suppose poverty causes crime, or that a remedy for crime can be found by piling largess on the "disadvantaged." Such efforts, alternately exciting and assuaging material appetites, simply spin the cycle on another upward twirl. The intended beneficiaries will emerge from the experience more demanding than ever.

Anomie is, in sum, the product of a life-style in which impulse has broken free from precisely those inhibitions and repressions so offensive to practitioners of the "new morality." It is symptomatic of the fact that civilized society has lost its grip on the value consensus which is its central organizing principle.

A civilization is built up, as Freud observed, "under the pressure of the struggle for existence, by sacrifices in gratification of the primitive impulses, and it is to a great extent forever being recreated, as each individual, successively joining the community, repeats the sacrifice of his instinctive pleasures for the common good."[2] What is now in motion is an unwinding of this process. Rather than teaching people to control their impulses, we are preaching the doctrine of impulse release. We are by the same token disrupting the socializing mechanism by which new members of society are brought to share in the community of restraint.

The matters touched upon in previous chapters are an almost perfect illustration of this thesis—plainly suggesting that crime is rooted in deficiencies of character rather than in material circumstance. The statements of young people in the toils of modern "revolt" or outright criminality are, in particular, replete with the symptoms of anomie. This is most clearly seen in a restless and all-pervading boredom with the routine of life in which all pursuits "lose their savor"—a state of mind particularly conducive to crime. Two random news items from late 1966 suggest the nature of the problem:

In Perth, Australia, Heather Vincent, 16, and Patricia Burgess, 15, are taken into custody by a police constable for hanging head downward by their knees from a pedestrian footbridge over the Kwinana freeway. The headline of the news item relating this episode reads, "Aussie Teen-Agers Protest." What the two girls are "protesting": "There is nothing to do in this mad town."[3]

Half-way around the world, in Mesa, Arizona, an 18-year-old boy named Robert Smith walks into a beauty parlor and murders four women and a three-year-old girl. He is from a middle-class home, described as quiet and a "loner."[4] When arrested, he laughs and says he was trying to prove he was "somebody."

Except for the accented absurdity of the first item, and the special horror of the second, there is nothing particularly unusual about these news briefs. Similar explosions of youthful neurasthenia are visible almost every day in every advanced country of the world. If it is not youthful "provos" (provocateur-anarchists) hurling bombs at a royal wedding procession in Amsterdam, or outright gang violence in a large American city, it is in all likelihood a group of otherwise apparently sane teenagers rioting at Ft. Lauderdale or Daytona Beach or the Strip, or at a concert staged by Chuck Berry or the Beatles—kids with "nothing to do" erupting into sociopathic behavior.

Driven by loneliness and lack of purpose, the rootless youngster seeks shelter in the crowd or gang and identity in senseless
acts of violence. Frederic Thrasher wrote 40 years ago that "the
adolescent finds in the gang the desired escape from, or compensation for, monotony."[5] The same is true today. Slum kids who
do increasingly reckless things are, in Paul Goodman's phrase,
"raising the ante," to tell themselves they are really alive.[6] This
phenomenon is found with equal clarity among the more prosperous delinquents. And, as noted by a Michigan prosecutor who
put three young middle-class murderers behind bars, it leads to
similar results. Kids go bad, he said, by trying to outdo each
other. "For lack of anything better to do they'd throw rocks at
the windows in the high school . . . They hang around together, they brag, they talk about doing things—and there's always one guy in the crowd that will actually do it. It may be a
filling station stickup, it may be murder."[7]

The delinquents themselves have repeatedly confirmed this
diagnosis. In London, a rebellious young Briton says: "With a
gang you feel you belong somewhere, have a place in society.
Among a gang you can be somebody—the country is short of
police and robbery and violence are dead easy. The excitement
makes you feel important."[8] Another, arrested for participation
in a riot, agrees: "It was great being in the papers . . . Makes
you feel like you've done something, made people sit up and take
notice . . . The thing I hate most is people in authority—they're
idiots—they deserve all they get. I could kill them."[9]

A delinquent American girl offers similar comment. "School
is so monotonous," she says. "They flunked me in ninth grade
and I am repeating it now. It's so boring . . . I don't want to
get married until I am 30 years old . . . I want to have fun
first. Our gang has fun fighting . . . We are troubled because
we are bored . . . Stealing doesn't bother us morally . . . We
are not a bad gang, but there is quite a lot of stealing."[10]

Such themes are repeated at endless length in contemporary
surveys of delinquent or "angry" youth. In all Western societies,
there are apparently large numbers of adolescents unable to find
any purpose in existence, who have nothing to do, who reject
the notion of productive work, and who therefore seek to invest

their lives with meaning by joining a gang or indulging in point-less violence. The young lady quoted above tells us: "I love my gang." The experience of participating in something or going somewhere in company with other people who share her emotional state creates for her the illusion that her life has become significant. Because she is doing exactly what her colleagues do, she is having "fun." And since having "fun" is the only purpose she can discern, running with her gang, stealing and fighting, become the major objects of existence.

Prof. Erik Erikson describes this phenomenon as "identity-diffusion," in which young people "would rather be nobody or somebody bad, or indeed, dead—and this totally, and by free choice—than be not-quite somebody."[11] Salisbury quotes one observer of young delinquents as saying: "They have no interest in anything."[12] And at the other end of the youth spectrum, Irving Kristol says: "So many college students 'go left' for the same reason that many high school students 'go delinquent.' They are bored."[13]

As the Durkheim analysis suggests, this "boredom" springs precisely from the breakdown of internal restraints; it is the reverse side of that unquenchable thirst for "novelties, unfamiliar pleasures and nameless sensations" that results from concentration on the self and its untrammeled impulses.[14]

That today's young people are strenuously self-centered—more so apparently than their predecessors—is popularly acknowledged. Few of them, indeed, bother to deny this aspect of their personalities; they proclaim it rather proudly. As one teen-age hero quoted by *Look* magazine phrases it: "Oh, wow, what's so awful about feeling good?"[15] Other spokesmen are equally eloquent. A young Briton included in a survey of "mods and rockers" describes his existence as a "frantic process of living for kicks."[16] A youthful American beach bum, interviewed by *Time-Life*, asserts, "I'm more or less living for today."[17] And a young lady immortalized by *Newsweek* says: "Teenagers are out for fun. When you're young you might as well take advantage of it."[18]

In the opinion of Dr. Graham B. Blain, Jr., chief of psychiatry at Harvard University's health office, today's youngsters are "less disciplined, more destructive and morally lax" than their predecessors.[19] A *Chicago Sun-Times* survey concludes that "today's teen-agers are admittedly self-centered and, with few exceptions in this era of affluence, spoiled by parents, teachers and other adult figures who readily gratify their whims . . ."[20]

The quest for sensation is apparent in many ways. It is an obvious component of the strident rock-and-roll music which is the common teen-age idiom. Exaltation of self is notably a theme of folk-rock singer Bob Dylan, who has become a kind of symbol of youthful protest. As one sympathetic commentator opines, Dylan's music conveys the idea "that the only loyalty is to oneself," and that "the old-fashioned virtues of hard work and thrift and a clean tongue are obsolete."[21]

Most suggestive is the semi-religious consecration of some young people to ingestion of the hallucinogenic drug, LSD. The stated purpose of drug-taking is the emotional "kick," pushing society, obligations and responsibilities totally out of mind. The mentality of the drug cultist is suggested by one young "viper" who says: "Why do we try drugs? We really feel like we're limited too much . . . It seems hypocritical of older people to tell us not to try certain things."[22] Drug-taking creates an intensely private experience severed from the norms of society. This form of escape has long been a furtive resource of some troubled individuals. The difference today is that drug-users are not isolated escapists, but a defiant subculture proud of their break with the normal codes of social value.*

Exaggerated narcissism leads to one of the most alarming features of the "new morality" mystique—an insistence on having one's way now, with no waiting. The product of the "new morality," absorbed in Self, knows only the immediate point in time in which the Self exists. For such a mentality, neither past nor future has a great deal of meaning. *Esquire*, in a sardonic

---

* The *Washington Post* reports the Berkeley, California, "drug culture and the similar one across the bay in San Francisco, where the Psychedelic Book Shop is located, are like nothing America has seen in the past. They have their own music, painting, poetry, mores and group subdivisions . . . It is not apologetic. It is evangelistic, ideological and it proselytizes, not to hook people for money but because its members believe that drugs are a positive individual and social good." When such attitudes are purely escapist, they are difficulty enough; but when they are evangelized as a way of life for an entire society they assume the outlines of latent catastrophe.

review entitled "The New American Woman," describes this personality type as follows:

Possessing no sense of the past, no conception of history, she is possibly the first woman to be totally of her times, so plugged into the potency of the moment that nothing she says or does can be counted on to last . . . [She experiences] the feeling of rootlessness . . . She is the result of "the new leisure" . . . [She does not] have the attention-span for . . . training.[23]

Other commentators have noted the same phenomenon. Brandeis professor Lewis Coser, discussing certain members of the "new left," says one notices among them " a curtailment of time perspective, an immersion in the here and now of immediate experience. They often seem to be given to undifferentiated, almost visceral responses."[24] *Time* magazine, designating a composite figure called "Twenty-Five and Under" as the "Man of the Year" for 1966, observes: "Theirs is an immediate philosophy, tailored to the immediacy of their lives." Buell Gallagher of the City College of New York says: "This generation has no utopia. Its idea is the happening. Let it be concrete, let it be vivid, let it be personal. Let it be *Now!*"[25] And a perspiring "soul-singer" reputedly an idol of the young declaims: "Heaven? We want love and meaning *now.*"[26]

One's notion of time is of course conditioned by experience. To the very young, a year seems an infinity; as one gets older, a year seems very short indeed. The time perspective of youth is necessarily compressed—a phenomenon most clearly seen in the much-satirized instant nostalgia of the popular music field, wherein a song hit of six months past becomes a "golden oldie." This foreshortened vision—which it should be the function of the civilizing process to enlarge—makes the assessment of antecedents and consequences extremely difficult. The fun-ethic takes this disability as an asset, declaring the limited perspective of the young the only one worth having. A normal and heretofore temporary handicap is thus transformed into a life-style with ominous implications, tending, among other things, to preclude the development of abstract intelligence.

The net meaning of these tendencies has been summed up by Yale psychologist Kenneth Keniston as the "cult of the present." Among "alienated" students he examined, Keniston writes, past and future are dismissed in a relentless concentration on the experience of the moment. Even though the present often seems dull and "boring," these young people can conceive no antidote to its shortcomings either in reflection on the past or in planning for the future. Instead they hunger for emotional "breakthroughs," intensifications of experience, affirmations of significance through direct action. They seek to evade "the conventional categories of our culture" to achieve "self-expression." Keniston sums up these characteristics as examples of an "inability to tolerate any restraint or self-limitation."[27]

Extreme concentration on Self and servitude to impulse are social danger signs of the first magnitude. These are essential features of the infant mentality, and their increasing sway suggests the development of something which might be called the infantilization of our culture. Me, Want, Now are the chief coordinates of the child-mind, incapable of conceiving perspectives on existence other than its own.*

"Unlike more mature adults," the late Dr. Robert Lindner observed, "the child cannot wait upon suitable circumstances for fulfilment of its needs. Where the adult can postpone luncheon for a few hours, the infant expresses hunger-frustration by crying or other perhaps more aggressive techniques."[28]

That the assertedly revolutionary stance of the "now" people is merely childishness institutionalized goes far to explain the estrangement of many young people from the surrounding world of adults. Living for the "kicks" of the moment, the adolescent withdraws into a world of his own and shuts out adult society. This is a realm where costs must be reckoned and responsibilities shouldered. It is therefore to be avoided.

A young Californian interviewed in a journalistic analysis of

---

* As Jean Piaget puts it, "the child thinks for himself without troubling to make himself understood or to place himself at the other person's point of view." Anti-repressionist Norman O. Brown similarly comments that "infants are naturally absorbed in themselves and in their own bodies; they are in love with themselves; in Freudian terminology, their orientation is narcissistic."

the youthful psyche says of adults: "They're so stupid. They're so untrustful—you know, don't trust anyone. They think they've just got to clamp down . . . even if I become old and saggy, I'm still going to be young."[29] According to one British adolescent, "being young is being in an enormous like-minded club, with its own standards, and the most terrible thing in the world would be to be drawn into the adult world. Adults are to be pitied . . ."* [30]

Distaste for the adult world in the teeny-bopper subculture is an obvious motive behind fads of dress and musical taste. The *Newsweek* survey found that "knee-high boots and Prince Valiant bobs symbolize first, a declaration of identity with their peer group and, second, a declaration of rebellion against adult authority. Nearly half the girls and one-third of the boys surveyed bought certain clothes against the express wishes of their parents . . . nothing can solidify a fad faster than adult opposition."[31] Conscious alienation from adult society is even more strongly accented in the rapidly-growing world of LSD and marijuana users. The drug-culture is predominantly youthful, and its members view adult society as hostile, "square," hopelessly benighted. As a study by the University of California's School of Criminology puts it, youthful drug-users "are specially resistant to authority, paying more attention to their own kind than to adults."† [32]

---

* In the remarks of one young Briton, this estrangement flares into open hatred: "Old people accuse us of wallowing in self-pity. Nonsense, it's the old and the middle-aged who whine and rail against life. And against us, the young whom they choose not to understand. It's convenient for them not to accept the responsibility for our actions, to brush aside their own guilt by calling us vermin. 'Good luck to them.' They'll be in their graves long before most of us will; 'kicking up daisies.' Good luck, I say."

† How far this process can go is indicated by a teenage spokesman who remarks: ". . . when I'm older, I would like to look back to my teenage days and think of all the fun we had. Mods and Rockers I feel will be two different words that will go down in history as titles given to two very different youngsters who dominate the teenage world of today. The different clothes we wore. Great. The fun we had dressing up in our high-heeled boots and trying to keep our balances as we went around corners. Great. The Beatles, those four hairy lads from Liverpool who we used to rave about. Great. All part of history."

This young man views the adolescent years not as a period of preparation for more important tasks but as the sum and substance of existence. When he is an adult, the significant part of his life will be over; he will look back on his teenage years with misty-eyed nostalgia, a golden era that is "all part of history."

Dislike for adult authority thus becomes a positive determination to go on being adolescents—to enjoy the pleasures of self-indulgence, if possible, forever. This is the "persistence of infantilism" described by Marguerite and Willard Beecher—a condition in which young people were unwilling "to accept any restraints," found that "work on a job or in their home was a discipline they could not endure," and discovered after marriage "that bringing up their own children was such a limitation on their 'freedom' that they resented it and escaped it in any way possible." Keniston similarly notes, at the collegiate level, what he calls "the refusal of adulthood" by his "alienated" Yale students.[33]

If the chief purpose of the civilizing process is to bring impulse under control and "socialize" new members of the culture to the on-going corpus of value, then a society in which adolescents are not trained out of impulse release has ceased to perform its most critical assignment. Like a body which is no longer capable of manufacturing new cells, it is dying. The persistence and apparent hardening of infantile thought patterns indicates that our anomic civilization is undergoing a crisis of dissolution.

There are signs, moreover, that this breakdown of the civilizing process can ultimately lead on to a complete inversion—with adults accepting dominant value patterns from children, rather than the reverse. The new legions crossing over into the years of chronological maturity, unattuned to adult value and longing for the "important" years behind them, seem increasingly responsive to the whims and follies of the succeeding adolescents. We may in consequence wind up with a generation of adults who wish nothing more than to be teenagers again and who devoutly emulate teenagers in dress, behavior, and thought patterns.

That we have already proceeded part-way to this objective is indicated by Stanley Kauffman of the New Republic, who sums up the current mood in American art and literature as follows: "If it's young, it's good or potentially good; if it's Non-Young it's corrupt or blind or passé . . . The favor of the young is the great criterion; failure to please them is, in itself, proof of sterility or stodginess or reaction . . . I am not arguing . . . about the intrinsics of the art of aesthetics of the young. I am questioning the eagerness of the Non-Young to adore them."* [34]

Newsweek similarly notices "a curious new trend—the adoption of teen-age fads by adults," which threatens "not only to perpetuate the fads but the adolescent mentality as well." This is particularly apparent in terms of dress, dance, speech habits—a development which some observers see as a passing phase but which others view more seriously. The latter believe that the "youth cult" may "be leading the real youths to the wrong conclusions about how they should act as adults. Teen-agers of today . . . may grow up to imitate tomorrow's teen-agers—thereby setting up a cycle of permanent adolescence."

This reverse acculturation has been aptly described by Barrington Moore in his survey of the family's role in modern political development. Young people, Moore believes, are no longer willing to take their parents as models for emulation; they seek examples and values in an outside world characterized by sensationalism and impulsiveness and carry these back to the home. Moore concludes that the family thus constitutes "a 'transmission belt' through which totalitarian pressures toward conformity are transmitted to the parents through the influence of the children."

Examples of this effect are numerous in our society. Perhaps the most noteworthy is the increasing prevalence of the "now" psychology among adults—an apparent adoption by parents of the limited time perspective of their children. Richard Hoggart, for one, observes that a state of mind is developing among British adults which seems completely indifferent to past and future alike and is "particularly accessible to the temptation to live in a constant present." S. N. Eisenstadt opines that a growing emphasis on the present marks Western society generally. A prosaic example of this trend in America is the growth of consumer credit buying, which in 1967 reached the staggering total of $100

---

* Commenting on a decline in youthful respect for adults, John D. Black, director of the Counseling and Testing Service at Stanford, says: "It . . . may be that respect for elders was justified in those bygone eras when mere survival was a mark of competence . . . perhaps now, respect may be something which has to be earned regardless of age, or else something that all people deserve as human beings without reference to age or status."

billion—a figure Edwin Lahey of the *Chicago Daily News* believes to be a "measure of our steadily increasing tendency to
mortgage next year's wages for something we want right now."[35]

The spread of such attitudes and behavior patterns among
adults can of course only serve to confirm teen-agers in the essential correctness of their own preference for "now," driving
the cycle through yet another turn.

Adult imitation of youth may be in some degree traceable to a
normal distaste for getting old. But when it reaches the point of
reversing the acculturation process, it behooves us to inquire
whether special factors have not entered the equation. One of
these worthy of remark is the possibility that loss of internal
limits places a stronger than usual emphasis on what is "new."
Newness, in the absence of other value criteria, is the one hope
of the rudderless and de-racinated. It represents the other thing,
other place, other state of mind in which one hopes to escape the
pointlessness of anomic existence.

It is logical to suppose a society spurred by hunger for the new,
demanding change to escape from spiritual emptiness, will eventually pass cultural leadership to the young. As adult society
abandons adult value, it has little of cultural merit to transmit to
anybody, so acculturation becomes in a sense meaningless; and
since the young have at least something to transmit to adults in
the form of energy and enthusiasm, supply and demand tend to
pull the system inside-out. Adults in anomic society, on this view,
will look increasingly to the young as their rescuers from cultural
insignificance.

We are, of course, considering these matters in isolation. These
tendencies are interwoven with countervailing pressures gener-
ated by the old ethic and the old socialization system. In many
cases both the old and the new processes operate simultaneously
—with adults transmitting certain values (or non-values) to children, and the children transmitting certain other values (or non-
values) to the adults. The increasing evidence of "permanent
adolescence" suggests, however, that the second process is waxing in influence while the first is waning.

A special footnote is in order, finally, about that oft-repeated
demand for enjoyment "now." In most of the examples we have

quoted, "nowness" is presented as if it were somehow admirable —evidence of a vital zest for experience. In terms of the necessary pre-conditions of civilized life, it is not admirable at all. It is the most childish of character traits and, when it persists into the years of chronological maturity, the most criminal. Inability to defer gratification is in fact the hallmark of the morally illiterate —the leading feature of the delinquent and psychopathic personality.

Fritz Redl and David Wineman give this description of delinquent boys referred to them at their treatment home in Detroit: ". . . in moments of boredom . . . they again break out into wild, disruptive, and impulsive behavior. Then, too, they can't wait for anything; whatever they want has to be granted RIGHT NOW, and, if it isn't they again break down into seething hostility."[36]

In a study of modern homicide, Marvin E. Wolfgang notes the "now" bias of violent criminals. He concludes that capital crimes emerge from a "subculture of violence," in which direct physical aggression seems normal and natural, "middle-class value" does not obtain, and impulses are assuaged through instantaneous action. We find ourselves, Wolfgang says, in an ethical zone "where basic desires are less inhibited, restricted, or restrained; where reduction of tensions and satisfaction of needs are characterized by immediacy and directness; and where the social regulators of conduct are less omnipresent than in the large culture of which this collectivity is a part."[37]

Lindner similarly observes: "The psychopath, like the child, cannot delay the pleasures of gratification, and this trait is one of his underlying, universal characteristics. He cannot wait upon erotic gratification which convention demands should be preceded by the chase before the kill: he must rape. He cannot wait upon the development of prestige in society: his egoistic ambitions lead him to leap into the headlines by daring performances. Like a red thread the predominance of this mechanism for immediate satisfaction runs through the history of every psychopath."[38]

Through the history of every psychopath—and through the history, it seems, of a large and growing number of Americans.

Such, then, are the outlines of the anomic personality becoming so prominent in American society: Concentration on Self and sensation, rootlessness and boredom, demand for gratification "now," disruption and reversal of the adult-child socialization process. This is the source of our crime wave. Its constituent elements bear a striking resemblance to Durkheim's analysis—and, like Durkheim's studies, they occur in a context of plenty. They are the result, not of poverty and deprivation, but of breakdown in the realm of conscience.

FIVE

No Right, No Wrong

When confronted by evidence that crime springs from deficiencies of character rather than material circumstance, environmentalists move to a second line of argument. Their explanation is materialist nonetheless: Perhaps a breakdown of moral values is responsible for crime, but material conditions are in turn responsible for the change in moral values. So, in this view, it all comes out the same.

Thus the reasons for "anomie" and the "new morality" are persistently sought in such things as industrialization, the rise of "scientific" ideas, the clustering of population in urban centers, high-consumption economics, mass advertising, and so forth. Talcott Parsons remarks that "the general erosion of traditional culture and symbols . . . is inseparable from a scientific age."[1] Prof. Walter Metzger says the problem is one of "urban living" and "the process of industrial expansion," which weakens traditional codes of value. The Group for The Advancement of Psychiatry puts it that "geographical and social mobility, rapid technological change, urbanization, and increase in population have altered established patterns of behavior, with a resulting challenge to traditional attitudes."[2]

As has in part been seen in our study of the "poverty" question, this kind of analysis does not altogether come off. It is doubtful that material conditions *as such* form value patterns, whether those conditions be affluent or impoverished. In particular, the argument fails to account for the fact that, almost without exception, groups with strong religious convictions and cultural ties are not so susceptible to moral breakdown as are the irreligious.*

Because of scholarly and official preoccupation with material factors, we do not have a great deal of information on the relevance of religious belief to crime; the President's Commission, as noted by dissenting commissioner Genevieve Blatt, neglected the question altogether. There is nevertheless some impressive evidence available concerning the impact of religious belief on conduct—and the effects of changes in such belief in altering that conduct. In both categories, the available data belie the materialist argument.

There is, for example, the finding of the Kinsey researchers that religious devotion makes for continence in sexual behavior. The Kinsey report tells us that:

> The accumulative and active incidences of pre-marital coitus had been distinctly higher among those females in the sample who were less actively connected with religious groups, and lower among those who were most devout. This, in general, was true for the Protestant, Catholic, and Jewish groups. In many instances the differences between devout and inactive members of particular groups were very marked. The differences between Protestant, Catholic, and Jewish females of the same degree of devoutness were usually less than the differences between the various levels within any one religion. There appear to be no other factors which affect the female's pattern of pre-marital behavior as markedly as the decade in which she was born and her religious background. . . .
>
> For both the females and males in our sample, degrees of religious devotion did correlate with the incidences of the various types of sexual activity and devoutly religious backgrounds had

---

* The official view that "poverty" is the cause of crime has not been modified by the findings we have reviewed. Accepting most of the evidence we have set forward, the official theoreticians simply assert that both poverty *and* affluence are the cause of crime, and let it go at that. Their reliance upon material causes for crime is complete, and it never seems to occur to them that such a divergence in the "causes" could mean these are not causes at all—that there is some other element, not material but moral, at the root of our difficulty.

prevented some of the females and males from ever engaging in certain types of sexual activity. The incidence of nearly all types of sexual activity except marital coitus were, in consequence, lower among the religiously more devout females and males, and higher among the religiously less devout.[3]

These findings become the more impressive when we reflect that most of the traditional tabus about sexual behavior go counter to powerful primary instincts and are not generally backed up by the force of the criminal law. If religious belief can achieve such notable effects under these circumstances, it is reasonable to suppose it will be even more influential in cases where these drives are not involved, and the auxiliary support of the law endorses the preachments of faith.

Also noteworthy is the fact that, when religious belief is broken down, or codes of faith are radically altered, changes in vital areas of human conduct tend to follow suit. Even so ardent a relativist as Bertrand Russell acknowledges the baleful results of declining religious belief on the whole gamut of behavior. Lord Russell states:

> Those who advocate any ethical innovation are invariably accused, like Socrates, of being corrupters of youth; nor is this accusation always wholly unfounded, even when in fact the new ethic which they preach would, if accepted in its entirety, lead to a better life than the old ethic which they seek to amend. Every one who knows the Mahometan East asserts that those who have ceased to think it necessary to pray five times a day have also ceased to respect other moral rules which we consider more important.[4]

That the influence of religious faith carries over into the field of activities designated as criminal is also indicated by the Kinsey figures. The data show, as Edwin M. Schur observes in a study of abortion, "that for all religions there was a fairly clear inverse relationship between degree of devoutness and incidence of induced abortion. This was quite pronounced in the figures for Protestants . . . [and] in these discussions of abortion among married women, the researchers report: 'The percentage of devout Catholics with induced abortion experience is extremely low and [that] of the religiously inactive rather high.' "[5]

Similar results have been recorded with respect to suicide. Erwin Stengel notes that "suicide rates among Roman Catholics in predominantly Protestant countries have usually been found to be below the national average. The same applies to Jews and to Moslems. It appears, therefore, that it is religious devoutness rather than a specific religious faith which is decisive."[6] Stengel adds the further fact that mere formal religious designation does not always correspond to the suicide figures, since some predominantly Catholic countries have high suicide rates. Overall, however, the correlation of devoutness to low incidence of suicide is convincing. Herbert Hendin observes that "the Catholic countries . . . except for Austria, have very low suicide rates . . . In a country with a strong religious or moral prohibition against suicide, there is likely to be more concealment of suicide, but more importantly there is also likely to be less suicide . . . the society's attitude toward suicide has an important bearing on the suicide rate."[7]

The same influence of religious and moral ideas on behavior is suggested in studies of totalitarian political practice. Seymour Lipset notes, for example, that Nazism had a hard time making headway in strongly Catholic areas of Germany. Lipset shows, moreover, that religious affiliation in America often overrides economic circumstance in defining political allegiances and attitudes towards issues (this despite the fact Lipset himself is pretty much an old-style materialist).[8]

Johnstown, Penna., the law-abiding community previously referred to, also suggests the effect of strong religious belief in reducing criminal activity. The *National Observer* notes: "Johnstown is a religious community, almost equally divided between Roman Catholics and Protestants. Some clergymen estimate that 95 per cent of the population is church-going, and the dozens of church spires poking through the haze all over the city suggest they are church supporters as well." The head of the Catholic High School says: "Some of our children may seem to lack common courtesy, but their parents have grounded them solidly in morals, ethics, and religion."[9]

Nor are the Johnstowners alone in resisting the drift of the supposedly "inevitable" ideas, as is evidenced by Jewish and Chinese enclaves in some of our major communities. As Lowell Carr writes, "Jews have developed the firmest family and group traditions and the most adequate agencies for dealing with their own cases of social breakdown . . . ," with the result that they "not infrequently" will show a much lower delinquency rate "than white, native-born Protestants of the same economic level."[10] This persistent ability of groups with strong religious and cultural ties to withstand the asserted potencies of physical causation suggests the power of material change to compel moral change has been considerably overrated. Firmly rooted beliefs can and do countermand the alleged dictates of economic determinism.

This is not to deny that changes of thought in changing circumstances do occur. It is obviously necessary for new ideas to come into being, or for old ones to be modified, to take new data into account, and to enable the society to function better and to survive. But the particular change in ideas which concerns us is all too obviously not of this sort. The alteration of thought and value that has marked American society in recent years is distinctive precisely because it has *not* made us better able to survive; it has made survival for many individual members of society, and for society as a whole, increasingly difficult. To suggest that the "new morality" is a necessary adaptation to modern circumstance does not, therefore, make sense. It is like arguing that the process of evolution mandates the birth of deformed or vulnerable children. There is no logical—much less inevitable—reason why technological change *beneficial* to human life should dictate the birth of ideas *destructive* of human life. At least, there is no such reason compatible with the theories held by the poverty analysts and other environmentalists.*

---

* Belief in such a twist of irony might be derived from a Hardyesque cynicism about the cruelties of fate, or from conservative pessimism about the intrinsic evils of industrial society. The one species of thought from which it emphatically cannot be derived is the environmentalism we have been discussing, which views material and moral development alike through the lens of meliorism. The notion of moral change rooted in material change is founded, as Metzger suggests, in the idea that everything is constantly being altered for the better. The asserted connection between the two kinds of change is based, in short, upon a theory holding that both changes are *beneficial*. If it is conceded that the moral changes are not in fact beneficial, there is no reason to suppose them inevitable or even likely.

Perhaps the strongest argument for the materialist position is that founded on the disruptive effects of war—particularly the American experience in the aftermath of World Wars I and II. Yet it is not clear that all wars have had similar long-term damaging effects, and we know that some groups and individuals have emerged from recent wars and other crises with their moral sensibilities intact. The explanation may be that war or any other severe dislocation is the occasion for demonstrating what the ethical condition of the society or the individual already happens to be.

Albert Cohen suggests, with respect to individuals subjected to "strain," that this is often the case. One man in crisis will exhibit strictly law-abiding behavior; another will commit a crime. The difference, Cohen says, depends on the "symbols" and "normative reference groups" by which the two men guide their behavior; depends, that is, on the ideas about right and wrong which the men accept and the kind of behavior they believe is expected of them.

It is further noteworthy that the idea of instability and crime issuing specifically from the dislocations of World War II has not been validated by statistics. British researcher Leslie T. Wilkins, studying crime figures in relation to the war, remarks: "It has long been the opinion of many social workers and sociologists that evacuation and other disturbance of the lives of young children during the 1939–45 war would have a lasting effect upon the behavior of these children. So far as is known, this has not been confirmed statistically . . . Any theories regarding the lasting effects of war-time must, it seems, accommodate the fact that children *born* during the 1939-45 war have not as yet shown any tendency toward excess criminality [compared to the years immediately preceding]."[11]

Wilkins' figures suggest that children passing through the war at age five turned out to be more crime-prone than the average; the possible significance of this datum is obscured, however, by the fact that British youth experienced a vast jump in criminal behavior in the mid-1950s, a development Wilkins finds inexplicable in terms of the war.

The internal confusions in the environmentalist argument, together with the consistently superior moral performance of people with strong religious beliefs, suggest we should do well to look elsewhere for answers to our difficulty. They suggest, in fact, that we might reasonably look to the one source of distress which the environmentalists ignore: The power of ideas themselves.

On the environmentalists' own reading, the common denominator of all the baleful changes which have overtaken us is their effect on traditional belief. All these theories assume that an alteration of conditions will make belief change, and thus bring about a change in behavior. They therefore acknowledge, indirectly, the controlling influence of ideas on action. They simply dismiss the possibility that the particular ideas under discussion might be imparted to the nation for ideological rather than material reasons.

Let us, then, set up an alternative hypothesis. Our proposition is that, *when people are taught to think like criminals, it is reasonable to suppose that sooner or later they will start acting like criminals.* Or, to put the matter more specifically: When a group of influential members of society sets out to tear down standards of morality, preach that there is no objective measure of right and wrong, that religion is mumbo-jumbo and that deviant behavior should be looked upon with toleration, it is reasonable to suppose immorality, irreligion and deviant behavior will become increasingly popular.

Our hypothesis may seem reasonable but irrelevant. Perhaps such an effort would produce the harmful results alluded to—but what evidence is there to believe such a thing has been attempted? The answer is that there is a good deal of evidence indeed—showing that men of influence, fully aware of what they are doing, have taken it as their explicit mission to break down codes of value, and have, on the whole, done the job remarkably well.

To demonstrate this, one need only examine the ideas current among the people charged with instructing American youth in our colleges and universities. The attitude prevalent in these circles is profoundly hostile to traditional value. Thus, according to a study sponsored by an educational foundation and endorsed by a committee of nine college professors, the *purpose* of a college education is to "break or alter the mold of value." The study laments that college courses do not do more to achieve this objective, but makes it clear this is what the educators are after.[12] The same view is expressed by Prof. Metzger, who says "the conserving function of the college no longer [looms] so large," and by the late Carl Becker, who said the function of a modern education is "to undermine rather than to stabilize custom and social authority." Former President Charles Seymour of Yale, himself a determined Christian, put it that "an important aspect of the university function is to train its students in the habit of skepticism."[13]

The stated justification for this view is that it stretches the mind, making the college student aware of intellectual alternatives. This is as it may be. The obvious point is that to pursue such a relentless effort to *break down value*, in view of the value crisis confronting American society, is to crusade for catastrophe. At a time when the decline of value is issuing in crime and social agony, we are actually seeking to educate our young people to disbelieve in traditional conceptions of right and wrong.

Principal casualty of this new sophistication has been, inevitably, religious belief. Religion is typically described, in academic circles, as primitive superstition or utilitarian mythology very well in its place but not to be taken seriously otherwise. We have already noted the anti-religious, relativist currents running deep in Western society—the literary fads, the "new morality," the penetration of relativist notions into the sepulcher of religion itself. These influences are strongly reinforced by the formal instruction given American young people, and in large part derive from that instruction in the first place.

A great many academicians agree with the conclusion of John Dewey that "faith in the divine author and authority in which Western civilization confided, inherited ideas of the soul and its destiny, of fixed revelation . . . have been made impossible for the cultivated mind of the Western world."[14] As Prof. John Childs of Teachers College, Columbia, remarks, modern scholars have "reached the conclusion that religion itself is an historical affair," relative to time and place. In the intellectual climate suggested by that opinion, the claims of Judaeo-Christian revelation are necessarily disparaged. The religion of the West is seen as simply another cultural manifestation, as one time perhaps relevant to the needs of our society, but no more "true" in the abstract than voo-doo or Vedanta. What is true for us is not true for anybody else, and in that case—so the natural inference runs —is not really true for us either.[15]

In a review of anthropology textbooks, Margaret Mead summarizes the all-too-characteristic treatment of religion in modern education. ". . . the student of anthropology is confronted with a mass of detailed, often bizarre, rich description of religious behavior, which differs strikingly from anything which he has experienced in his own culture," she says. This strange perspective "is very likely to result in an alienation of the students' interest in religion as a subject for study, an alienation which is of course intensified by the secularization of psychology and sociology."[16]

That Miss Mead's references to psychology and sociology are justified is suggested by the observations of professors Gordon W. Allport and Kenneth W. Sutherland, who have undertaken reviews of textbooks used widely in these fields. Allport's summary of the treatment accorded religion in psychology texts corresponds closely to Miss Mead's observations in the field of anthropology. In one textbook, he notes, the subject of religion is handled against a backdrop of alien customs and eccentricities. He concludes that the author's "picture of religious activity is one of quaintness, superstition, escapism, and, on the whole, of prescientific illusion."

Summing up the total impact of the curriculum and associated influences of the typical university education on the mind of the student, Professor Merrimon Cuninggum observes: ". . . when we broaden our consideration to include all institutional interests and all aspects of college life, then we must perforce admit that the tone of higher education is secular and the total impact upon the majority of students is, if not anti-, at least non-religious."* [17]

---

* Ignace Lepp, who has studied the modulations of unbelief quite closely, sums up the problem as follows: "Contemporary atheism . . . is no longer a phenomenon of a few individuals protesting against the taboos of society . . . It is the common lot of at least a considerable portion, if not of the majority, of our contemporaries and is well on its way to becoming the common norm of society. The intellectuals were the first to break with traditional faith; the bourgeois followed them; then came the masses . . ." (*Atheism in Our Time*, Macmillan, 1964; p.11.)

Concerning the personal attitudes of the professoriate, Prof. Lipset refers to a study indicating the majority of scientists and social scientists listed in *American Men of Science* in two test years "did not believe in God or immortality," and adds that "studies of American religious behavior suggest that these professors and scientists were far more irreligious than the general population." Further inquiry, Lipset concludes, "confirmed the fact that scientists and various professorial groups are much less religious than businessmen, bankers, business people, and lawyers, and also indicated that writers eminent enough to be listed in *Who's Who*, and presumably not as affected by the conflict between science and religion as those in the natural and social sciences, held irreligious views."[18]

That this development goes hand-in-hand with profession of a relativist and "permissive" outlook is confirmed by Paul Lazarsfeld and Wagner Thielens in *The Academic Mind*. The authors discovered the vast majority of social scientists on the college campus are "people who critically scrutinize institutions like religion and the family" and are "hospitable to unorthodox possibilities." In an explanatory paragraph, Lazarsfeld and Thielens say: "The social scientist faces an additional situation deriving from the nature of his work, which is likely to strengthen a basically permissive attitude," and is therefore able "to visualize a state of human affairs radically different from that of today."[19]

These findings document what will be readily attested by anyone familiar with the prevailing opinion on American college campuses. The intensity with which the relativist creed is professed varies, of course, from place to place. But the notion that one point of view on moral questions is in general about as good as another has by now become standard doctrine in the academy, only slightly chastened by time and consequence. The ancient

---

Why "intellectuals" hold such views is a complicated matter which cannot be explored adequately without a full-scale analysis of Western thought over the past century and more. In brief, however, it seems apparent that the anti-religious bias of the intellectuals is at least in part an occupational hazard. The man of reason often finds religion "unreasonable," opposed to scientific or rationalist orthodoxy. It supposes a supernatural order superior to human intelligence, and it imposes limits upon the powers intelligence can arrogate to itself. Utopians, scientific planners, and those who hope to reconstruct humanity through the instruments of secular power do not find the chastening dictates of religion congenial.

house gods having been pulled down, we are confronted by a democracy of assumptions in which right and wrong, truth and falsehood, are levelled into a common mediocrity.

Such are the views of the men entrusted with instructing American young people. What have been the results? On the whole, it would appear that the professors who feel their value-breaking efforts have been wasted are far too modest.

In a May, 1965 survey of college students on the question of whether their campus experience had intensified or weakened their religious faith, *Newsweek* concluded: "Next to his high-school class ring, the first thing today's impressionable college freshman learns he can do without is his old ideas about God. For most students, it is less a sudden traumatic loss of faith than a gradual fade-out of their adolescent concept of deity . . . the question of God is more likely to seem *passé* than problematic . . . *Almost 40 per cent of the students said that their experience in college had made them question their faith. Almost twice as many seniors as freshmen said college had raised questions about their faith.*"[20] (Italics added.)

A survey taken at a dozen major colleges by the Educational Reviewer in 1963 similarly reflected a downward trend at all the institutions save one (the Catholic school, Marquette) in religious conviction, in each case setting in during secondary school and college. Other surveys confirm this and show a marked deterioration in standards of right and wrong to accompany it. Describing today's characteristic student as a "professionalist" interested in attaining an austere technical competence, Yale psychologist Keniston says: "Although most students believe at least nominally in God, and some attend church, religion plays no important role in the professionalists' attempt to 'find out what really matters.' Exposed from early childhood by schools and mass media to the vast variety of human conviction, such students are likely to be ethical relativists . . . [They] wish they could find some principled purpose, but accept the fact that, in modern American society, such purposes are hard to come by."[21]

A like verdict emerges from a book called *The Unsilent Generation*, consisting of essays by eleven Princeton University students. The common theme of these essays is that the students had lost whatever religious faith they had when they got to Princeton, had at best a tenuous hold on morality, and that both those things were in large part owing to the effect of their education.

One student described the goal of the university as "the realization that there are many different viewpoints and many different approaches to human problems, and that no set of values or ideas need be the only 'true' one." This student, who refers to himself and his colleagues as "superbly educated," concludes by saying that "there cannot, at least as I see it, be any absolute or unchanging moral law."

Other quotations from other contributors include: "I figure I can be indifferent to an indifferent God . . . it is this world, not the next one, that I'm concerned with." "I seldom think of God, and only pray when I am exceptionally troubled. Even when I pray, I don't consider myself to be asking for help or advice. I simply find I derive a measure of comfort and self-assurance." Another says that "religion plays almost no part at all" in his outlook on life. Still another says he is indifferent to religion, except for the Catholic Church, "which I regard with disgust." Others opine that God "must be a pretty nice guy" and that "the objective existence of God has been made irrelevant by the industrial revolution."* [22]

Of similar tendency is the following statement, written by a Harvard University student in the spring of 1967: "In the years of adolescence, our understanding of Communism has been hindered by nationalistic cliches; Communism is to be feared (the Red scare), yet I would be surprised if 10 per cent of the population of the United States is aware that the ultimate values and goals of democracy and Communism are the same. Communism is not the answer, but neither is pure democracy . . . [At Harvard and in American college life generally] we see that there are alternatives to the absolute maxims that we accepted as children. Many choose to doubt God. We see that democracy is not

---

* Among the small minority of the contributors who had retained a semblance of religious belief, one says "Princeton has been a terribly corroding experience," and another adds: "At Princeton, the willing initiate is taught that self-interest and disloyalty are valuable qualities, and he soon becomes proficient at varying his beliefs and purported commitments to suit the social situation at hand."

the knight in shining armor and that the American government is confronted with a multitude of problems. The blinders of grade school and college no longer exist . . ."[23]

The young man who wrote this passage is of the opinion that Harvard has taught him to see "both sides" of the question. The resemblance of his statement to Newsweek's findings, the Princeton essays, the Yale analysis, suggests he is in fact part of a rather substantial conformity which has been trained to disparage religious belief and traditional values as a species of benighted ignorance.

A less subjective confirmation of the impact of relativist teaching emerges from a study comparing the moral attitudes of freshmen with the parallel attitudes of seniors at Vassar College. "The senior is not so critical as the freshman," the survey concludes, "of persons who become intoxicated, who don't vote, who have intercourse before marriage, are lawbreakers, or don't take things seriously enough. She tends not to set arbitrary standards of right and wrong conduct, and judge others by them . . ." Nor, as noted in Chapter II, to judge herself by them, since she displays far more willingness than the freshman to break rules, countenance civil disobedience, betray her country rather than her best friend, lie, steal, engage in premarital relations, have an abortion, or sneak into a movie.

Studies at Antioch, Colgate, and Michigan State, comparing freshman and senior ideas, yielded the same result. In each case the trend was heavily toward "permissiveness" and relativism—and away from belief in religious values or fixed moral ideas of any sort. As author Philip Jacob concludes, the net impact of an American college education today is to produce a whole echelon of young people who tend to adopt a "liberal attitude" in which they refuse to "let fixed moral standards or ingrained prejudice govern their relations with other people."[24]

The GAP similarly finds, in its conspectus of student attitudes, that youthful views on sexual behavior have changed enormously in recent years, in part because young people "find ample evidence not only that the adult world lacks consensus on acceptable standards of sexual behavior but that the underlying values of human relationships are murky as well." The study adds that "threats of social ostracism and religious rejection do not mean as much as they once did" as controls on adolescent impulse.[25]

These findings are endorsed by the Newsweek survey quoted above. It tells us that: "A high degree of tolerance pervades campus attitudes toward morality—a mixture of inhibition, realism, cynicism, and jittery concern. Two-thirds of the boys and girls polled believe that prevailing campus standards encourage promiscuity . . . *and more than four out of five said that their experiences in college had made them take a more tolerant attitude toward those who defy traditional morality.* Fifty-eight per cent of the girls said they feel current attitudes make it harder for them to say 'no.' Presumably, the same permissive climate encourages the boys to ask the question more often. And 37 per cent of both the boys and girls approve the prescription of oral contraceptives in student health centers, a practice already followed at the University of Chicago."[26]

In like fashion, as we have already observed, cheating on the campus has been increasing markedly. Discussing the failure of "honor systems," Prof. Ralph Raimi writes in Harper's that "far from being horrified at the sight of a cheating student, the average student would be horrified at the suggestion that he reprimand or report such cheating when he sees it . . ." A student at William and Mary, in a letter to the Richmond Times-Dispatch, confirmed this assessment. "Although few of the students are engaged in cheating," he said, "I think it would be a fair estimate, by the use of the student's views and the campus situation, to say that 75 per cent of the student body would not report a friend for violating the honor code."[27]

These conclusions about classroom cheating apply, as the Vassar results suggest, to the notion of cheating in general—that is, to the idea of fulfilling one's desires through some kind of dishonesty. How broad the new "tolerance" on this subject has become was indicated by student reaction to the famous Charles Van Doren case of the 1950s. In that episode, students at Queens College were asked what they thought of Van Doren's performance in pretending to be a quiz-show genius while being prepped on the answers—as close an analogue to classroom cribbing as one is likely to find in the grown-up world. The students responded overwhelmingly in Van Doren's favor, a flat majority considering him to be a "tragic hero."

Also indicative is the growth of the previously mentioned "drug culture" at leading American universities. Jeremy Larner comments that "while there are no significant statistics—any more than there are on virginity, and for the same reasons—drug-taking is becoming increasingly popular on American campuses. A variety of drugs can now be easily obtained at any college which draws its students from metropolitan areas—which means that the problem is most acute at the biggest and best universities and at some of the most prestigious small colleges. Marijuana is generally the drug of choice: a young man from an Eastern college claims, 'I have yet to see a college party anywhere in the last two years where at least one-third of the kids have not been turned on.' "[28]

Finally, in our brief mention of the "new left," we have seen what is perhaps the premier instance of collegiate lawlessness in response to permissive teaching. Although there are many aspects of this movement which deserve comment, its most significant feature is the manner in which it makes explicit certain tendencies latent in the common run of academic thought. According to its own spokesmen and sympathetic observers, the "new left" is an almost perfect expression of philosophical nihilism. Its advocates proudly assert the movement has no clear-cut philosophical convictions, no firm ideas about things, no program beyond the release of impulse. They are not interested in thinking, they say, they are interested in *acting*.

A leader of the radical group Students for a Democratic Society says, for example, "We prefer action to worthless sectarian debate." Similarly, Phillip Abbott Luce, a former leader of the Communoid Progressive Labor Party, has observed: ". . . I have never been particularly interested in theoretical politics and the fine points of ideology . . . I feel that instead of becoming a part of the system—and inevitably becoming an accomplice in its crimes—a man should take direct action on his own."[29]

A year after he made this statement, Luce brought out a book in which he revealed that his own position had changed perceptibly, but his observations still stressed the young radicals' lack of philosophic conviction. "They are more romantic than political," he wrote, "and they cover up their ideological lag with excessive emotion . . . the SDS represents the height of New Left unconcern for theory and is apparently too involved in its activities to realize this . . . SDS is more preoccupied with action than with theory, as is so much of the New Left . . ."* [30]

The yen for "action" and the absence of ideas are, obviously, related; if one has no clearly defined philosophy and yet must repose his faith in something, he is likely to repose it in cultist emotion—some cry of the heart or spasm of the reflexes. And certainly the mixture of nihilism and activism leads on, by an irrational logic, to some form of lawlessness; if one is committed merely to the rightness of "acting" in obedience to impulse while dismissing all questions of theoretical restraint, it follows that representatives of authority seeking to check the impulse should be defied.

What is this revolution against values if not an expression of the preachments which dominate the academy? A determination to disbelieve in objective truth, a one-eyed skepticism which delights in challenging religion and traditional morality while ignoring the sins and omissions of agnosticism and non-commitment—these are the staple diet of a whole generation of American undergraduates. Non-belief, on major college campuses today, is all too often an article of faith. Given the evidence that loss of religious conviction and erosion of value contribute strongly to deviant behavior, is it any wonder that a segment of the college population should translate this nihilism into lawless action?

Most students subjected to relativist notions do not of course go on to commit overt violations of the law. But they do go on to

---

* Irving Kristol comments in *The Atlantic* that the student radicals are "in the historically unique position of not being able to demand a single piece of legislation from their government—their 'platform' is literally without one legislative plank." Concerning student outbreaks at the University of California, Kristol remarks: "Even in the single area where one would most expect specific and tangible proposals of reform, the organization of the multiversity, these have not made their appearance. For an entire year the students of the University of California at Berkeley have given dramatic evidence of dissatisfaction with their university experience—and does anyone know specifically what they would like, by way of improvement? The university officials certainly don't know, nor do the regents, nor do the faculty."

become influential members of society—lawmakers, judges, clergymen, civic leaders, social workers, teachers, parents. In those capacities, they take with them their conception of impulse-
release and tolerance imbibed when they were students; they set
the intellectual and moral pattern for the society as a whole.
They are the models for less privileged members of society, for
their own children in suburbia. The exhilarating philosophy
urged by professors in the classroom becomes, in them, the "new
morality." What it then becomes in society at large we may discover in the FBI statistics.

In a prophetic novel, *The Brothers Karamazov*, Fyodor Dostoevsky spells out an appropriate parable. Among the book's
many characters are a fiery intellectual, Ivan, and his presump-
tively dim-witted half-brother, Smerdyakov. Ivan preaches that
there is no God, no truth, no right and wrong, and that everything is relative. Being an intellectual, he doesn't particularly do
anything about these ideas; he simply preaches them. Smerdyakov, however, is not an intellectual. He listens to Ivan's preachments, accepts them, and acts on them. He murders their father.
When the horrified Ivan confronts him, Smerdyakov explains:
"I was only your instrument, your faithful servant . . . You
said, 'everything was lawful' . . . For if there's no everlasting
God, there's no such thing as virtue."[31] So why not kill?*

When value is annihilated and the standards of belief pulled
down, why should it surprise us if people begin acting as if there
were no such thing as right conduct? When we are instructed by
highest authority that everything is relative, why shouldn't we
expect augmented crime and a breakdown of morality? What,
indeed, is "crime"? What is "morality"? And why should anybody worry about its breaking down?

---

* It is noteworthy that William Hamilton, one of the "God is Dead" theologians, takes Ivan as one of his culture heroes.

SIX

Permissives and Progressives

If there is one subject on which all students of crime seem to be agreed, it is the crucial importance of the family. A strong family relationship, according to the available evidence, is one of the best defenses against the outbreak of youthful criminality. A weak or otherwise deficient family relationship is the cause most frequently discovered at the root of delinquency and juvenile disorder.

As usually conceived, the breakdown in family relationship occurs in a slum background where the father has packed up and left, or is habitually drunk, or in jail. Present theory generally treats the "broken home" as a subdivision of "poverty." Cure slums and material deprivation, we are told, and we will cure deficiencies in the family relationship. The Crime Commission states the case directly when it says: "Every effort must be made to strengthen the family, now often shattered by the grinding pressures of urban slums."[1] No other source of family breakdown is indicated.

According to the evidence we have reviewed in the matter of "poverty," and according to a considerable body of data on the present condition of the American family, this view of the matter misses the point. Not all families in slum backgrounds are broken; indeed, "ghetto" families with strong religious and cultural ties are generally a good deal more successful than the more affluent. Nor do all families outside the slums perform even the minimal functions they are supposed to perform.

It is a fact, for example, that juvenile delinquency in the suburbs is growing even faster than juvenile delinquency in the ghettos. The FBI tells us that "suburban crime has [the] sharpest trend, up 17 per cent . . . Young people comprised 54 per cent of the total arrests for the serious crimes in the suburban communities."[2] Which suggests that suburban homes must, in their own way, be quite as "broken" as those in the slums, and that mere libations of money will not correct things. As Harrison Salisbury puts it: "Behind an apparent facade of normality many a suburban home conceals just as broken a home as the Red Hook family from which the father has long since vanished."[3]

The purpose of the family, construed as a social institution, is to mould the new member of society to an understanding of social value. It is the chief instrument of cultural and ethical assimilation. If this function is not performed, for whatever reason, then the family situation is to all intents and purposes "broken"—the family unit is no longer working as, from society's point of view, it is supposed to.

It becomes apparent that a family can be "broken" quite easily if parents abandon their role as preceptors of value to their children. And evidence that precisely this development has occurred, in slums and suburbs alike, is overwhelming. Every available survey shows that parents in all income brackets are letting their children do as they wish, with a minimum of supervision and control, and that too many young people are not being inculcated by their families with the necessary standards to guide their behavior in the outside world.

Although adhering to the notion that "broken homes" are principally a result of poverty, the Crime Commission acknowledges that delinquency is increasing among the well-to-do (it passes this off, in a single paragraph, as an insoluble dilemma) and tacitly concedes that the central feature of family breakdown is characterological rather than material. The Commission introduces as an exhibit of parental failure in the slums the following statement from the mother of a delinquent youth:

. . . we'd try to keep him from something he really wanted to do. But he usually goes out anyway . . . I told him he was wrong going against his parents like that, but he keeps sneaking out anyway . . . [Her husband] don't do much. I'm the one who gets upset. My husband, he'll say something to Mel and then he'll just relax and forget about it. (Husband and wife laugh together.) There's little we can do, you know. It's hard to talk to him 'cause he just go ahead and do what he wants anyway.[4]

Is that sort of parent-child relationship a function of poverty? Compare the behavior of a divorced father toward his daughter in a middle-class home as described by Jules Henry:

Lila's father does not seem to object to his cute daughter's efforts to swindle him; when he caught her, it was merely that he had won and she had lost . . . The Green home is pretty, and the children are comfortable. Mr. Green's giving Lila twenty dollars and not insisting on an accounting may be part of a total pattern of behavior in which, out of desire to make amends [for the absence of the mother] and the need to be loved himself, he lets things go. . . In doing this he gives Lila no moral fiber for though he enables her to compete, to spend money on clothes and grooming, he presents her also with provocations to cheat.[5]

There is no common *material* factor between these two episodes. In the first instance, both parents are present but there is an absence of money. In the second instance, one parent is missing but money is readily available. The common factor is *moral* —an absence of parentally sanctioned value. These homes are "broken," not because of poverty *per se*, because of divorce *per se*, but because the parent has resigned his function as the preceptor of value.

Cases involving such permissiveness by parents abound in juvenile court records. One ready to hand, chosen at random, is summarized in a rather routine news story out of Chicago. The story tells of two delinquents being sentenced by an irate judge as the mother of one of them stands by in tears. The judge remarks: "All the tears in the world won't wipe out this act of violent vicious destruction." The mother says she has given her son "too much," and the judge replies: "That's the whole trouble—too much for nothing, too much because they don't believe it, too much because they have no responsibility."[6]

Similar reflections on the fruits of permissiveness are provided by an article on the Caryl Chessman case by Elizabeth Hardwick. Miss Hardwick writes, in puzzled accents:

> Chessman's family, his early years, are not what one would expect. He was an only child who loved his parents and was loved by them . . . the affection on both sides was real and lasting. Chessman was spared the blight of neglect, abandonment, beatings, drunkenness . . . His parents urged him to 'do the right thing,' to return to reform school when he had escaped and so on, but he does not record any pressure more coercive than their mere hopes and pleas. They were feeble and trusting people. They believed whatever excuse their son gave for staying out all night and were always surprised and dismayed to learn he had been 'getting into trouble.'[7]

Miss Hardwick cannot understand how such parental complaisance could lead on to crime, since it does not fit the prototype in which tender loving care can avert repressions and therefore hostilities. The obvious conclusion is that the failure of the family does not always occur through harshness and brutality; it also occurs when parents are "feeble and trusting" and believe every excuse their children give them for their behavior and are perpetually amazed that their children "get into trouble."

Such parental indulgence is no doubt traceable to many influences. It is obviously related to the impulse-release doctrines of the "new morality" and to other general factors previously discussed. But there are also more particular influences at work—influences specifically aimed at forestalling the socialization function of the family. They are a result of the so-called "permissive" movement in raising and educating children.

While conscious adherence to permissive doctrines has waned in recent years, there is reason to believe the chief precepts of permissiveness have got themselves woven into the national psyche, and plenty of evidence that permissive practice continues in many American homes.

The point of permissive child-rearing doctrines, however modified, is to let the child do as he wishes. The theory holds that the child is basically "good," and that what is necessary is to prevent him from becoming corrupted by external pressures. The desired objective is the flowering of impulse, the absence of baffling constraint, a chance to "express" the promptings of one's inner nature. Since human instincts are not automatically oriented toward law-abiding behavior, and since the shattering of value systems by unbridled impulse is the root of crime, the results have been predictably grim.

"Today's parents themselves are the products of somewhat permissive parents of the time before the second World War," the Gluecks note. "There was much support for the philosophy of child rearing which said that, since a child is 'creative,' it should be permitted to experiment more or less at will, and so on." As a result young people generally receive plentiful helpings of the material things in life without having to work for them. "Today the tendency is to hand everything on a platter to the adolescent. Very little effort is required on his part, so he really becomes bored with life, in a sense . . ."[8]

The Gluecks conclude that:

> Life requires a certain amount of discipline. You need it in the classroom, you need it in the home, you need it in society at large. After all, the Ten Commandments impose a discipline. Unless general restraints are built into the character of children, you can arrive eventually at social chaos . . . Not only parents but others are uncertain in many cases as to what is morally right or wrong, and that makes discipline harder to enforce . . . [9]

Marguerite and Willard Beecher offer similar observations. "A whole generation or more of parents," they write, "have been led to believe that there is something wrong or evil about indoctrination and the exercise of any authority over children. The folly of this campaign now greets us in newspaper headlines and screeches at us from the airwaves. We are now confronted with a Pandora's box of evils—evils much worse than the one parents were supposed to be avoiding. Where is it to end:—the rising incidence of illiteracy, the school failures, the juvenile vandalism, sex orgies, dope addiction? What shall we do to prevent an increase in this army of children in search of limits?"[10]

It is precisely the object of permissiveness to do away with limits, to let the child do whatever his impulse tells him. The result is therefore to invert the normal function of the family relationship and to short-circuit the principal agency of "socialization." The child, trailing clouds of glorious impulse, sets the pace and presumes to instruct. It is the adult who must orient his behavior to the norms of conduct demanded by the child. Permissiveness thus gives intellectual sanction to the upside-down value system of the "new morality" and the adolescent troubadours who celebrate the Golden Age of Puberty.

It also gives sanction to the mental and emotional attitude characteristic of the most violent delinquents. Redl and Wineman, whose experience in superintending a treatment home for pre-adolescent delinquent boys forms the basis for two instructive books on the subject of youthful aggression, repeatedly emphasize the need for limits upon impulse to forestall violence. Stressing the requirements of affection and reasonable freedom in the rehabilitation of wayward youngsters, the authors nevertheless come down hard on the calamitous effects of permissiveness. The child, they note, expects the adult to perform a "protective" and limiting role, defining the boundaries of acceptable behavior. If this role is not performed, the child is lost, and his impulses carry him beyond the bounds of reason. They comment: "It is easy to see how this 'protective role' of adults renders highly questionable some of the sentimentally generalized theories of total permissiveness. It is our conviction, and this conviction has been solidified during all of our experiences, that children either do not perceive total permissiveness as an affection symbol or that, as far as they do, an affection symbol of that sort constitutes only half the basis which they need for security in a treatment home."[11]

These conclusions are roundly seconded by law enforcement officers who have to deal with permissively untrained youngsters. A prosecuting attorney scores the "general feeling that there's an easy solution—if a person gets in trouble, he's sick, he needs treatment. They do it in nursery schools these days. 'Don't stunt the child's personality.' When he gets older and gets in more serious trouble, they say 'Let's not be hasty . . .' These kids know this. They trade on it. Everybody wants to rush in and salvage the wrongdoer."[12]

Police official Harry Taylor of New York is of a like opinion. "In thousands upon thousands of instances [of delinquency] the parents are at fault," he says. "There is a worsening breakdown of the family unit. It is in the home that respect for authority must first take shape . . . In the slum areas, there are too many broken homes, too many working mothers, too many kids running loose on the streets . . . But the crime crisis doesn't affect just the slum areas. In the suburbs you have a growing crime rate, too. In the homes of the well-to-do there seems to be, increasingly, a lack of parental supervision. There's a chain reaction. Disrespect for parents results in disrespect for policemen and the law generally."[13]

Children brought up on impulse release, accustomed to compliance with their every whim, are ill-equipped to live in harmony with society and its laws. Permissiveness, says Richard LaPiere, "teaches the child to want, need, expect, *etc*. . . . prompt and willing conformity by others to his own whims and fancies. No society, not even our own, is prepared to cater to the infinitely varied and contradictory wants of adults brought up in the permissive mode. What is even more important, no society, including our own, can maintain a very high proportion of members who have been inducted into the view that they are inherently frail and must therefore be given all and required to give nothing in return."[14]

Permissiveness in the home has met its counterpart, and then some, in the philosophy of "progressive education."

The net purpose of "progressivism," as Richard Hofstadter has put it, is "a crusade to exalt the academically uninterested or ungifted child into a kind of culture hero."[15] In keeping with prevalent academic authority, progressivism seeks to level out standards and erase distinctions, to exempt the pupil from the stultifying rigors of discipline. It is well-suited to a social-political style which rejects the notion of personal responsibility and transfers blame for wayward behavior from individual to environment.

Exactly how many schools have acceded to "progressive" doctrine is difficult to calculate; because of the merciful autonomy of local schools, the Dewey-eyed theoreticians made only partial headway in some areas and in others none at all. In recent years, moreover, progressivism has suffered the same fall from intellectual grace that has afflicted permissive child rearing. "Progressive" ideas have nonetheless permeated the "educationist" bureaucracy in the United States, the National Education Association, the teachers' colleges, and the large metropolitan school systems of our major states. Like "everything for baby," the aftereffects of "life adjustment" linger on and work important results even when the formal underpinning in the realm of doctrine has been swept away.

Under "progressive" theory, the student is not punished if he does something wrong; quite obviously, his misbehavior is the result of some flaw of circumstance or crippling of the psyche; he must be "counseled." And if he cannot do his work and obtain a passing grade, he must be passed anyway. In the interest of life adjustment the child who is the product of a "permissive" home may thus be subjected to an equally "permissive" school.

How all this works out in practice has been recounted by disillusioned teachers who have been through the "progressive" mill, and count themselves fortunate to escape with their lives. Miss Joan Dunn, a former teacher in the New York public schools, tells of the tough young ladies over whose activities she was asked to preside. "A group of them congregates in the cafeteria during one of the regular periods," she says, "and under cover of the noise and confusion seize upon some nice little girl, force her into the washroom, and take her lunch money. If she refuses, they beat her up. Very few refuse; they know it is wiser to give up the money."[16]

To pupils like these, Miss Dunn says, "school is a clubhouse, a place of amusement, a convenient place for getting cheap lunches, meeting friends, and settling grudges. If nothing else happens to engage their interest, they can always smash a few windows so that their trip will not have been in vain."[17]

The author traces these agonies to various aspects of "progressivism," group therapy, absence of disciplinary guidelines, child worship. The net result, she says, is an environment in which "ignorance is accepted as the norm," children are encouraged in delusions of "something for nothing," and respect for authority is replaced with a species of contempt.[18]

Miss Dunn concludes that "some schools today are in such desperate shape that they can take a good child and corrupt him. The school today can serve to infect the family"—as with the children of deeply religious immigrant parents. Such children learn the "new ways" in school "from teachers whose mission in life seems to be destruction of all the old gods, from teachers who rattle on endlessly about the rights of youth . . . who cheerfully resign all their prerogatives as elders and teachers and encourage children to run wild."[19]

Similar testimony comes from Robert Kendall, who taught in the public schools of Los Angeles. Kendall provides a graphic and dismaying chronicle of daily chaos, with pupils fighting, spitting on the floor, hurling threats and obscenities. And an even more dismaying picture of flat refusal by school authorities to back necessary disciplinary measures or to support those teachers who attempted to mete them out. The losers, Kendall asserts, are the good or aspiring pupils who want to get something worthwhile out of the school, and the teacher who wants to impart knowledge and the ability to think rather than to drift aimlessly with the system.

Modernist views on education contribute to delinquency in more subtle ways as well. A common element in many delinquency cases is the fact that the youngster has dropped out of school. If we could find a way to correct the dropout problem, we would be a long way down the road toward solving the delinquency problem. But, it develops, modern educational trends have accentuated this difficulty rather than correcting it.

Some dropouts are youngsters who, at 15 or 16, might be gainfully employed but who have limited aptitudes for classroom work. Modern compulsory education holds them in school doing things that don't interest them and keeps them idle when they could be working or at least learning job skills in a vocational training class. These young people quit school at the first opportunity, ill-prepared for productive citizenship.

In a second category, some students with intellectual potential drop out because they simply are not motivated; the vapid subject matter and method of presentation do not engage their interest. They chafe under the makework of the classroom and become increasingly drawn to mischief outside it.

In yet a third category, a large percentage of dropouts are incapable of absorbing classroom material because, in their progress through school, they simply have not learned to read. Unable to learn, they were nevertheless passed along from one grade to the next under the prevailing "age and poundage" theory of achievement.

These tendencies have become intertwined with still another influence: The increasing secularization of the schools. Permissiveness in home and classroom confronts, of course, one great obstacle: the primal influence of religious sentiment. Habits of reverence and obedience to a higher moral authority act as powerful inhibitors to lawless or immoral action. Even at the best of times, it goes without saying, these sentiments are imperfectly observed. But people accustomed to reverence for Holy symbols are subjected to a powerful interior restraint. The leaching away of such reverence is an obvious corollary to the "new morality" and to true modernity in education. Moral breakdown in the colleges has been accompanied by a sustained effort to achieve secularization of American thought, and to pull down ancient habits of religious veneration, in the elementary schools.

Under current doctrine, mention of the Deity, religious teaching, or the simplest statement of gratitude to powers higher than the earthly state are banned from American classrooms. Pupils are no longer allowed to say Grace, to recite the Lord's Prayer, to give thanks to the Supreme Being.*

---

* These prohibitions are justified on "constitutional" grounds, on the argument that all mixtures of "church and state" are ruled out by the First Amendment to the Constitution. Although this is not the time to go into that particular argument, it seems clear this "constitutional" plea is essentially beside the point— since the opponents of classroom prayer vehemently object to a constitutional amendment on the subject, which would itself be the final determinant of constitutionality.

Thus, under modern theories of education, the child is compelled to spend the intellectually active hours of his formative years in state schools, where he is subjected to a regimen which does not impart basic intellectual skills, is exempt from ordinary discipline, all too often learns to disrespect authority, finds achievement and excellence frequently proscribed, and is insulated from the symbols and substance of religious sentiment. Having subjected him to this, we wonder how it is he becomes a juvenile delinquent.

Finally, to make matters official, the same outlook is carried over into the law itself. In almost all jurisdictions, a youthful offender—no matter how drastic his crime—is considered a "juvenile" and is treated with lenient concern. The idea is that these young people are salvageable and should be rehabilitated rather than punished, a reasonable theory which law-enforcement officers charge has been carried far beyond reason. Because many young hoodlums realize that as "juveniles" they will receive conciliatory treatment, they lose all restraint. Former Washington, D.C., Police Chief Robert V. Murray says:

> The young criminals who commit these serious crimes on the street—a great many are juveniles, but they're as big as any man in this room. They knock down people on the street and it is necessary to hospitalize them.
>
> They are very defiant and arrogant, particularly if they've had any court experience at all.
>
> We've had cases many times where we've had maybe two, three or four in a group who have committed robberies on the street—purse snatchings and what we call yoking of men, particularly elderly men. We would send the cases to court and the next thing you know, we'd pick the same juveniles up. Their first cases hadn't been called yet.[20]

The failure of this approach is certified by the Crime Commission, which notes that the "optimistic assumptions" of the juvenile justice system simply have not proved out. The report tells us that juvenile courts,

> reflecting the philosophy that erring children should be protected and rehabilitated rather than subjected to the harshness of the criminal system . . . substitute procedural informality for the ad-

versary system, emphasize investigation of the juvenile's background in deciding dispositions, rely heavily on the social sciences for both diagnosis and treatment, and are committed to rehabilitation of the juvenile as the predominant goal of the entire system.

Studies conducted by the Commission, legislative inquiries in various states, and reports by informed observers compel the conclusion that the great hopes originally held for the juvenile court have not been fulfilled. It has not succeeded significantly in rehabilitating delinquent youth, in reducing or even stemming the tide of delinquency, or in bringing justice and compasssion to the child offender.[21]

FBI chief Hoover similarly observes that realism toward juvenile offenders has given away too often to false sentiment. "Under the pretext of rehabilitation," he says, "far too many young thugs have been released prematurely to continue preying upon society. Pampering, overprotection, fawning indulgence—these set a pattern of weakness which breeds contempt for the law and for those charged with the administration of justice . . . We mollycoddle young criminals and release unreformed hoodlums to prey anew on society."[22]

The net impact upon young people of permissiveness in the home, the school, and the courtroom should be apparent. As Professor Becker notes, the process of joining society is "a series of progressively increasing commitments to conventional norms and institutions. The 'normal' person, when he discovers a deviant impulse in himself, is able to check that impulse by thinking of the manifold consequences acting on it would produce for him."[23] Under the ministrations of permissives and progressives, this series of commitments is systematically precluded; the child is both encouraged to act on impulse and relieved of the manifold consequences. The result is vastly to increase the level of deviant behavior.

SEVEN

The Unethical Ethic

In one of his several critiques of American education, Paul Goodman remarks that the purpose of the school is to undo the bad effects of the home, and that the purpose of life in general is to undo the bad effects of the school. The evidence suggests, however, that the correction and adjustment implied by that sardonic formula don't always come about. In particular, the adolescent cry for "rights" without responsibilities, the shortening of the time perspective, the hunger for immediate comforts without pain or labor, are becoming notable features of adult society as well. These things are apparent in a number of ways, but are crystallized most directly in the modern-day phenomenon known as the welfare state.

The virtues or demerits of welfarism in general do not lie within the province of these pages. But its points of impact upon the present discussion are numerous. Foremost among these is a deadening effect on the ideas of personal responsibility, control of impulse, and respect for the rights and property of others. In these categories, the welfare state has very effectively transformed the standards of behavior once dominant in American life.

The old incentives were plain, if not always meticulously observed: Work hard, be responsible and honest in your behavior, labor to improve yourself, and things will go well. Break the law, steal something, injure someone, fritter your time away in idleness, and you are liable to public disgrace or certain legal penalties. Benjamin Franklin's homilies on thrift and enterprise, as Max Weber noted, are the classic statement of this position.

Lewis Yablonsky, in his study of gang behavior, suggests the relevance of this "middle-class" value system to the problem of crime. He lists the values cherished by the middle class, which represent deterrents to crime, as follows: "(1) Ambition is a virtue, (2) an emphasis on the middle-class ethic of responsibility, (3) a high value on the cultivation of skills and tangible achievement, (4) postponement of immediate satisfactions and self-indulgence in the interest of achieving long-term goals, (5) rationality, in the sense of forethought, planning and budgeting of time, (6) the rational cultivation of manner, courtesy, and personality, (7) the need to control physical aggression and violence, (8) the need for wholesome recreation, and (9) respect for property and its proper care."[1]

Following Albert Cohen, Yablonsky attributes much juvenile crime to "lower-class" reaction against and rejection of these values. Cloward and Ohlin and other sociologists offer a similar argument. Interestingly enough, all of these value traits are today condemned by our nation's reigning ideology. They are, as we have noticed, consistently disparaged in the education imparted to young people, with a corresponding decline in personal values. And, of equal importance, they are being disparaged, by the welfare state, in everyday practice.

The welfare orthodoxy is an institutionalized effort to turn "middle-class values" inside-out—an elaborate attempt to remit penalties for nonperformance, to level out the differences between the productive and the nonproductive, to bestow comforts upon those who cannot or will not win them through effort. As welfarism spreads, the positive incentives in our society put a diminishing premium on effort and personal responsibility, while the negative ones no longer punish improvidence and sloth.

The Reverend H. H. Brookins of the First African Episcopal Church, chairman of the Los Angeles United Civil Rights Committee, says: "People get on welfare, but they don't get any help to get off. The result is that welfare trains whole families to live

on the handouts of relief. In fact, welfare often seems designed
to make sure that people stay chained to its handouts. They get
to thinking they're just a number, and since numbers can't have
morality, it's easy for a woman to say, 'I'll have another baby because it'll mean a little more money.' When welfare gives people
no sense of human dignity, no stake in society, you can't wonder
why it is itself a cause of social explosion."[2]

That the welfare system encourages idleness and immorality is
attested by Juanita Kidd Stout, the first Negro woman elected to
a judgeship in Pennsylvania. "The tragedy of relief," she says, "is
that it takes away from people the drive to work. When a person
is capable of earning only $45 a week, he may be all too willing
to accept $45 from public assistance for doing nothing. I have
the deepest sympathy for the good mother struggling to bring up
her children on a welfare grant, and for the father who wants but
cannot find work. But I deplore a system that regards the hand-
ing out of checks as its prime function, that subsidizes the lazy
and immoral home with the taxpayer's dollar."[3]

Judge Stout urges that welfare programs be revamped to make
receiving a check contingent upon some effort at self-improvement. "I know as well as any social worker," she says, "that the
deplorable homes in our urban centers are breeding and multi-
plying indolence, illegitimacy, disrespect for law. I know, too,
that the collection of relief checks is becoming one of the big
occupations in this country. I believe strongly that a moral atmosphere in the home should be a factor in determining eligi-
bility for welfare. An immoral home should not be subsidized."[4]

Examples of the sort mentioned by Judge Stout are apparent
in almost all big-city welfare systems. After investigating social
conditions in the Watts section of Los Angeles the McCone
Commission discovered it was far more profitable for some people
there to be unemployed than to work. "A job at a minimum
wage," the report noted, "pays about $220 per month, against
which there would be transportation, clothes and other expenses. When the average AFDC [Aid for Dependent Children]
family receives from $177 to $238 per month (depending on the
welfare program) the financial incentive to find work may be
either negative or nonexistent."[5]

A like conclusion was revealed in a *New York Times* article which discussed a case in which a man left a job he already had to go on the welfare rolls. He had given up an $85-a-week position as a tow truck driver because "after deductions, lunch money, and car fare, he was left with $60 a week in take-home pay. He is drawing $55 a week now in unemployment compensation."[6]

In California, welfare enthusiasts have refined the pleasures of not working into something of an art. *Los Angeles* magazine reports the high level of opulence achieved by certain smart operators through the workings of unemployment compensation: "Twelve unemployed young swingers from the new Sunset Strip put up $55 every week to live in luxury . . . how this one works: On unemployment insurance you collect $55 a week. Twelve times $55 is $660 a week, or nearly $2,800 a month. For $2,800 a month you can rent a six-bedroom home with sauna bath and swimming pool, and still have a bundle left over for eating and entertainment. By happy coincidence, Club 55 now includes six guys and six girls. When a job thrusts itself upon you, or when your unemployment insurance runs out, you have to leave the club. But there's a waiting list a year ahead."[7]

The ultimate variation on this theme is the "welfare union" concept, reported by Washington columnist Don Maclean. "An increasingly popular idea," Maclean wrote, "is that welfare recipients should band together into unions. These unions, which might collect dues directly from the poor's welfare payments, would see to it that they got increased benefits . . . Already several big cities have poverty unions and plans are afoot to place the headquarters of the National Association of Welfare Recipients right here in Washington . . ."[8]

Case histories of welfare bilking multiply in direct proportion to the increase in such programs. Under the war on poverty, for example, a married couple with a combined income of $11,000 a year secured a Federal loan of $25,000 to open a combined sandwich-shoe repair-export-import emporium in a "depressed area." The husband of the family actually left a paying job at the Ford Motor Company to take part in this welfare project. In another "poverty" example, it was found that an unemployed auto worker named Ozie Bulock was pulling down $160 a week, tax-free, through two different Federal programs. The most he had made while working was $104 a week. Bulock was receiving $72 a week from the Michigan Employment Security Commission as part of a Federally supported job-training program and another $190 once every two weeks from a "war on poverty" project. He acknowledged that he was making more this way than he expected to earn when he got back to work.

A similar story emerges from Harlan, Kentucky, an "Appalachian" area which has been a prime target of the war on poverty. Cloyd McDowell, president of the Harlan County Coal Operators Association, said good jobs paying $2 and $3 an hour were going unfilled because workers preferred the welfare programs offered by the government. Chief culprit, McDowell said, was something called the "Happy Pappy" project, which offered a training program and other assistance to unemployed fathers.

"If they [the government] come up with any more giveaway programs," McDowell commented, "we may have to close down. I know of some men with mining experience who are out cutting bushes if they are on their feet at all . . . the people in charge get the men on their rolls and then undertake to protect them from private employment. In any event, they are overprotective to the extent that they don't send them around to talk jobs."[9]

How far this development may go in the future is suggested by a bill presented to the 89th Congress, under which it would be possible for people who don't like the idea of working to relax for a year and three months, totally unemployed, while being paid $85 a week. Under this proposal, an unemployed person could pull down an annual wage of $4,420 without doing anything more strenuous than going through the motions of checking in at the unemployment office.

Equally instructive is a spin-off from the Federal "medicare" statute of 1965, wherein the state of New York created an aid program for the "medically indigent" which would allow people of substantial income, bills paid and money in the bank, to take a free ride at taxpayers' expense. The Wall Street Journal reported that under terms of the New York program, a family of four with a net income of $6,000 a year ($7,000 in some circumstances) "also may own a home and a car, have $3,000 in the bank, insurance of up to $1,000 cash value on each family member and unlimited term life insurance and still be considered too poor to pay medical bills."[10]

As that example indicates, the spread of the welfare psychology is not limited to the "poor" members of society. A case in point was the 1966 experience of Dr. Owen Hand Browne, a college professor residing in Raleigh, N.C. Dr. Browne was informed by a government functionary that he was eligible for unemployment compensation. According to the reasoning of the government clerk, Dr. Browne's three-month summer vacation was a period of "unemployment." Incredulous, Dr. Browne decided to fill out the appropriate papers. In short order he received an unemployment compensation check for $400. Finding himself the beneficiary of a system of which he disapproved, Dr. Browne contributed the proceeds to conservative groups and publications working to eliminate such abuses.*

The ultimate result of these tendencies is apparent. In a 1965 survey, U.S. News and World Report calculated that a family with an income of $5,000 a year would be well-advised to forego that stipend and go on relief. By quitting work, the head of the family would have no taxes to pay. In addition, he could secure for his family various government-supplied benefits through ADC, unemployment comp, food stamps, rent subsidies, free medical and dental care.

Because living on welfare can be an attractive proposition, the number of people who choose it as a vocation is moving rapidly upward. Richard M. Elman, himself a partisan of welfarism, notes the proliferation of welfare recipients. "In a period of unsurpassed national prosperity," he writes, "their numbers are still increasing by an average of 5,200 persons a month. Even as the

---

* Also interesting is the history of a government agency called the Area Redevelopment Administration, which came into being in 1961 for the alleged purpose of diminishing the number of communities in the economic doldrums. The effect has been totally the reverse. When the ARA first set to work, there were 103 areas in the United States officially listed as "depressed." In two years' time, the number had zoomed to more than 1,000. With millions of dollars available to cities earning this designation, many communities found it in their interest to get themselves enrolled as economic disaster areas.

unemployment percentages drop, the relief rolls increase."[11] Welfarism is in fact expanding at more than twice the rate of population growth. Relief costs between 1954 and 1964 almost doubled—from $2.7 billion a year to $5.1 billion. The number of people on relief in this period moved from 5,500,000 to 7,800,000 —a 42 per cent increase. U.S. population in the same span increased by only 18 per cent.

The result of this system is a kind of natural selection in reverse. It selects out the strong and productive for special punishments, the weak and nonproductive for special favors. And, if we pay a premium for indolence and degrade responsibility, we can reasonably expect the indolent to increase in numbers and influence.

There are other problems as well. As Prof. Charles Rice of Fordham observes: "There appears to be a definite, though not fully ascertained, relation between indiscriminate welfare and the rising crime rate." Rice notes the high correlation, in a sampling of one ADC program, between ADC payments and criminal records. The results showed that "of 65 males (other than husbands) who were involved with the mother of the dependent children, 40 had arrest records totalling 247 arrests . . ."[12]

The ADC formula places a premium on illegitimacies, broken homes, abandoned mothers, and runaway papas. Aid is not supposed to go to families where there is a "man in the house" capable of working, so many of the men leave the house. Efforts to trace these men down and exact support for their wives and children are often perfunctory at best.* We have in effect offered a bounty for fatherless children, and told the mothers that, for every illegitimate child they can certify to the authorities, they will get an extra stipend. We have in consequence produced a bumper crop of illegitimate children.

One interesting statistic on what is happening as a result of ADC was revealed by Dr. John T. Atwater, public health director of New Haven, Connecticut. Atwater predicted that by 1971

---

* And, under regulations issued by welfare officials in Washington, such efforts are expected to be less than perfunctory. The Federal officials have instructed local welfare departments to stop checking up on suspected drifters, and to accept relief applicants' statements at face value.

this New England city would be blessed with a rich harvest of illegitimate children—greater than the number of children born in wedlock. The doctor made this prediction after a survey showing illegitimate births increasing rapidly in New Haven with the total birth rate declining. The survey disclosed, among other things, that a total of 100 women in New Haven had, over a five-year period, given birth to no less than 340 illegitimate children.

The same trend is apparent on a national scale. In the 20 years between 1945 and 1965, illegitimate births in the United States increased rapidly—from 10.1 per 1,000 unmarried women to 23.4. Between 1961 and 1966, illegitimate births increased even as the total number of births declined. Precisely as in New Haven, fewer legitimate and more illegitimate babies are being born each year. All this despite the fact that the number of poverty-stricken families in the U.S. has been steadily decreasing.

Professional sociologists, we are told, "are at a loss to explain the sharp and persistent rise in illegitimate births."[13] Their puzzlement might diminish if they glanced over the number of illegitimacies encouraged by ADC. It was discovered, for example, that in Los Angeles' south central district "80 per cent of the fathers of children getting AFDC welfare are not in the home. Of all the district homes getting AFDC, 69 per cent have one or more illegitimate children." In nearby Watts, the McCone Commission says, "we were told that [an] 18-year-old girl who is no longer eligible for assistance when living with her mother may have considerable incentive to become a mother herself so as to be eligible as head of a new family group." And: "The welfare program that provides for a man's children is administered so that it injures his position as head of his household, because aid is supplied with less restraint to a family headed by a woman, married or unmarried. Thus the unemployed male often finds it to his family's advantage to drift away and leave the family to fend for itself."[14]

It is as a result of these practices that America's relief rolls have in the past decade of prosperity taken an astonishing leap upward. The bulk of rising relief costs since 1954 have been in this category—an increase of some two million ADC recipients, or 104 per cent. And still more are on the way. *U.S. News* tells us:

Aid to dependent children proliferates because jobless men lacking skills required to get new jobs are found, in growing numbers, to be deserting their families. Many of these men, welfare officials say, are drifters who father illegitimate children. Deserted wives, sometimes turning to any man who comes along, add to the high rate of illegitimacy in the self-perpetuating "breeding grounds of city slums." Result of all this is a growing "welfare society." Unless some answer is found, this "subsociety" is destined to increase in size, dollar costs, and indirect costs—because, sociologists say, it is certain to breed more criminals, more mental defectives, more unemployables of almost every type.[15]

ADC is a tangible and direct expression of what has been implicit in wholesale welfarism from the start—the undermining of the father as a source of livelihood and of authority, and the resulting disintegration of the family. The effects in terms of criminal behavior are notorious. Lord Bertrand Russell, himself a strenuous advocate of welfarism, illustrates the point:

. . . it is quite likely [Russell writes] that the substitution of the state for the father . . . will ultimately extend to the whole population. The part of the father, in animal families as with the human family, has been to provide protection and maintenance, but in civilized communities protection is provided by the police, and maintenance may come to be provided wholly by the state, so far, at any rate, as the poorer sections of the population are concerned. If that were so, the father would cease to serve any obvious purpose . . . all the traditional reasons for traditional morality will have disappeared, and new reasons will have to be found for a new morality.*[16]

One does not have to accept Russell's notion of purely biological reasons for morality to see that these new arrangements place major practical incentives in opposition to moral behavior. When

---

* Russell says the growth of state welfarism will also encroach upon the functions of the mother, who "may continue her ordinary work and have her children cared for in institutions," or else "be paid by the state to care for her children while they are young." We have of course seen explicit steps toward both of these things in such projects as ADC and the "Head Start" program—although the former has been arranged in the opposite way from Russell's forecast. In the case of the state's paying the mother to take care of the children, he says, "traditional morality" can be maintained by denying payment to a woman "who is not virtuous." Under ADC, of course, it works just the other way around; the less virtuous a woman is, the greater the payment. The effect on "traditional morality" is obvious.

the family tie is strong, and when family relationships are respected, value also tends to be strong and respected. When the family breaks down, morality and public order break down with it.

Equally harmful is the "something for nothing" premise of the welfare enthusiasts, a premise which can all too easily convert itself to criminal uses. Taking what one wants by force is, of course, one of the chief characteristics of criminal behavior. To the criminal it seems perfectly just that he should get his provender at someone else's expense—that the world, or some segment of it, owes him a living.

A point the Beechers make about permissive indulgence of children is equally applicable here. "It makes no difference," they say, "whether one wants only to ride the merry-go-round at Coney Island or tour the country in his own Cadillac—someone has to pay for it. Everything and every service in the outside world has a price tag on it. The rule of payment for value received is much more than a cold, hard unpleasant pill to force down the throats of unwilling children. It is a law of life that applies to all of us. Those who go through life trying always to *get*, without giving in return, lead bitter and discontented lives."[17]

Across-the-board welfarism encourages getting without giving. Increasingly, the recipients of welfarist largess are made to feel they have some proprietary claim on the resources of the community and, to the extent they understand the transaction, on the property of other people. Consider the following statements:

> The obstacles that must be removed are the 'respectable' interests that get their income from the deprived and the defenseless; employers who want cheap labor, 'nice' people who don't want to be disturbed. They play rough and you have to play rough against them.[18] (*Saul Alinsky*)

And:

> The deep rumbling of discontent . . . today is the thunder of disinherited masses rising from dungeons of oppression to the bright hills of freedom . . . What the main sections of the civil rights movement in the United States are saying is that the demand for dignity, equality, jobs and citizenship will not be aban-

doned or diluted or postponed. If that means resistance and conflicts we shall not flinch.[19] (*Martin Luther King*)

When such exhortations are addressed often enough to people who have no property; when people are told they are miserable because those who have property have willed it; and when these preachments are combined with the notion that everyone is by right entitled to his quota of something for nothing—what, exactly, are we supposed to expect?

The translation from welfarist psychology to direct commission of crime was most obvious in the Watts riots of 1965. Here the "disadvantaged," long told they were being victimized by the well-to-do, urged to claim what was rightfully theirs, drew the obvious conclusion. They rioted, killed, burned, broke into stores in massive looting forays. They got their share of something for nothing by the direct route.

Bobbi Hollon, a welfare worker in Watts, expands on the "take it away" theme of the Rev. King and Mr. Alinsky. "I'm not for instigating violence," she says, "but I'm not for turning the other cheek either. Maybe I should shine you on, tell you what you want to hear, but that whole Christian bit has been used against the Negro people too long. *These people here could loot for ten years and not get back half of the money they've been robbed of in these stores all these years.*

"These people here tried legal means of getting help, and they got nothing. They begged the white people to listen to them, and nobody listened. Now the whole world is listening to Watts. I'm glad the riots happened." (Italics added.)[20]

All of this vengeful fury came, interestingly enough, *after* massive injections of welfarism in the Watts area. The McCone Commission found welfare spending prior to the outbreak of the 1965 riots had been ascending rapidly. Whereas Los Angeles County's population had grown 13 per cent between 1960 and 1964, welfare spending for ADC rose by 73 per cent. As a survey in *Reader's Digest* notes, "in the very month of the rioting, in fact, welfare poured $2,977,306 in AFDC checks alone into the riot area, which comprises only ten per cent of the county's population but swallows 36 per cent of the AFDC money . . .

Thirty-seven per cent of the juveniles arrested in the Los Angeles riots were being supported by welfare, overwhelmingly provided by AFDC funds."[21]

In 1967, riots surpassing the carnage of Watts occurred in Detroit, replete with systematic looting aimed at merchants who had allegedly robbed the rioters in some unspecified fashion. This outburst, too, followed a heavy binge of welfarism. As *Time* magazine put it, "no city has waged a more massive and comprehensive war on poverty."[22] Detroit had received some $42 million in Federal funds for anti-poverty efforts and had budgeted an additional $30 million for 1967. It has extensive medical aid, job training and Head-Start school programs, all costing in the tens of millions of dollars.

From New York to Los Angeles, welfare projects of every description have been similarly attended by crime, vice, kickbacks, and violence. It is difficult to single out any program which has not been so afflicted. In one Washington, D.C. welfare program, Senator Robert Byrd, D-W.Va., found 60 per cent of the recipients in the Aid to Dependent Children program were flagrantly violating the program's "man-in-the-house" rule.

The New York Times reported: "There were the usual swindlers collecting relief while holding full-time jobs, and comfortably fixed clients taking the dole while living in two-telephone flats with stereophonic sound. Study of a sample of 236 cases of aid-to-dependent children payments showed nearly 60 per cent were ineligible under the rules. The rate of abuses was not significantly lower in the other assistance categories. Even the program's warmest defenders were shocked at the scale of violations."[23]

Such things are by now routine in large cities like Washington, New York, Chicago, and Los Angeles. But the evidence is strong that they are spreading elsewhere too. Parallel developments showed up in Abilene, Kansas, a tidy midwestern community with virtually no poverty but a swelling relief list. Angry taxpayers discovered that, although the population of their county had increased a bare 2 per cent since 1955, the welfare budget had increased 120 per cent—mandating sizeable increases in the tax rate. A little checking revealed that among the disbursements were money for bailing a man out of jail, payments to families that had moved to other states, aid to dependent children for mothers who had not yet had the children, and $500 in ADC payments to a woman whose husband owned property and operated a business in another city.

Nor is ADC the only offender. Public housing programs, which are supposed to reduce crime, have also helped increase it. Harrison Salisbury describes the Fort Greene public housing project in Brooklyn as a "$20 million slum" ideal for breeding criminals. Fort Greene and places like it, Salisbury says, "are forcing centers of juvenile delinquency. They spawn teen-age gangs. They incubate crime."

The trouble starts, Salisbury adds, "when slum clearance begins . . . Bulldozers do not understand that a community is more than broken-down buildings and dirty storefronts. The wreckers tear this human fabric to ribbons." The old families move out, disgruntled and confused. New ones come in, brought together to live at public expense and segregated from the rest of the community by reason of their impoverishment. Suddenly the gangs begin to blossom. One housing man is quoted: "The first thing that happens is the kids begin to destroy the property. Even before it is built. They steal the place blind. As soon as the windows go in they smash them. They smash them again and again. What difference does it make, it's public ain't it? That's what they say."[24]

Haynes Johnson notes that crime in Washington, D.C. is particularly rampant in the Eastern quadrant of the city which "contains nearly two thirds of the public housing units in the District." He adds that "while the National Capital Housing Authority continues to talk about the long waiting lists of more than 5,000 families for public housing, in one such housing unit alone . . . 109 out of 350 apartments are vacant. The windows now are boarded up and the entire development is as much a slum as any group of buildings on the south side of Chicago or the west side of New York."[25]

More and more frequently, comments Jane Jacobs, "children engaged in [street fights] turn out to be from superblock projects

. . . The highest delinquency belt in New York City's Lower East Side . . . is precisely the park-like belt of public housing projects. The two most formidable gangs in Brooklyn are rooted in two of the oldest projects . . . The worst girls' gang in Philadelphia has grown up on the grounds of that city's second oldest housing project, and the highest delinquency belt of that city corresponds with its major belt of projects."[26]

Like the Washington, D.C. project, the Pruitt-Igoe housing development in St. Louis has been afflicted by an exceedingly low occupancy rate traceable to rampant crime, much of which went unreported because the victims feared retaliation. A grand jury disclosed "there is a considerable amount of crime" unreported in the housing complex and that "the fundamental reason for the failure to report crimes is the fear of reprisals on the part of the tenants." According to liberal sociologist Lee Rainwater of St. Louis' Washington University, Pruitt-Igoe has become "an embarrassment to all concerned."[27]

By 1966 officials were prepared to concede Pruitt-Igoe hadn't worked, and decided to pour in still more millions to fix it up as a more suitable welfare emporium. At that time, the *Wall Street Journal* reported, conditions in Pruitt-Igoe were as follows:

> To reach her eighth-floor apartment, Mrs. Julia Boyd, a slim young mother of seven, risks a trip on an unlighted, urine-stenched elevator (if it's running) to the seventh floor, then up a dark stairway strewn with garbage, and finally down a tunnel-like hall often haunted by muggers. Her children must scramble with 5,000 other project youngsters to find even a patch of dirt play space free of broken glass. Crime and vandalism are so rampant that the housing authority spends $91,000 a year for private guard service to augment the 24-hour city police patrol.[28]

Equally lugubrious results have followed on Federal efforts at "urban renewal," ironically advertised as a method for improving living conditions and curing city blight. According to Prof. Martin Anderson of Columbia University, the Federal urban renewal program, through 1960, had succeeded in tearing down some 126,000 dwelling units while building a mere 28,000. The result has been fantastic overcrowding of people evicted from their former homes, creating chaotic conditions where they have not previously existed.

Anderson's view is confirmed by such authorities as Richard Cloward, Scott Greer, Nathan Glazer, and several other students of urban problems. Cloward says urban renewal and related Federal programs have managed to destroy about one million dwelling-units overall, while encouraging construction of an estimated 700,000—a net loss of over a quarter of a million. Greer says that "at a cost of more than $3 billion, the Urban Renewal Agency has succeeded in materially reducing the supply of low cost housing in American cities."[29] The results of this demolition work have been all too frequently disastrous. A case in point is the Hough neighborhood of Cleveland, a slum created by Federal "urban renewal" and the scene of intense racial violence in 1966.

As reporter Ross Hermann describes the situation, infusion of Federal "urban renewal" into Cleveland meant the uprooting of thousands of families from other parts of the city and the movement of these people into the Hough neighborhood: "The bulk of the approximately 4,000 families shoved aside by Federal projects crowded into the Hough area, the only place they could find moderately priced housing. The density of occupancy became so great that neighborhood values collapsed." Out of this situation grew resentments, protests, and, ultimately, riots.

This verdict is seconded by the U.S. Commission on Civil Rights, which denounced the conduct of the "urban renewal" program in Cleveland. The Commission confirmed the charge that the Federal projects had razed homes and forced people into the Hough neighborhood. As William Schulz writes, the Commission found that "urban renewal in Cleveland has decreased the amount of housing available to low-income Negroes and increased overcrowding in the ghetto."[30]

In hearings on the Cleveland situation, father Theodore Hesburgh, President of Notre Dame and a member of the Civil Rights Commission, evaluated the results of the "urban renewal" effort this way:

> These enormous Federal programs . . . are coming in, supposedly to help the community. They want to rebuild our so-

ciety. What has happened in many cases is that people who are presently in the worst situation have their houses swept out from under them by bulldozers, they are given very little help in finding other houses and they generally go to worse than where they came from. This is immoral.[31]

Results fully as counterproductive have issued from the "war on poverty." In New York City, some $6 million of Federal tax money have been funneled into a "poverty" organization called Mobilization for Youth, the stated purpose of which is to combat juvenile delinquency. The evidence suggests it has been more successful in spawning delinquency than in combatting it. Among other ventures, Mobilization for Youth has participated in rent strikes and school boycotts, printed literature distributed at the scene of riots, and provided a haven for some three-dozen ultra-leftists, including two openly identified members of the Communist apparatus.[32]

Related difficulties popped up in another welfare venture called HARYOU-ACT, which in June 1965 received $1.5 million from the "war on poverty" to assist it in battling juvenile delinquency. According to a report issued by the New York City comptroller's office, this antipoverty agency developed into one of the most scandalous episodes in the history of governmental mismanagement. Literally hundreds of thousands of dollars taken from the taxpayers and turned over to HARYOU-ACT were unaccounted for, and there is evidence those dollars in many cases found their way into some influential private pockets.

As developed by inquiring reporters and confirmed by New York authorities, HARYOU-ACT had the following items in its record:

More than $700,000 was spent for "miscellaneous and unclassified" matters, which auditors had a hard time tracing.

The agency withheld $200,000 in taxes from employees which it had not, as of April, 1967, turned over to the state and Federal governments.

A sum of more than $425,000 was spent for "guard services," although this outlay was supposedly disapproved by the government.

A private accounting firm was unable to track down $569,000

in payments made by the organization and had to apportion out these expenses on a formula basis.

A HARYOU-ACT revolving fund of $550,000 was not listed in any of the agency's books or records.

Nearly $20,000 worth of equipment disappeared in the first 16 months of HARYOU's operation, but virtually none of this loss was reported to the police or insurance companies.

HARYOU turned equipment over to the hate-preaching "Black Arts" repertory theater of LeRoi Jones, despite Federal disapproval. The equipment, at the time of the New York comptroller's report, had not been recovered.

What might have happened to the disappearing money and equipment was suggested in a report by the *Wall Street Journal*, which disclosed that tax dollars funneled through HARYOU had a way of gravitating to people related to officials of the program. The *Journal* noted that expenditures included payment of $350 a week for "cleaning services" to individuals related to officials, and the leasing of eight vehicles at $90 a week from a travel agent who was himself renting them for less from another agency. The agent was on the HARYOU payroll at $175 a week as a "consultant." Another episode involved the use of tax funds to fly an official and three staff assistants to Chicago to arrange a protest march.[33]

Outright violence has also occurred quite frequently in certain phases of the national "poverty" program. Exhibit A in this respect has been the various Job Corps Centers, where young men induced to believe they should follow their impulse and that society is the cause of their distress have waged a long guerrilla campaign of tax-supported lawlessness.

Riots, physical violence, and outright crime have been the rule at Job Corps centers rather than the exception. At Camp Breckinridge, Kentucky, bloody riots drew headlines. At Camp Atterbury in Indiana, seven corpsmen were arrested on a charge of sodomy, two others on charges of possessing dope. In Texas, five Job Corpsmen were arrested for allegedly shooting down two Lackland Air Force Base airmen in San Antonio. In St. Petersburg, Fla., continued rowdyism at a girls' Job Corps Center caused the city council to vote to have this "poverty" program booted out of town. In Lewiston, California, local residents said prison parolees among the Corpsmen terrorized the community.

Things got so bad in the Job Corps that even Senate Democratic Leader Mike Mansfield of Montana felt compelled to speak out. In April, 1966 Mansfield described an incident which, in Job Corps annals, is far from unusual. "Some months ago," he said, "a juvenile in Billings [Montana] with a most unfortunate background was selected for the Job Corps. However, before he could be transported to camp in the Midwest, he was involved in a barroom brawl and shot a patron. His defense was immediately taken over by the Job Corps officials; he was then taken to camp and returned to Billings when required by the courts. He was given better counseling, care and attention than the average individual.

"Within the past week or so he escaped from camp with a colleague, stole a car, and in Indiana was involved in a car accident taking the lives of two people and hospitalizing others in critical condition, including himself. I am well aware that there can be bad apples in every program, but it seems to me that there is something wrong. Perhaps it is a matter of lack of know-how and inefficiency on the part of the administrative Job Corps personnel involved."[34]

That still other "bad apples" have had a way of turning up in the Job Corps barrel is noted by Rep. Paul Fino, R.-N.Y., who cites these examples:

In Kentucky, 150 enrollees wrecked the Breckinridge Job Corps camp in a riot set off because of a protection racket run inside the installation. Dozens of youths dropped out of the program in terror.

In Camp Kilmer in New Jersey, officials in nearby towns complain bitterly about the rising crime rate which they blame on the corpsmen. The people say that the streets are unsafe and unfit for any young girls.

In Kalamazoo, Michigan, a group of Job Corps trainees clashed with a rival group in a riot that spread over several city blocks and required 50 policemen to quell.

At Charleston, W. Va., Women's Center, there were reported drunken fights, thievery and immoral conduct.[35]

In 1967, numerous instances were documented in which anti-poverty workers had helped to inflame sentiment against local governments in various cities where riots had erupted. An effort to mobilize "the poor" into a militant "power bloc" has in fact been one of the poverty program's main objectives.

These are only samples from a voluminous body of data—which continues to expand even as these words are written. (A recent news report tells of an arsenal of weapons uncovered at one Job Corps Center, etc.) They are sufficient, we believe, to show that welfarism, far from curing crime, can frequently be the cause of it.

EIGHT

The Courts and the Criminals

Among the elements in American life which have contributed to the growth of crime, one of the most obvious and immediate is judicial leniency. This has long been true in the case of juvenile offenders. It is becoming increasingly so in the case of adults.

Although the soaring juvenile crime rate strongly suggests the need for less permissiveness in dealing with youthful criminals, the trend is in the other direction. Instead of treating juvenile criminals as adults, the courts have begun treating adult criminals as juveniles. Thanks chiefly to the U.S. Supreme Court, concern for the psychic comfort of the offender and leniency in dealing with his crimes are rapidly becoming established parts of American jurisprudence.

The court has issued a long series of decisions weighting the scales of justice heavily in favor of criminal defendants and against society. Its most dramatic move in this direction was the *Mallory* decision of 1957, in which the justices ordered the release of a convicted rapist on the grounds that his seven-and-one-half hour detention before arraignment violated his constitutional right to be brought before a magistrate "without unnecessary delay." The result of this decree was to make the securing of before-arraignment confessions in Federal courts exceedingly difficult.

In a 1961 case the court limited the right of local police agencies to conduct searches in quest of incriminating evidence, a domain previously within the discretion of state law.

In 1963, the court handed down the *Gideon* decision, in which an indigent Floridian was turned loose on the premise that he should have been provided counsel by the state. He received a new trial and was acquitted.

On the same day, the court also delivered itself of a revolutionary but little-noted ruling in the case of *Fay v. Noia*. It held that the appellant, who had served 20 years of a sentence for murder, should be released from a New York prison because he had not retained an attorney at his original trial or appealed his case to a higher court.

In 1964, the court held that a criminal should be exonerated because the justices disagreed with the "search and seizure" methods employed by the police, who had discovered firearms and burglary tools in the suspect's car.

Also in 1964, the court ruled that a man named Danny Escobedo, convicted of murder, should go free because he was not allowed to see his counsel at the station-house before he confessed to the police.

In 1966, in a group of four cases now identified under the rubric *Miranda v. Arizona*, the court extended its previous rulings to new dimensions. It decreed that police could not question a suspect at all if he demurred, and that a lawyer's services must be energetically pressed upon him and financed by the state if he were incapable of paying for one.

The *Miranda* majority said that if a defendant "indicates in any manner and at any stage of the process that he wishes to consult with an attorney before speaking there can be no questioning. Likewise, if the individual is alone and indicates in any manner that he does not wish to be interrogated, the police may not question him."* [1]

---

* The court acknowledged that the principal beneficiaries of its ruling would be those who are in fact guilty—a fact highlighted by its use of the "self-incrimination" argument and its statement that, with counsel present, the innocent person would in all likelihood tell the truth to clear himself. He who remains silent, on the court's own reasoning, is most likely to be guilty. It is precisely this defendant who is the object of the court's solicitude.

In effect, the purpose of *Miranda* is to reverse the psychological equation—away from the police interrogator, arrayed with authority in behalf of society, and toward the criminal. It is to add to the normal motives in favor of silence or falsehood the preponderant weight of legal authority. The net impact has been to put a virtual halt to police interrogation of suspects and therefore to inhibit confessions.

That confessions are necessary for the solution of many crimes is indicated by Justice John Marshall Harlan, who states: "We do know that some crimes cannot be solved without confessions, that ample expert testimony attests to their importance in crime control, and that the court is taking a real risk with society's welfare in imposing its new regime on the country. The social costs of crime are too great to call the new rules anything but a hazardous experimentation."[2]

How hazardous the experimentation is may be gathered from the statement of one police official interviewed on the subject of confessions by the Scripps-Howard newspapers. "Ninety per cent of serious crimes," this official stated, "are solved from a man's own lips at headquarters. A body is found in the woods. A vague description of someone seen in the neighborhood may lead to several suspects. Questioning is the police way of singling out the right one."* [3]

The court additionally reasoned that if the defendant is in fact guilty and reluctant to confess, the work of the police in getting a confession is a violation of the privilege against self-incrimination. Confession after long interrogation, the court said, *ipso facto* suggests the confession is not "voluntary." In this logic, the very efficacy of police interrogation is a compelling reason for doing away with it.

It is apparent that no guilty person motivated by the instincts of self-preservation would, under these circumstances, confess to anything. The only confessions likely in the conditions prescribed by the court would be from resigned perpetrators of passion crimes, suicidal types, or pure psychopaths; it is also likely that a large percentage of such confessions would be of the "Black Dahlia"variety— false confessions by eccentrics. The one kind of confession most unlikely to emerge from such a combination of factors would be a true confession from a professional criminal.

* This backfiring of permissive methods appears to motivate some of the attacks on crime statistics. "Fearing that some people may make a connection between more crime and more experimental methods of dealing with criminals," Miss Ottenberg notes, "these sociologists have solved the problem by attacking the crime statistics. The sociologists are also embarrassed because the latest FBI crime figures clearly demonstrate that poverty and deprivation are no longer the sole answer for crime."

On the testimony of numerous law-enforcement personnel and distressed judicial officers, the Supreme Court's sustained venture in relieving the criminal of psychic discomfort has contributed heavily to the current upsurge of lawlessness. As Harlan's statement indicates, the point has been made most emphatically by several of the Supreme Court justices themselves.

In dissenting from *Miranda*, Justice Byron White said: "There is . . . every reason to believe that a good many criminal defendants who otherwise would have been convicted on what this court has previously thought to be the most satisfactory kind of evidence, will now . . . either not be tried at all or acquitted . . . In some unknown number of cases the court's rule will return a killer, a rapist, or other criminal to the streets and to the environment which produced him, to repeat his crime whenever it pleases him."[4]

Concerning the argument that the police should be able to break cases without confessions, executive director Quinn Tamm of the International Association of Chiefs of Police says: "It would be grand if the officer could play Sherlock Holmes and contemplate all aspects of a case for hours on end. But he has 15 cases, and, in the real world, some of them simply cannot be solved without questioning."[5]

Some advocates, of course, say otherwise. When a hue and cry was first raised over *Mallory*, Democratic Senator Thomas C. Hennings of Missouri proclaimed that "none of the spate of predictions that those who have committed crimes would roam the land in vast numbers, and that the doors of our jails and penitentiaries would be flung wide open to release malefactors of predatory crimes in large numbers to continue their depredations have materialized . . ."[6] In the wake of *Miranda*, Sidney Zion of the *Times* set forward a similar argument. If the court's rulings had hampered law enforcement, he said, "why have we not heard about killers, rapists, muggers and burglars walking freely out of the precinct houses?"[7]

A review of the record indicates that, if Mr. Zion has not heard about criminals going free, he has not been listening very carefully. Convicted rapist Andrew Mallory, for one, did indeed "walk out of the precinct house," journeyed to Philadelphia, committed virtually the same crime for which he had originally been convicted, and was sentenced to a long term in a Pennsylvania prison.

The *Mallory* rule took immediate effect in Federal courts, and since Washington is the only city in which ordinary justice is handled in these courts, the effects of the new permissiveness have been more apparent there than elsewhere. As a result, quite a few criminals have been walking free from courtrooms and precinct houses. Shortly after the *Mallory* rule was handed down, for example, a suspect who confessed to beating up and robbing two men was released. The judge attacked the interrogation at the police station because "under the Mallory decision you should not have done this."[8]

In 1958 a man named James Killough who confessed to murdering his wife was released because his confession had been given at the station house prior to arraignment. The judge who ordered his acquittal said: "In this case defendant on three separate occasions voluntarily confessed . . . Yet the U.S. Court of Appeals has seen fit to throw the confession out. We know the man is guilty . . . but we sit here blind, deaf and dumb and can't know these things."[9]

In 1966, Judge Burnita Matthews ordered acquittal of a 23-year-old defendant who had confessed to murdering his father. The *Washington Post* reported: "After a non-jury hearing, Judge Matthews threw the confession out, basing her ruling partially on the Supreme Court's *Miranda* ruling . . . With no confession, no eyewitness, and no murder weapon in evidence, the prosecutor's case was washed out."[10]

In still another Washington case a man confessed to setting a fire that nearly killed a woman and her children. His lawyer argued, according to *Reader's Digest* editor Eugene Methvin, "that the mere presence of a uniformed policeman psychologically coerced him, thereby violating his Fifth Amendment privilege against self-incrimination."[11] The confession was ruled out— although conviction was obtained on other grounds.

The number of cases in the nation's capital affected by such considerations is large. The *Post* reports that "officials in the U.S. Attorney's office said it is impossible to calculate how many pending cases involve confessions obtained before *Miranda*. The number is 'considerable,' said one official. Others point out that confessions most frequently occur in major crimes such as rape, murder, and robbery. There are more than 50 pre-*Miranda* cases of that sort awaiting trial now. Many contain confessions or other incriminating statements. It is doubtful that many of them will be used, however, one prosecutor said, because of the shaky constitutional grounds on which they were obtained."[12]

A similar travesty of the judicial process has occurred in New York. In early 1967, a defendant confessed to murdering two women, but because he had not been informed of his right to counsel the confession was disallowed. The prosecutor remarked: ". . . if it were not for assaults upon eight other women, many of whom are prepared to testify against the defendant, I would now by virtue of the Supreme Court decisions hailed and praised in many circles be recommending that your honor return this admitted killer to a community that he ravaged for more than eight months."[13]

In Brooklyn, one Mrs. Joan Powe was accused of murdering her four-year-old son by tying him up, covering his mouth with adhesive tape and then beating him with a rubber hose and broomstick. Mrs. Powe confessed all this to police without benefit of counsel. The prosecution subsequently felt called upon to dismiss the case. When Mrs. Powe thanked the judge for releasing her, he replied: "Don't thank me, thank the United States Supreme Court. Don't thank me at all. You killed the child and you ought to go to jail. The trouble is there is insufficient evidence because of the Supreme Court decision, and so that is that."[14]

According to Brooklyn District Attorney Aaron E. Koota, there was a 40 per cent increase in a two-month span in the number of suspects who refused to make statements in his jurisdiction, a result he traced to the Supreme Court. Koota said that since *Miranda*, 96 of 239 suspects in major criminal cases had refused to make statements. Previously such refusals had run about 10 per cent. "Most of these men," Koota said, "will walk the streets as free men. These vicious crimes will never be solved. Recent Supreme Court rulings have shackled law-enforcement agencies, making it possible for vicious criminals to escape punishment."[15]

The same kind of thing has been occurring all over the country. In Columbus, Ohio, a confessed murderer was released after he had told police where to find the murder weapon. The gun was found and established as the instrument which had inflicted death. But because the gun had been discovered as a result of the confession, and because the confession was inadmissible, both statement and weapon had to be ruled out as evidence. The murderer walked free.

In Cleveland, a young man on probation admitted a killing, but because police had not warned him of his Supreme-Court-established rights, he was released. The presiding judge stated: "There is no question in my mind that this is anything but a willful, deliberate act of murder without any justification. Someday members of the Supreme Court will engage themselves in the practical problems of life in a modern urban society, and deal with realities rather than theories that place individual rights far above the community."[16]

Senator John McClellan cites still other examples in the same vein, as follows: "In Evansville, Ind., a murderer was seen leaving his victim's apartment. Later he admitted the crime. No coercion was exerted over him. Yet, under the *Miranda* decision, the prosecuting attorney felt the confession had to be excluded, and therefore allowed the murderer to plead guilty to manslaughter. Numerous prosecuting attorneys in our major cities have [stated] that this decision has had similar effect in their jurisdictions.

"In Seattle, Wash., on March 19, 1966, a hotel clerk was shot and killed during the course of a robbery. He was shot twice with different caliber pistols. A suspect was questioned and given all the warnings required by the *Miranda* decision, including advice as to his right to counsel, but was not furnished with an attorney before being questioned, although he was told that the court would appoint an attorney for his trial. He freely confessed to the robbery and murder. The confession was corroborated by the finding of the guns, but it was excluded on the basis of the *Miranda* decision.

"The guns were likewise excluded as derivative evidence, and so was the testimony of three witnesses who saw the murderer borrow one of the guns and later return it. Thus, the state had to capitulate to the unrealistic technicalities of the *Miranda* doctrine and dismiss an otherwise open and shut case of murder and robbery."[17]

If *Mallory* and *Miranda* have helped free criminals to allow them to strike again, the effects of *Gideon* are plainer still. George J. Jaffee, writing in *This Week* magazine, calls the aftermath of the *Gideon* case "the greatest prison break of all time." Across the country, Jaffee wrote in 1964, "hundreds of prison-hardened criminals are walking out of their jail cells scot-free . . . The prisoners escaping are not minor criminals. They have committed serious crimes in 15 states of the U.S. In Florida, for example, a random sampling of the criminals released would include: A man, 36 years old, sentenced to 30 years in prison in 1961, for murdering his girl friend with a pocket knife. A woman, 22, who had been convicted and sentenced in 1961 to five years in prison for armed robbery. A man, 28, convicted in 1960 to six months to life for assault with intent to murder. A man, 24, sentenced in 1961, to 20 years for armed robbery . . ."[18]

Currently accepted search-and-seizure and probable-cause doctrines have had similar effects. In a Tucson, Arizona case, a policeman's action in crawling under a stolen car to check its serial number was ruled "unreasonable." And in Washington, a like verdict was handed down because police had looked in a garbage can under a suspect's porch and found narcotics. The defendants in both cases were set free.

In various New York rulings, "probable cause" has been carried to hitherto unsuspected lengths. In one case a policeman arrested a man who had been engaged in a burglary because he thought the man's movements were suspicious. The officer's surmise was right and the man confessed. The New York court turned the defendant loose on the grounds that there had been no "probable cause" to suspect a theft even though one had in fact occurred.*

---

* In matters of evidence, the Supreme Court has said that if the prosecution chances across evidence favorable to a defendant it must turn the material over

Measured in aggregate terms, the court's handiwork is even more alarming. Prior to *Mallory*, Washington, D.C., ranked 12th among cities in its population class in number of serious crimes per 1,000 of population. By 1965, it ranked fourth. In 1958, there were 13 victims of serious crimes in Washington per 1,000 of population. By 1965, the number had risen to 28 per 1,000. In 1957, there were 509 apartment burglaries. In a comparable span in 1964, there were 2,788.

Methvin notes that "in the five years before *Mallory*, with crime rising nationally, Washington's police had reduced serious crimes 37 per cent. But thereafter the rate began to climb sharply, and in nine years it has gone up 24 per cent. Holdups, purse-snatchings and muggings, down a third before *Mallory*, sky-rocketed 305 per cent—five times the national increase. Worse, the rate of police success in solving crimes has been cut in half, to an all-time low."[19]

The report of the Washington Crime Commission confirms the last-cited item. It shows that in 1957 there were 15,554 criminal offenses reported in the District, down from 20,163 in 1950. The clearance rate was 49.5 per cent, compared to 48.5 per cent seven years previously. By 1966, the number of offenses had more than doubled—to 34,765—and the rate of clearance had dropped to a rock-bottom 26.3 per cent. (The Washington Crime Commission, which professes to believe judicial leniency is not responsible for increased crime, can think of no certain reason why this state of affairs should exist.)

The Senate Committee on the District of Columbia gave this 1965 precis of the *Mallory* era: "The upsurge in crime has been Washington, D.C.'s foremost local problem in recent years. Even more alarming is the fact that criminal activity has climbed year by year since 1957. The present crime rate trend for 1965 will make this year an all-time record high for the nation's capital city . . . The increasingly acute problem is pointed up by the Federal Bureau of Investigation statistics showing that for the first quarter of 1965, Washington, D.C. had a 10 per cent in-

---

to the defense attorney. This decree was elaborated upon by a lower court which held that witnesses known by the prosecution to be favorable to the defendant's case should be made available to the defense.

crease in crime compared to a 2 per cent average increase for 18 other cities of comparable size . . . By another comparison, FBI statistics show that crime in the District of Columbia in 1964 increased by 25.1 per cent over 1963, while the increase for 18 other cities of comparable size in the same period was only 13 per cent . . . June, 1965 marked the 37th consecutive month with an increase in crime in Washington . . ."* [20]

In response to these conditions, Congress in 1966 passed a law to give District police powers to deal with hoodlums. Civil liberties advocates, fearing a rebuke to the Supreme Court, urged President Johnson to veto the bill. He did. And the terror continues.

Emphasis on "rehabilitative" justice has affected law enforcement at all levels, above and beyond the specific mischief of *Miranda, et al.* Sociologists and academic criminologists have long urged, and various jurists have agreed, that commission of crime is not the criminal's fault, and that correction should be sought in improvement of his surroundings, removal of repressions and frustrations, and the like. As the sociologist interviewed by Miss Ottenberg puts it: "For the past decade . . . an increasing number of offenders have been put on probation or sent to psychiatric clinics rather than to jail or released early on parole. And the FBI's index of serious crime has risen . . ."[21]

The President's commission on crime in Washington similarly observes, from a different perspective, that "the national trend in recent years has been toward more liberal parole practices." It chides the Washington parole board for not following this trend, noting that the percentage of first release applications granted in the nation's capital was 39.2 per cent—not considered anywhere near high enough. The commission states that "thirty-three states had higher percentages—Ohio and Washington had over 95 per cent and California 87 per cent." The dominant official view is summed up in the commission's suggestion that the

---

* The FBI statistics also showed post-*Mallory* Washington with the following ranking among cities of comparable size in various categories of major crime: First in aggravated assault; first in robbery; fourth in housebreaking; fourth in murder; fifth in auto theft; ninth in rape; ninth in larceny.

purpose of parole is "to make supervised freedom a productive experience."[22]

That parole has indeed been a "productive experience" for large numbers of criminals is indicated by the 1965 testimony of FBI chief J. Edgar Hoover. Discussing criminals who had been involved in fatal assaults on policemen, Hoover said: "Convictions have been recorded for 70 per cent of the 294 responsible persons on some criminal charge and one-half had received some form of prior leniency during their criminal careers. Almost one-third of the killers were on parole or probation when they murdered the police officer."[23] *U.S. News and World Report* likewise observed that of "265 murderers released on parole, many continued a career of crime accounting for 737 additional offenses—including 12 new murders."[24]

Countless such stories are in the record, including that of a Newark, New Jersey man who attempted to rape two nuns, and beat them so badly that they were hospitalized. This man had been arrested 14 times previously but had never served time in jail. In a similar episode, two New York youths were arrested on a charge of kidnapping and rape. One was on probation from a term for assault and robbery, the other on parole after conviction for attempted murder. Yet another beneficiary of permissiveness was one Ronald Dessus of Philadelphia, who attacked a man with an iron bar and mutilated him so badly doctors feared the victim might never recover his sight. A Philadelphia magistrate released Dessus on $500 bond. Not long afterward, Dessus was arrested again and charged, in the company of two confederates, with raping and beating an 80-year-old woman, her 44-year-old daughter and 14-year-old granddaughter. The eldest woman died and the three defendants were charged with homicide.

Clemency based on pleas of insanity has produced equally startling results. Some of the things which have occurred under this heading are difficult to believe. There is, for example, the case of a defendant in Washington, D.C., who pleaded not guilty by reason of insanity and was committed to St. Elizabeth's Hospital. He then secured a writ of habeas corpus, on the grounds that he was *not* insane, and walked forth a free man.

The "insanity" plea is an abuse of long standing, and one which seems to be getting worse with the passage of time.

In one episode of the '30s, a murderer named Martin Lavin feigned insanity, was committed to an institution, and escaped conviction. When his partner was acquitted by reason of a technical flaw in the evidence, Lavin realized he could go free altogether. He stated that he was sane, and was released. Dr. Frederic Wertham, the psychiatrist who examined Lavin, subsequently told a legislative committee looking into crime: "Martin Lavin was sent to an institution for the insane, although he was merely feigning insanity. He is free now—and I tell you, he will yet commit another murder." Three months later, Lavin shot and killed a New York police officer while robbing a pawnshop.

In a later New York case, a young architect named Orman was shot and paralyzed by a mental patient who had been paroled from Central Islip State Hospital. Concerning this case, editor James J. Kilpatrick writes: "It appeared that the patient had an obsession against germs. He somehow got it into his head that Orman threatened him with contagious disease; so he shot him. Orman's young wife, the mother of two children, asked the anguished question: 'Why did the hospital give this man parole?' "[25]

In the famous Arizona case of Winnie Ruth Judd, who murdered two women and mutilated their bodies, the defendant was committed to an institution. Over the course of 30 years, Mrs. Judd escaped from the Arizona State Hospital for the Insane at Phoenix no less than seven different times. Her last breakout was in 1962, and as of this writing no one knows where she is.

Even more incredible is the 1967 case of a woman in Maine, acquitted by reason of insanity of the drowning murder of her three small children. The same woman had similarly been acquitted, 12 years earlier, of murdering three of her other children. In 1962 she had been released from a mental hospital as "cured," raised a new family, and then repeated her original crime.

Among the more celebrated beneficiaries of psychiatric clemency was William D. Hollenbaugh, the "Mountain Man" who kidnapped a high school pupil and fled with her through the

Pennsylvania hills. In the course of the subsequent chase, Hollenbaugh shot and killed an FBI agent, seriously wounded another law enforcement officer, and was at last shot and killed himself on the lawn of a farmhouse. It developed Hollenbaugh had been locked up in the Fairview State Hospital for the Criminally Insane, but was released in 1959 and declared cured of schizophrenia. In two months' time he turned up in Virginia and was arrested for breaking and entering. He was jailed for this back in Pennsylvania but was freed once more in 1961.*

Another unbalanced criminal freed by judicial leniency was Emmett Hashfield, convicted of the butchery-slaying of an 11-year-old girl. Hashfield had spent no less than 28 of his 53 years behind bars. Like countless other criminals across the nation, he had been freed repeatedly by clemency-minded courts. Gladys Denny Shultz records a conversation with a lawyer concerning the Hashfield case. The lawyer told Miss Shultz that, if Hashfield were released again, "I personally would rejoice," because such a result would prove the high impartiality of the law in protecting the constitutional rights of even the lowliest member of society.

"But what," Miss Shultz asked him, "about the constitutional rights of children? Not to be tortured to death, for instance?"

"Of course," she records the reply, "if he were to kill another child he would be tried again."[26]

Of course.

The question of "insanity" is admittedly a difficult one—a legal rather than a medical conception. Under what is known as the McNaghton rule, the word is taken to mean the ability to distinguish the difference between right and wrong. Psychiatrists do not ordinarily use the term "insane," dealing instead with various degrees of mental disturbance in their own technical vocabulary. In general, they have argued that tests of mental disability broader than the right-wrong criterion should be used. An important step was taken in this direction in 1954, when the U.S.

---

* The effect of this kind of thing on the overall crime problem is prodigious. A 10-year check of Washington, D.C. court records reveals, for example, 588 people charged with serious crimes committed to the mental hospital by reason of insanity. Of these, 562 were either released outright or escaped. Of those who were released, 134 were subsequently involved in further crimes.

Court of Appeals adopted what is known as the "Durham rule," declaring that "an accused is not criminally responsible if his unlawful act was the product of mental disease or mental defect."[27]

The issue is complex and has yet to be clarified by the courts. Suffice it to say that the "Durham rule" has spread its influence in widening circles, making insanity pleas a good deal easier to come by than they used to be. We are approaching a point where the defense of mental illness or unbalance per se may, through a kind of circular logic, be sufficient to exculpate almost any criminal. Since no normal person would commit a murder or other heinous crime, anybody who does such things must be unbalanced; and since anyone who is unbalanced is not responsible for his actions, no one who commits such a crime can be held accountable for it. While we have not yet reached this point, we are already well past the stage where recidivist criminals can pop in and out of custody by using the "insanity" defense.

The danger posed by such criminals is confirmed by various authorities, academic and professional. Marvin E. Wolfgang, in a meticulous study of homicide in the city of Philadelphia, concludes that recidivism is a principal element in the occurrence of murder. "Contrary to many past impressions," he writes, "analysis of offenders in criminal homicide reveals a relatively high proportion who have a previous police or arrest record . . . The Philadelphia data have shown that 64 per cent of offenders have a previous arrest record, that of these 66 per cent have a record of offenses against the person, and that of these 73 per cent have a record of aggravated assault. Many of the persons previously arrested were convicted but given relatively light sentences and probably little constructive attention. The facts suggest that homicide is the apex crime—a crescendo built upon previous assault crimes."[28]

The researches of the FBI disclose that such repeaters are the chief source of crime in America. The Uniform Crime Report says: "For the 92,869 offenders processed in 1963 and 1964, 76 per cent were repeaters; that is, they had a prior arrest on some charge . . . Leniency in the form of probation, suspended sentence, parole and conditional release had been afforded to 51 per cent of the offenders. After the first leniency this group averaged more than three new arrests."[29]

In other words, *three-quarters of the crimes recorded in these two years were committed by people who had already been in the clutches of the law and got free; and more than one-half were committed by people who had been let off from their appointed sentence.* Our crime rate for these years could have been cut in half merely by requiring criminals already convicted to serve out their time.

U.S. News observes that, in the famous Brinks robbery case, no less than 10 of the 11 gang members had been in previous trouble with the law and received leniency. "Of the 176 hardened criminals who have appeared on the FBI's '10 Most Wanted' list since 1950," the magazine adds, "148 had at one time or another received some form of leniency. As of June 1, 1963, the FBI had 'wanted' notices posted for 84,000 criminals. Of these, 18,629 were parole violators and 5,077 were probation violators."[30] That is to say, there were at that juncture almost 24,000 criminals loose in the land who had already been caught once, were released, and allowed to repeat their illegal actions.

"For the criminal repeaters," the FBI comments, "those with 2 or more arrests, the average criminal career (span of years between first and latest charge) was 10 years during which period they averaged 5 arrests for different criminal acts . . . The average criminal career . . . and the average number of arrests for these repeaters disclose the high volume of offenses being committed by a relatively small criminal population."[31] The criminals, in sum, are going free in droves, permitted through the curious logic of judicial leniency to threaten the lives and liberty of law-abiding citizens again and again.

NINE

Civil Disobedience

We have been discussing a wide range of indirect inducements to crime. If the record ended there, the situation would be bad enough. But there is, unhappily, more. The impresarios of the responsibility-free society have been exceedingly thorough, and have gone on to include direct inducements as well. These still more blatant encouragements to lawlessness are generally comprehended under the title of "civil disobedience."

The doctrine of "civil disobedience," as currently expounded, holds that if you don't agree with a law you are entitled to break it. You are, in fact, *obliged* to break it. To do anything less is a compromise with conscience, an offensive restraint upon one's own intuitive knowledge of what is good and what is evil.

Promotion of this doctrine under almost any circumstances would hardly be congenial to law enforcement. Even in the hands of learned philosophers, slow to anger, it poses enormous complexities. But its impact when preached repeatedly by political agitators to a populace already strong on the notion of impulse-release is predictably cataclysmic.

When a society has been instructed in the individual's lack of responsibility, enjoined to believe everyone is entitled to his share of something for nothing, and told there are no fixed objective standards of value, the tinder of social conflagration is obviously there. "Civil disobedience" is the direct spark needed to send this flammable mass into eruption.

The chief advocate of "civil disobedience" theory in America is the Rev. Martin Luther King, who has made it his personal mission to go about the country telling people to disobey laws they find "immoral." "I think we have moral obligations to disobey unjust laws," Dr. King says, "because noncooperation with evil is as much a moral obligation as is cooperation with good . . . "[1] Since the definition of an "unjust" law is a highly subjective matter, this formulation reduces itself in practice to a self-appointed commission to pick and choose among the laws one will obey.

In his famous "Letter from Birmingham City Jail," King makes the point quite clearly. "An unjust law," he says, "is a mode that is out of harmony with the moral law . . . Any law that uplifts human personality is just. Any law that degrades human personality is unjust . . . *So I can urge men to obey the 1954 decision of the Supreme Court because it is morally right, and I can urge them to disobey segregation ordinances because they are morally wrong.*"[2] (Italics added.)

But there are some people who hold the reverse view of which laws are moral and which are not—who say segregation ordinances are just and the '54 Supreme Court decision is unjust. By King's logic, these people are entitled to break de-segregation laws according to *their* interpretation of what is just and what is not—and some of them, of course, have done precisely that. In which case, with King breaking laws on one side of the issue and segregationists following suit on the other, the whole matter comes down to a test of who is the stronger. All law goes out the window, and the reign of might begins.

King's early "civil disobedience" advocacy was not reprehended in some circles because it was directed at local segregation ordinances in Southern communities; these ordinances, it was felt, were destined to be overturned by the Federal courts anyway, so in a sense King was only anticipating the new shape of the higher law to come. But it has become increasingly apparent that King is also willing to violate Federal court orders, including Supreme Court orders, if necessary, when these do not suit his standards of justice.

On two separate occasions, King was questioned on this point by Southern editor James J. Kilpatrick. Each time King spoke somewhat vaguely, but said enough to make it clear that if he did not agree with a Supreme Court ruling he would disobey it. Asked if in some instance where the Supreme Court might rule against the interests of the demonstrators, "would you then regard such an opinion of the Supreme Court as an unjust law to be disobeyed?" King refused to say he would obey such an order.[3] In early 1965, King made the matter explicit when, in defiance of a Federal court injunction, he staged an abortive march between Selma and Montgomery, Alabama. "I have made my choice," King said. "I have got to march . . . There is no alternative in conscience or in the name of morality."[4] *

King has consistently employed the "civil disobedience" strategy even when the existing legal system offered him plentiful means for redressing grievances and was inclined, in almost every relevant particular, to favor his position. To resort to "civil disobedience" when the Federal executive and Congress are busily passing civil rights laws of every description and the courts are thoroughly congenial to the aspirations of the civil rights movement suggests the employment of the tactic is not moral affirmation but threat.

Further implications of the King view came to light in July, 1966, when King was leading a protest rally at Soldiers Field in Chicago. He told his followers there: "This day we must decide to fill up the jails of Chicago, if necessary, in order to end slums." King's group also showed motion pictures of the rioting in Los Angeles—an enterprise King said was designed to "demonstrate the negative effects of the riots." The opinion of Chicago's Mayor Richard Daley was that the films in fact helped stir disorder. Daley charged members of King's staff "came in here and have been talking for the last year of violence and showing pictures

---

* *Time* magazine asserts that, when he made this statement, King had already made a "deal" with Federal authorities to the effect that he would defy the court order only up to a point.

and instructing people in how to conduct violence. They are on his staff. They are responsible in great measure for the instruction that has been given for the training of youngsters."[5] King denied these charges, but rioting did in fact break out in Chicago in connection with his protests.

The lengths to which "civil disobedience" advocacy can go are suggested by King lieutenant Bayard Rustin, a former member of the Young Communist League who says: "The Negroes must stay in the streets . . . if the Federal government does not give black men and women and tiny children protection, they would not be men with red blood in their bodies if they did not take whatever weapons were at hand . . . I call now for an uprising, non-violently, in 100 cities, where we will sit and stand and stand and sit and go to jail again and again, until there are no color barriers, until the government is forced to recognize us to carry on business and to accommodate us."[6]

John Lewis, official of the Student Non-Violent Coordinating Committee says: "If we don't get meaningful legislation out of this Congress, the time will come when we will not confine our marching to Washington . . . We will march through the South, through the heart of Dixie, the way Sherman did . . . [Negroes upset with the judicial appointment of Mississippian James P. Coleman] may be forced in the name of freedom to carry on mass social dislocation and civil disobedience through the South . . . Mass demonstrations have to become a type of force . . . Aggressive non-violence is noncooperation, it is civil disobedience on all levels."[7] *

Lewis' SNCC colleague, James Forman, was even more straightforward: "There's going to be a considerable amount of violence," he said, "if major changes are not made. I daresay that 85 per cent of the Negro population, if not 95 per cent, does not adhere to non-violence or does not believe in it."[8]

Other spokesmen have elaborated on this view as follows: "We need 100 skilled black revolutionaries, dedicated men ready to die." (Jesse Gray, leader of the Harlem rent strikes.) "If you

---

* It is worth noting that this SNCC leadership group has more recently been replaced by Stokely Carmichael of "black power" fame, on the grounds that it was too "moderate."

tell the white man you're not going to do him in, you're not going to give us anything to fight for." (Percy Sutton.) "We're
going to have a demonstration, and don't say it is going to be
peaceful because the cops have declared war on the people of
Harlem. Every time they kill one of us, damn it, we'll kill one of
them." (Self-styled Communist leader William Epton.)[9]

The last-quoted of these, Epton, provides a link between the
"civil disobedience" advocates and the votaries of the "new left,"
since he served as an official of the Progressive Labor Party in
New York. During the turmoil in Harlem in 1964, which PLP
helped stir up, Epton stated: "We will not be fully free until we
smash this state completely and totally. Destroy and set up a
new state of our own choosing and our own liking . . . and in
the process of this smashing we're going to have to kill a lot of
these cops, a lot of these judges, and we'll have to go up against
their army. We'll organize our own militia and our own army."[10]

In and of themselves, such statements would be inflammatory
enough. But their impact has been vastly increased by the fact
that "civil disobedience" theory has received both passive and
active endorsement from high-ranking officials in government.

In 1963, for example, urging passage of that year's civil rights
bill, President John F. Kennedy said that "in too many parts of
the country, wrongs are inflicted on Negro citizens for which
there are no remedies at law. Unless the Congress acts, their only
remedy is in the street."[11] His brother Robert, in a 1965 statement, put it that "there is no point telling Negroes to obey the
law. To many Negroes the law is the enemy."[12] The late Adlai
Stevenson, in 1964, alleged that "in the great struggle to advance
civil and human rights . . . even a jail sentence is no longer a
dishonor but a proud achievement."[13]

Vice President Hubert Humphrey similarly asserted that while
sit-in demonstrations might be "technically" in violation of the
law, "that was not the point."[14] In 1966, Humphrey expanded on
these sentiments by remarking that if new welfare programs were
not passed, "we will have open violence in every major city and
county in America." He added that if he personally had to live
under slum conditions, "I think you'd have more trouble than

you have had already, because I've got enough spark left in me to lead a mighty good revolt under those conditions."[15]

Parallel utterances came from Rep. Emanuel Celler, D-N.Y., who said that if the Johnson administration's housing bill were not voted out of the House Rules Committee, that omission would invite "violence in the streets."[16] Robert Kennedy voiced a like opinion concerning the prospect of cuts in antipoverty spending by the Federal government. A December 1966 press dispatch revealed that Kennedy had warned of "an explosion among Negro youth" if such cutbacks were made. "We have raised their expectations," Kennedy said, "and unless we make major steps . . . we will reap a whirlwind that will be completely uncontrollable."[17]

To these governmental statements have been conjoined high-level pronouncements from other opinion-forming elements in our society, most notably some members of the clergy. In May, 1964, the Methodist Church approved a report which explicitly affirmed King's "civil disobedience" doctrine. The relevant paragraph stated: "In some instances, where legal recourse is unavailable or inadequate for redress of grievances from laws or their applications that, on their face, are unjust or immoral, the Christian conscience will obey God rather than man."[18]

In the Selma demonstrations, the question arose of obeying or defying the Federal court injunction against the March to Montgomery. Several ministers and other prominent citizens strongly urged that the order be defied. Rabbi Israel Dresner of New York said: "There is a higher law in God's universe and that is God's law. There is a time when man must choose between man's law and God's law."[19] Others who advocated a similar course, according to a sympathetic account in Time magazine, were Mrs. Paul Douglas, wife of the former Illinois senator, a Protestant clergyman, and a Catholic priest.

In the spring of 1966, the Center for the Study of Democratic Institutions, a richly endowed group featuring a number of prominent citizens on its letterhead, published a study which came to the net conclusion that disobedient behavior was a "duty" of citizens who felt their conscience or the Natural Law being violated by the positive law. One contributor, Richard Lichtman, opined that, if society is corrupted, the system may need changing by "general obstruction or violent revolution . . . depending on which is most likely to lead to a significant change." Another contributor, Scott Buchanan, averred that civil disobedience was a good thing because political systems are "born in revolution and they are kept alive and responsible by the permanent possibility of revolution."[20]

Following the pattern of this advocacy, there have in recent years been an increasing number of violent outbreaks. In 1963, '64, '65, and '67, flare-ups occurred in Harlem, the Bedford-Stuyvesant area of Brooklyn, Rochester, Philadelphia, Chicago, Watts, Detroit. In several of these cases, what began as demonstrations under the direction of various "civil rights" leaders evolved into outright riots, complete with looting, assault, various kinds of violence, murder, and open battles with the police.

The most celebrated of these outbursts were the August, 1965 riots in the Watts section of south Los Angeles, in which 38 people were killed, 201 buildings were completely destroyed and 536 others heavily damaged, $200 million worth of property damage was inflicted, and police and national guardsmen fought pitched battles with rioters and waged a five-day war of attrition against looters and snipers. Watts, at last invested by some 16,000 law enforcement officers, was a battlefield in a new kind of civil war.

How the riots were viewed in Watts was suggested by a young Negro, a star athlete and Rhodes scholar, interviewed by Shana Alexander of *Life* magazine. "As a riot," he said, "it was a masterful performance. I sense a change here now, a buzz, and it tickles. For the first time people in Watts feel a real pride in being black."[21]

Identical sentiments were expressed by Bobbi Hollon, the previously quoted welfare worker in Watts. "People here used to be ashamed to say they came from Watts," she is quoted. "They used to mumble it. Now they say it with pride." She added that "I'm glad the riots happened. I'm glad to see anything happen that can help make this whole thing better. And people are making a serious mistake if they think the riots are over."[22]

Outbreaks of violence in Newark, Detroit and some 70 other American cities in the summer of 1967 were even more clearly tied to incendiary agitation. In Cambridge, Md., H. Rap Brown of SNCC told an assembled crowd: "If America don't come around, we're going to burn America down, brother. We're going to burn it if we don't get our share of it." Shortly thereafter a large chunk of Cambridge was indeed burned down. Later Brown asserted that "violence is necessary. It is as American as cherry pie. If you give me a gun and tell me to shoot my enemy, I might just shoot Lady Bird."

In the Detroit rioting, the looters were characterized by what was described as "nihilism" and a "carnival spirit." The resulting disaster included 41 dead, 347 injured, 3,800 arrested, 5,000 people homeless, 1,300 buildings burned to the ground, 2,700 business establishments pillaged, and property damage estimated at $500 million. In the wake of all this, Harlem Congressman Adam Clayton Powell declared that such riots are "a necessary phase of the black revolution—necessary." UAW President Walter Reuther remarked that "only when they get their fair share of America will they respond in terms of responsibility."[23]

Among the most flamboyant representatives of "civil disobedience" doctrine are the members of the "new left," whose record is dotted with appeals to lawlessness in theory and practice alike. In the 1960 San Francisco riots against the House Committee on Un-American Activities, "new left" students (not called such then, but of the same unfriendly persuasion) interfered with the hearings of the committee, disrupted the proceedings of adjacent courts, and ignored the orders of police to evacuate the premises. Similar uprisings against the committee were staged in Washington and Chicago; in the latter exercise, demonstrators threw themselves under police vans to keep them from moving.

Phillip Abbott Luce documents the violent activities and even more violent intentions of some of his former cohorts in this movement. He describes the efforts of the Progressive Labor Party, in which he was a leader, to force a "confrontation" with the police, its stashing of arms, its program to send revolutionary cadres underground. He notes the outlook of the "new left"-related Black Nationalists who attempted to blow up the Statue of Liberty and quotes the statement of one "new left" fringe leader: "We'd assassinate the President if it suited our ends."

Luce also quotes one Progressive Labor Party chieftain as saying during the Harlem riots of 1964: "I advocate precisely that people disturb the peace . . . Let us not run and let us not pray —let us fight back . . . There is no lawful government in the country today. Only a revolution will establish one. If that is a civil rebellion, let us make the most of it."[24]

The most famous instance of "new left" disobedience has been the long guerrilla action staged at the University of California by undergraduates and others who conceive themselves to be latter-day Paines and Jeffersons vindicating the cause of "free speech." In September, 1964, university authorities decreed students should confine their campus politicking to a certain specified area. This ruling was protested by a series of "sit-in demonstrations" by the students at the university administration building. At one such demonstration, when Berkeley city police arrested a demonstrator, students surrounded the police car and "captured" it. On another occasion, the students were removed from the administration building on the orders of the California governor. Still later, the Free Speech Movement added a new dimension to its protest when one of its leaders declared the right to unrestrained expression also encompassed the use of obscenities in public discourse.

The "new left" Viet Nam protests of 1965 were marked not only by the conventional marches and defiance of the police, but by such additional furbelows as the burning of draft cards, extended discussions on ways and means of evading the draft, and attempts to halt the movement of troop trains. These adventures produced some interesting symptoms of highmindedness in the pursuit of illegality. At the Berkeley teach-in, satirist Paul Krassner advised students who wanted to burn their draft cards to do so with facsimiles. "They say nothing about photostats," Krassner told the students. "So those of you who have access to photostatic machines, you can just make photostats of your draft cards and destroy them in public if you like." This suggestion outraged "purists" among the students, whose sense of honor would not allow them to do something so unethical. "Burning a photostat of your draft card," said one, "is like kicking over a toy locomotive and then saying you derailed a whole troop train. It's insincere."[25]

While the "new left" tumult is the best-publicized instance of campus disaffection from received notions of law and order, there are other examples as well. The apparent belief of the students that they are entitled to riot if they are unhappy spreads beyond the confines of explicit politics. Recent years have seen outbreaks of student violence at various resort spots like Geneva-on-the-Lake, Ohio, Laconia, N.H., and Ft. Lauderdale, Fla. On a single weekend in 1965, student rioters at five resort towns broke windows, fought police, threw rocks, damaged automobiles and other property. It is estimated that 100 people were hurt and $20,000 worth of property was damaged.

The nation's chief law enforcement official, FBI Director J. Edgar Hoover, has hit hard at "civil disobedience" advocacy. To show contempt for law and order and promote pride in lawbreaking, Hoover said, "can only result in an acceleration of our serious crime problem. In some quarters, it already appears that the social stigma formerly attached to lawbreakers is being replaced by sympathy for their actions and an irrational hostility to law enforcement . . . Where is the line to be drawn against the snowball effect of civil disobedience? Willfully disobeying misdemeanor statutes today and committing felonies tomorrow is a logical regression from a government of law to an anarchic society."[26]

Other law enforcement officers echo Hoover's sentiments. Edmund McNamara, police commissioner of Boston, says, for example, that when mixed in with other pressures to criminality "the theory that if a law or ordinance does not fall in with your beliefs it should be broken" can only result in "a major crisis." Similar views are expressed by officials in St. Louis, Denver, Minneapolis, Kansas City, Washington, D.C., Honolulu, Memphis, Seattle, and Houston.[27]

As we have seen in our discussion of the courts, the "civil disobedience" idea is not always expressed in the precise language favored by King. It shows up as well in the continued suggestion that law violators in underprivileged circumstances cannot be expected to obey the law and should not be punished for violations. In place of an outright attack upon the law as such there is substituted a plea for "understanding" the needs and hardships of the criminal. This outlook is suffused throughout our society, as noted, in everything from permissiveness in the home and school to judicial leniency for juveniles and adults alike.

Thus, even as "civil disobedience" has reached its most violent phase, it has met with ambivalent response from academic and other authorities. When Los Angeles police chief William Parker (now deceased) moved to put down the Watts rioting, he was attacked for "brutality"; various spokesmen in the public media sought to work out extenuations for what had happened; and even President Johnson addressed himself to the problem in ambiguous terms. Although condemning the violence, Johnson sought to fix blame on sources other than the rioters themselves, and had nothing to say in condemnation of the "civil disobedience" doctrines which contributed to the violence. He instead waved the threat of further Watts-like outbreaks, including possible violence in Washington, D.C., as an inducement to having one of his favored programs enacted.

Speaking on the question of home rule in Washington shortly after Watts, Johnson said: "Those of you here in the District of Columbia, I want to warn you this morning that the clock is ticking, time is moving, that we should and must ask ourselves every night when we go home, are we doing all that we should do in our nation's capital, in all the other big cities of the country? . . . Let's act before it's too late."[28] This statement was welcomed by a spokesman for the National Association for the Advancement of Colored People, who said race tension was "seething beneath the surface" in Washington and Johnson's utterance was therefore "very appropriate."* [29]

---

* Less enthusiastic was Republican leader Gerald R. Ford of Michigan, who said Johnson's warning "amounts to an invitation to trigger terrorism in the streets." And syndicated columnist Don Maclean, who lives in downtown Washington, expressed his misgivings about the possibility of violence. ". . . President Johnson wouldn't know any of this," Maclean said, "because he has never lived in a section of town such as this. He simply wants to get the home rule bill passed and if it takes a friendly little warning about a riot to do it, well what's power for if you don't use it?"

Pat extenuations for lawless behavior, whatever the crime, are seldom wanting. When Senator Robert Byrd made his disclosures about violations of the welfare law in Washington, he was roundly attacked as a monster oblivious of the plight of the needy. What was required, said Byrd's critics, was to change and liberalize the law—in order to avoid penalizing the children.** We encounter the "new morality" formula all over again. To keep the aid dollars flowing despite violation of standards, the thing to do is to get rid of the standards.

A massive national campaign to broaden abortion laws, as we shall see in a succeeding chapter, is based on the same kind of reasoning. Since people will not obey these laws, we are told, the laws should be rescinded or drastically revised.

In the Job Corps troubles, Federal officials resolutely refused to impose standards of discipline, barring even the elementary step of ejecting a recalcitrant youngster from the program. As one official put it, the philosophy of the program was: "Spoil these boys—they have never been spoiled before."[30] When the program erupted in violence, disorder, and repeated criminality, Federal officials attempted to place the blame anywhere but on the corpsmen and on the absence of discipline. When the Camp Atterbury troubles first broke to the surface, Job Corps Deputy Director Christopher Weeks said the problem was the "hostility" of the local citizens, and that the corpsmen's misbehavior resulted from their feeling of "rejection" when they visited surrounding communities. Weeks said that "if they're rejected, they'll react accordingly—and who can much blame them?"[31] Who, indeed?

In various outbreaks of violence by "Vietnik" and other radical agitators—starting with the May, 1960 riots against the House

---

** Byrd pointed out by way of rebuttal that, in purging the relief rolls, only 6 per cent of the children involved wound up in the city orphanage, "so about 94 per cent of the children continue to receive care. In most cases the children aren't receiving much of this money anyhow. In most cases, most of it's going to this woman and her paramour." Byrd added that "if we change the man-in-the-house rule, we are going to subsidize open, overt, public immorality. I don't think this should be done. I don't believe that the taxpayers of the Congress ever intended for the public welfare program to become a program that would foster and subsidize and encourage illegitimacy and immorality."

Committee on Un-American Activities—adult apologists have come forward to say the blame for the episodes did not rest with the students, but with the committee, the police, *etc.* In the 1960 riots, the student agitators were made the center of an elaborate morality play enacted in many national periodicals and from many lecterns and pulpits, in which the terrible forces of "police brutality" were depicted as overriding honest dissent. When documented evidence was brought forward to show the students had been deliberately disrupting the orderly proceedings of the law, the defense was that they had been unjustly "provoked."

After the Watts rioting of 1965, a concerted effort was launched to place blame for the disorder, not on the individuals involved, but on "conditions." The rioting occurred, said the explainers, because of "poverty," *de facto* segregation, ghettoization, absence of welfare measures—this despite the fact that, as we have seen, welfarism in the area had been at a very high level indeed. Responsibility for the rioting was fastened just about anywhere, in fact, except upon those who had engaged in it.* The Reuther position on the Detroit mayhem of '67 was cut from the identical pattern.

Perhaps the most striking of all official extenuations for lawless behavior was the performance of the University of California faculty toward the "civil disobedience" tactics of the Cal students. In an official vote, the faculty refused to condemn the lawlessness of the Free Speechers, and called for an amnesty for stu-

---

* A Baltimore, Maryland attorney named Leonard J. Kerpleman, who had been active in "civil rights" matters as a member of the NAACP and who had argued before the Supreme Court in favor of banning classroom prayer, wrote a letter to a Baltimore newspaper saying the Watts riots "disgusted me and sickened me as a human being." Kerpleman added that he could not accept "the manner in which Negro leaders have drawn the Watts carnage to their bosoms and have declared it to be not their shame but their glory. Gentlemen of the Negro community, by expressing pride, complacency or satisfaction in the Watts riots, you have lost me."

The chairman of the Maryland NAACP rejoined that "no one in his right mind hugs bloodshed and killing to his bosom, whether it is Watts or Viet Nam. Watts was a rebellion against long standing oppressive conditions which have not been corrected." Similar comments and disclaimers came from other Maryland "civil rights" leaders, none of whom, however, focused on statements such as those from the Watts spokesmen who felt a "tickle" after the 1965 disturbance and were "glad the riots happened."

dents who had been arrested. Prof. Sidney Hook offers the following comment on the faculty position:

It is this approval of student lawlessness on the part of the faculty . . . which constitutes the most shocking aspect of the role of the faculty in the Berkeley episode. The misled students have the excuse of youth, and the administration that it didn't understand until too late the fundamental political orientation of the FSM membership. But the faculty took its position on the only issue that was clearly defined in the situation, viz., whether the complex of problems . . . should be resolved by educational means or by student resort to civil disobedience. Its vote can only serve to encourage further lawlessness.[32]

The psychiatrists tell us that one of the chief elements in prolonged deviant behavior is the effort at self-justification. Not even the most hardened criminal will persist in lawless conduct without in some way rationalizing his actions. In his study of several warped and violent murderers, Dr. Wertham says that even the most psychopathic found it necessary to devise rationalizations for what they had done. He suggests that among the topics which must be taken up for discussion in such matters is "not only why one does it, but how one justifies it to oneself."[33]

In the case of "civil disobedience" advocacy, of course, the question is not difficult to answer. Those who engage in lawless behavior have already been assured that what they are doing is right; they need only to act, and countless theoreticians will come forward to proclaim that they could not have done otherwise. The crime is justified before it is committed.

What all this reminds one of is the French Revolution: Violence in obedience to theory, theory in justification of violence, and the Rev. King our modern Robespierre. King has supplied the doctrine and the leadership, and King above all can take credit, if credit it be, for the consequences. As theologian Will Herberg comments:

Shall we wreak our wrath upon [the] "punks" and "hoodlums" and allow those ultimately responsible, the Martin Luther Kings, the inciters to law-defiance in the name of "conscience," to go immune in their self-righteousness? They stand horrified at the rioting and violence. But isn't it all the handiwork of the demons they themselves raised? They are the guilty ones—despite the best intentions. If they have any conscience left beside that which they use as justification for the violation of law, let them search it now.[34]

TEN

People Brutality

Judicial lenience and contempt for authority converge on the policeman. It is the policeman who is called on to apprehend the criminal and who is hampered in that effort by the courts. As the visible and immediate symbol of law and order, he is also the target of repeated charges of "brutality" and the victim of political harassments.

"Brutality" is a reflex charge in some areas of "civil liberties" advocacy. The Supreme Court, for example, has indicated it believes police routinely use coercive techniques on suspects—although the *Miranda* decree which assumes this cites no example of such practices. One complaint against law enforcement officers says: ". . . the police accept and morally justify their illegal use of violence . . . such acceptance and justification arise through their occupational experience; and . . . its use is functionally related to the collective, occupational, as well as legal ends of the police."[1]

The spread of such ideas may be noted in the increasing number of complaints registered about "brutality." In fiscal year 1963, the FBI received 1376 such complaints; in 1964, 1592 complaints; and in 1965, 1787 complaints. By way of contrast, from January, 1958 to June, 1960, there were only 1328 such allegations. The large majority of these are registered by Negroes in the South;

but many of them have come from Northern states as well.

It is obvious that policemen are as liable to human frailties as anyone else, and it would therefore be surprising if some policemen did not exceed their authority. It is entirely fitting that close watch should be maintained to insure that police "brutality" does not occur and if it does occur that corrective steps are taken.

A review of the evidence indicates, however, that the balance in law enforcement has tipped entirely the other way. Under the impact of "civil disobedience," judicial permissiveness, and political improvisation, the officer who oversteps his limits is rapidly getting lost in the crowd of policemen who are themselves being knocked about, roughed up, and prevented from taking proper steps to defend themselves and their communities.

Consider, for example, a bizarre case which arose early in 1965. Two Chicago policemen, wearing civilian clothes, rushed to the scene of a disturbance and found a man armed with a broken beer bottle. They advanced on him, identified themselves as policemen, and ordered him to drop the bottle. His reply was "Come and get it, you —— —— coppers."[2] When one officer tried to get the bottle away from him, the suspect jabbed it in the policeman's face. The officer spent 23 days in the hospital.

When the case came to court, Chicago Judge George Leighton released the assailant as an injured party well within his rights. "The right to resist unlawful arrest," Leighton said, "is a phase of self-defense. What is a citizen to do when he is approached by two officers with a gun?"[3] What, indeed? Apparently, under the new code of judicial lenience, he is to slash them across the face with a broken beer bottle.

In another case, a group of young toughs jumped a policeman, knocked him down, kicked him, and took away his revolver. When they came to trial on charges of robbery and aggravated assault, the youths pleaded guilty. The judge, however, refused to accept the plea. He said the suspects were not in fact violating a law when the policeman approached them, that seizure of his gun could not be construed as robbery, and that their attack on the officer was not really an assault. The judge placed them on probation for the relatively minor charge of battery.

Ironically enough, such episodes have themselves been converted into charges of brutality by the police. Among the most famous of these was a 1964 case, in which an off-duty New York policeman named Thomas Gilligan tried to apprehend a Negro boy threatening a man with a knife. The boy attacked Gilligan, cutting his right arm; as he continued to attack, Gilligan shot and killed him. A grand jury—with two Negroes serving on it—examined the case and found Gilligan innocent of improper action. One of the Negro members remarked: "I did the right thing and so did the rest of the jury."[4]

This incident was greeted by posters saying "Wanted for Murder—Gilligan the Cop," and "When Will Gilligan Kill Again?"[5] Also by picketing of Gilligan's home and by the accusation from James Farmer, then head of CORE, that Gilligan had killed the boy in cold blood. The patrolman was secretly transferred to another precinct.

In still another such encounter, New York patrolman Sheldon Liebowitz tried to quiet a man acting boisterously on a street corner. The man attacked Liebowitz with a knife, and in the ensuing struggle got hold of the policeman's gun and wounded him with it. Liebowitz finally regained his pistol, shooting and killing his assailant.

The upshot of this episode was a rally by the Congress of Racial Equality, denouncing Liebowitz. *Life* magazine reported that "threats and abusive phone calls flooded into Liebowitz's hospital room, and police put the hospital under special surveillance and placed a 24-hour-a-day guard outside the patrolman's room. A few days later he was secretly moved to another hospital. The day after the shooting, CORE demonstrators marched on police headquarters chanting, 'down with the killers in blue' and 'the next cop's bullet may be yours.' "[6]

Of similar kidney was the furor over "police brutality" in the San Francisco student riots of 1960. According to partisans of the student demonstrators, the police set upon and beat the students without provocation. The *Washington Post* alleged that "the San Francisco police acted with altogether needless brutality, turning fire hoses on students whose protests were not flagrantly unruly."[7] But the record reveals that, despite intense provocation, there was no police brutality of any sort, and that the students inflicted considerably more damage than they received.

When the students disregarded a police order to vacate San Francisco's City Hall where they had been staging a mass sit-in and creating an uproar so loud the courts could not conduct their business, the police turned hoses on them, then slid, lifted, and carried them down the city hall steps into waiting patrol wagons. The simplest way of figuring out who was brutal to whom in this transaction is to tabulate the casualty figures. According to the *San Francisco Chronicle*, eight policemen were injured in the rioting, compared to four students. The students themselves, in self-justifying literature got up after the demonstrations, estimated six policemen were injured as opposed to five students.

Subsequent to the San Francisco uprising, it was revealed that one purpose of such demonstrations is to provide an occasion for "confrontations" with the police, from which charges of "brutality" can be spun to gain sympathy for the demonstrators. Reporting on the 1960 riots, J. Edgar Hoover disclosed that Communist leader Archie Brown, who had helped spark the demonstrations, rehearsed at a party meeting "how the party intended to use a follow-up campaign with campus students as the target." He stated that the party "planned to emphasize 'police brutality' as a rallying cry to attract the sympathy of student groups . . ."[8]

Phillip Abbott Luce, describing tactics of the Progressive Labor Party, quotes one leader of this group as saying: "If the cops allow you to speak, then afterward try to get the kids to follow you out into the center of Broadway and stop traffic. This will force the cops to come after you, and we will have a confrontation."[9] In another demonstration in New York City, Luce adds:

> I was one of two people in charge . . . and, after seeing the huge squad of police officers in the square, I agreed to their suggestion that we move our 300 demonstrators to the United Nations under police supervision. As we started east on 47th Street, some of the Progressive Labor members, who had given us orders to create an incident the week before, came screaming up to me and demanded that we turn back and stay in Times Square to "fight it out with the cops." When I refused, some of them be-

gan to try to turn the marchers back, and en route to the U.N., 47 demonstrators were arrested.[10]

Similar plans were revealed concerning the 1965 Viet Nam demonstrations in Berkeley. *U.S. News* gave this summary of the demonstrators' actions:

> In preparation for trouble, students formed a "Police Brutality Committee." It began grinding out propaganda before the first arrest, and students were primed to start chanting "brutality" as soon as the police appeared on the scene. Students were also instructed to go to the university hospital and report injuries . . . Students and sympathizers overlooked no chance to raise the "brutality" cry . . . During the rioting, police said, a Berkeley radio commentator helped the "brutality" theme along by slapping the wall with his hand near the microphone and describing the noise as "blows" raining down on students.[11]

Also of interest in this respect are the figures assembled by the Federal Bureau of Investigation, to which such charges are addressed and which has the responsibility for looking into them. The figures reveal that, of the more than 1,700 complaints of "brutality" received by the FBI in 1964, a total of 47 were presented to grand juries for action under Federal law making it a violation for police to deprive someone of his constitutional rights. Of these, five cases resulted in conviction. The vast majority of complaints concern "verbal brutality," hard looks, "tone of voice," and so forth.[12]

All states and major cities have provisions and procedures for checking such complaints and for dealing with officers who are out of line. A spot check in mid-1965 found 289 such complaints had been received in Chicago, of which 281 were determined to be without substantial basis; in Los Angeles, 242 out of 314 complaints were not sustained; in New York, 194 out of 231 cases failed to vindicate the charges brought against the policemen.

A Los Angeles police official says: "Most of the complaints are of a pretty minor nature, such as discourtesy or handcuffs put on too tightly. It has come out many times that there isn't any physical brutality. It's verbal brutality. Some even say: 'I'm not complaining about the ticket or what the officer said. It is the way he said it, his tone of voice.' " A Chicago official adds that "some people seem to think they have a right to resist arrest at all times. So a degree of force has to be used to bring them to the station."[13]

What is often alleged as brutality, in fact, is anything the arrestee doesn't like concerning his arrest. *U.S. News* notes that the Berkeley demonstrators used "brutality" to describe "the stench of the crowded buses that took them to jail. Placing of two intractable students in isolation cells also was held to be 'brutal.' "[14]

Official comments on the inhibiting effects of the anti-brutality campaign were obtained by the authors in a survey of police officials from communities of varying sizes all over the nation. These officials were asked: "Are the decisions of the Supreme Court, such as the *Mallory* decision, hampering the work of the police in your city?" The answers, excepting those of two men who said they did not feel free to comment, were overwhelmingly in the affirmative. Representative replies include:

From Kansas City, Kansas: "Yes, some of the officers are afraid to do their duty because of possible repercussions. Many think a search warrant cannot be obtained until too late."

From Tucson, Arizona: "Recent precedent-setting decisions by the Supreme Court have of course had a direct effect on police operations throughout the country. In more recent months the decisions have changed police practices in investigation, interrogation and search procedures. While the decisions in themselves have been somewhat restrictive, they have also brought about a retraining of police officers across the nation which has resulted in police agencies all following the same rules of evidence and interrogation."

From Pittsburgh, Pennsylvania: "The *Mallory* rule has not been applied to state cases by the Pennsylvania Supreme Court. If it were it would eliminate incriminating statements in all but a few cases. Would make successful prosecution virtually impossible in a great number of trials."[15] *

---

* Other comments in similar vein include: Louis M. Kulpa, Chief of Police, Wheeling, West Virginia: "Yes, because it makes the police officers more cau-

Moreover, with the "constitutional rights" of the criminal affirmed, our jurisconsults have moved to impose severe penalties on police officers who assertedly violate them. As one lawyer puts it: "An officer who makes an illegal arrest or search and seizure which violates the constitutional rights of the person arrested must steel himself to a greater hazard of civil suit for damages, for it is now the law that a state officer who violates the constitutional or civil rights of the person against whom his action is directed can be sued personally for damages in the Federal courts, regardless of any right which the victim may have to sue in the state courts."[16]

The impact of these and other rulings on policemen required to arrest, book, and interrogate suspects may easily be imagined. An occasional tough and ingenious officer can devise means for getting his job done without finding himself faced down by some junkie or hooker waxing eloquent about "constitutional rights"; but the majority are naturally inhibited from moving against even the most likely and obvious suspects by the legalistic barbed wire the courts have draped over law enforcement.

A startling example of the difficulties under which police now labor is the story told by a New York patrolman who, off-duty, was confronted by a knife-wielding hoodlum. A uniformed officer standing by flatly refused to do anything to help his colleague until the potential victim of the attack insisted at length. "This guy is standing there with a knife on me," says the off-duty patrolman, "and the cop becomes a spectator . . ." When the assailant was at last disarmed and brought in, cooperation at a higher level was scarcely better.

---

tious in making arrests and they hesitate more and back off some." Police Chief, City of Reno, Nevada: "Yes, to protect the rights of criminals in relation to regard for the rights of victims. The armed robber doesn't have to advise his victim that he has the right to summon police prior to robbery, et al. . . ." Chief of Police, Baton Rouge, Louisiana: "Yes, to some degree, in that some cases are dropped due to insufficient evidence caused by the officer's hands being tied legally." Cleveland, Ohio, Chief of Police: "Yes, they are causing a crisis in law enforcement." Minneapolis, Minnesota, Chief of Police: "Yes, it takes more manpower on each case; we have to prepare them fast and get charges placed more rapidly." Philadelphia, Pennsylvania, Chief of Police: "Recent Supreme Court decisions have caused this department to step up the training program of constitutional law. These decisions have caused a lowering of morale for all law enforcement officers. People do not readily accept rapid and severe changes."

The officer who had been attacked says: ". . . then I get to the station house and the lieutenant down there wants to know what I'm doing. He wants to know if the guy actually *hurt* anyone or not. He knows I put my resignation papers in last week and that I'm leaving soon and so he says to me, 'Look, you're leaving anyway, so why bother about it?' Here this guy has just tried to knife someone—tried to knife me—and this guy, a lieutenant, is telling me not to bother."[17]

A New York detective sergeant tells an equally appalling story. "A woman OD'd [collapsed from an overdose of drugs] on Broadway," he relates, "and there's a guy there who is built like a cigaret machine and he has six cops at bay, just standing listening to him swear at them. There's a crowd and the cops are afraid to do anything, even question him, because he's yelling about brutality and swearing at them and the crowd is watching and he feels like a great man because everyone's seeing him abuse those six cops who are afraid to go near him . . . Maybe he gave her the OD. Maybe he killed her. And the cops didn't even know his name. They wouldn't even talk to him.

". . . I can tell you that now that he's told six cops where to go in public and got away with it, I feel sorry for the next lone cop who sees him making a disturbance and tries to stop him. The cop'll get killed . . . the important thing is that those cops weren't afraid of *him*—they were big enough to eat him up—they were afraid of the crowd, of someone who might accuse them of brutality and get them kicked off the force."[18]

Current statistics show that American policemen today are being killed and injured in record numbers. The FBI reveals that in 1964 "the number of law enforcement officers murdered in the line of duty reached a new high with 57 killings reported by local and state agencies. These deaths bring the total of such murders to 225 for the five-year period 1960–64."[19] In New York City alone seven policemen were killed and 1,602 were injured in the line of duty in 1964. The total number of assaults on policemen, both on and off duty, came to a whopping 2,493.

The recommended corrective for alleged police brutality is a further restraint on the police—a "civilian review board." Law-enforcement officials fear this device would be loaded in favor of minority or other interest groups, to impose still more impediments to effective police performance. J. Edgar Hoover says such boards would necessarily have political overtones and that "these panels would consist of appointed individuals who are . . . inexperienced and uninformed in law enforcement and police administration. This drive for external boards is an ill-advised maneuver."[20]

Los Angeles Police Chief Parker said of the review board idea:

If they get one in Los Angeles, then I will walk out. I would not share my administration of this department with a group of persons who are selected primarily from minority elements— many of them demagogues with axes to grind. When they have control over the force without any regard to responsibility for its performance, that's time for someone else to take over.[21]

Chicago's O. W. Wilson expressed the same opinion. A review board in his city, he said, "would destroy discipline in the Chicago police department . . . If we have a civilian-review board, that board creates a situation where I, as the head of the police department, am confronted by an adversary group which the entire department will tend to unite against. Therefore, if we had a civilian-review board, my discipline would be less effective than it is today."* [22]

Thomas F. Coon, editor of the official bulletin of the Society of Professional Investigators, writes that where the review-board idea is accepted, police morale "will take off upon a toboggan of descent." Coon adds that "the man in the field would not be human if he did not avoid certain ticklish law enforcement incidents, taking cognizance of the composition and persuasions of the board." Coon quotes the 1953 opinion of the New York

---

* Former New York Police Commissioner Vincent Broderick comments that "it is vital when the police officer's action is reviewed it be reviewed by one who has a capacity to evaluate the propriety of the action in terms of the police crisis in which it was taken and who, at the same time, has a disciplinary responsibility which extends not only to the propriety of the action but also to its complement, the propriety in the same situation of the officer's having failed to take action."

FBI Chief Hoover likewise comments that the review board concept "undermines the morale and saps the efficiency" of the police. "They deter officers in the proper performance of their duties for fear of having charges placed against them which would be judged by individuals wholly unfamiliar with police work."

Civil Liberties Union that disciplinary functions "are best exercised within the department itself rather than imposed by an outside agency."[23]

When he ran for his office in the fall of 1965, New York Mayor John Lindsay promised institution of a "review board" in the Empire City. When the board was launched, it fulfilled the worst fears of its opponents. The membership was heavily loaded with representatives of "civil liberties" and other protesting groups, chief among them being board chairman Algernon D. Black, a veteran "civil liberties" activist. John J. Cassese, president of the Patrolmen's Benevolent Association, commented, "they couldn't be impartial if they wanted to. You can see that by the board's composition."[24]

Police morale after the Lindsay investiture plummeted to new lows. Three of the department's top officials were bounced in moves which had as their barely-veiled motive an obvious appeal to New York minority-group voting blocs, and more than 700 patrolmen turned in their badges during the first six months of 1966. The resignation rate was triple that of the previous year. In the 1966 elections, New York citizens had a chance to sit in judgment on all this. In a referendum on the Lindsay review board, they voted by a margin of almost two-to-one to cashier the whole arrangement.

Confronted by danger to life and limb, judicial hindrance, and a growing tide of public abuse, police are finding it hard to recruit new members. Almost every city, in addition to its other difficulties in law enforcement, could use more and better-trained policemen.* These are becoming exceedingly hard to find.

---

* It is rather astonishing to discover that, with so much crime and general anarchy confronting them, the "brutal" police are forced to spend an inordinate amount of time running errands for the citizenry. The authors, checking the statistics for their home city of Indianapolis, found that in a representative month, the police had to make some 20,000 runs to deal with such matters as lost dogs, children falling out of trees, escaped Mynah birds, getting a 300-pound woman into a cab, and rescuing cats. Compared to this staggering burden of minor service runs, the police answer "only" 3,000 or so calls a month for major crimes.

The strain on police resources by matters only indirectly related to crime is seldom understood by the citizens who call on these alleged monsters in every conceivable circumstance. In a single month, the Indianapolis police conducted 171 dog investigations, received more than 1,000 dogs at the municipal dog kennels, and destroyed more than 1,000 dogs a month throughout 1965. In addition police

Washington, D.C. police found themselves in mid-1965 with 144 vacancies on the force, and sent recruiters around the country to try to get men to join up. Former Police Commissioner Thomas J. Gibbons of Philadelphia observed: "Back in 1953 we had the first examination for police recruits under my command . . . We wound up with about 2,000 applicants to draw from. We hired almost 1,000 . . . But by 1960 things have changed . . . The simple truth is that hardly anyone wants to be a policeman. In my city it's got so bad that we now have a new plan—instead of giving one exam for four or five thousand men each year, we give the test a couple of times a week for just a handful."[25] Police official Joseph Martin of New York City sums it up when he says: "I don't know why anyone would want to be a cop today."[26]

---

in every city must contend with the massive problem of traffic safety. Indianapolis police made some 51,657 traffic arrests in the first half of 1965.

ELEVEN

Matters of Life and Death

The practical meaning of the doctrines we have reviewed, and the darkening of counsel which can result from them, are well illustrated in certain specific topics of contemporary dispute. Three of these in particular are much controverted these days in the popular press and before legislative assemblies—abortion, capital punishment, and firearms control. A brief examination of each will serve to dramatize the subjects previously discussed.

The campaign for relaxed abortion laws illustrates the powerful head of steam which has been built up behind the notion that people should be exempt from the consequences of their actions. On analysis, the overriding purpose of this agitation is to save people from the results of irresponsible behavior.

In most American states, abortion is permitted only if it is necessary to save the life of the mother. Under proposed alterations constantly being brought before state legislatures, these laws would be changed to allow termination of pregnancy if there is a threat to the "mental or physical health" of the mother, if there is likelihood the baby will be retarded or deformed, or if the pregnancy is the result of "felonious intercourse" (incest or rape).

The principal reason alleged for these changes is that figure of 1 million criminal abortions each year, previously referred to.

For one or another of the motives suggested in the various amendments, we are told, women are going to have the abortions. It is better to have such operations performed under clinically hygienic circumstances than in furtive abortion mills.

A typical statement on this subject by Edwin M. Schur notes that "even the fairly conscientious abortionist works under imperfect conditions, and must for his own safety get the woman to leave his place of work as soon after the operation as possible. Hence the inadequacy of aftercare, the frequent lack of necessary medicines and emergency equipment, and the danger inherent in the abortion itself . . . combine to make the criminal abortion highly dangerous . . ."[1]

The proposed solution to this problem is to legalize abortions —in order, as most arguments have it, to spare the mother the anguish of bearing the child of rape, or a deformed baby, or a threat to her life—the factors abortion advocates most frequently stress. An article on abortion in a popular magazine begins, for example, by citing two cases: That of a young housewife victimized by rape, and that of Mrs. Sherri Finkbine, who flew to Sweden to terminate a thalidomide-endangered pregnancy.[2] This is a characteristic presentation, conveying the idea that broadening of abortion laws is chiefly demanded to alleviate such tragic situations. This is emphatically not the case. The overwhelming majority of criminal abortions in the United States have nothing to do with either of these episodes—illustrating the truth that hard cases make good rhetoric but bad law.

What, in point of fact, are the major reasons for which women seek abortions? Although the evidence in such matters is sparse, it suggests most induced abortions are inspired by considerations such as having too many mouths to feed, embarrassment from an extramarital adventure, or the impending birth of a child to an unwed mother. The recommended phrase "mental or physical health" is intended to cover contingencies of this sort. "Mental health" can be roughly translated as "absence of anxiety"—and any unwanted pregnancy, from whatever cause, is understandably a source of considerable anxiety to all concerned.

Although it is difficult to estimate such things in the underground world of criminal abortion, it is believed the vast majority of pregnancy terminations spring from motives of this kind. One pro-abortion essay quotes, as a typical case, an 18-year-old girl who did not want to give birth to an illegitimate child: "It wouldn't be fair to the child . . . and it wouldn't be fair to me or my family." Another example of abortion hardship is a married woman who had indulged in an affair and become pregnant: "I didn't love the man. I didn't want his child. Neither did I want to have the baby and let my husband believe it was his. For the sake of our four children, I just couldn't say anything to my husband."[3]

The late David Lowe, author of *Abortion and The Law* (from which the above quotations are taken), gave this summary of the reasons for which many women seek abortions:

> Many women . . . worry, quite rightly, that their shame will never be completely safe from prying eyes . . . Many women, too, are deeply distressed by the thought of turning the care of their child over to strange hands from the moment of its birth . . .
>
> . . . a girl still struggling to complete her schooling sometimes rejects the man's offer [of marriage, not of intercourse] because she feels that she ought to finish her education before starting out to raise a family. Sometimes, too, an older woman with a well-established career, or a divorcee, will steadfastly refuse to allow her freedom to be curtailed by marriage and a family, even though she finds herself unexpectedly pregnant . . .
>
> The surprising statistic . . . is that four-fifths of all criminal abortions are performed to terminate pregnancies in married women . . . What moves such a woman to ask for an abortion is, indeed, often a feeling that her *real* responsibility is to her husband and to the children she has already borne. She may feel that there is just not enough money to support an increased household . . . she may be disturbed at the thought of having to neglect her husband and other children in order to give proper care to the new baby. In sum, most married women who seek abortions are moved by the fear that, for one reason or another, they will not be able to cope with the responsibilities of running a household that includes an additional member.[4]

Thus, the indicated reasons for abortions are shame, a desire to continue schooling, the yen for continued freedom, responsibility to one's husband and other children. These are all serious matters of inconvenience and embarrassment. But do they justify the taking of a human life in embryo? According to the dictates of the "new morality," they do. Dr. Joseph Fletcher, whom we have previously quoted, demonstrates the relevance of his "situation ethics" by remarking that the unenforceability of laws against abortion "shows the dubious moral grounds on which they rest"—an interesting way of determining moral questions. Dr. Fletcher further explains that "really, there is no act that is intrinsically good or evil. The morality of any act depends on the circumstances under which it is performed—the motives of those involved."

The widespread use of the "mental health" argument for abortion could and undoubtedly would be construed to allow pregnancy terminations in the cases listed above. Dr. Alan Guttmacher comments: "I myself would allow abortions whenever they become necessary to preserve the life or the health of the mother. And I think health should be interpreted quite broadly. In 1960 the World Health Organization spelled out what I think is a perfectly splendid definition of health: Health is a state of complete physical, mental and social well-being, not simply the absence of illness and disease."[5] Under this construction, it is not hard to see that abortion in the cases referred to would be readily sanctioned. Which would be tantamount to saying one may indulge in pre-marital or extra-marital intercourse and be relieved of the consequences by extinguishing the life thereby created.

That the real object of the abortion campaign is to permit pregnancy terminations in any and all cases where the mother desires it is not merely a matter of derogatory inference. Like Dr. Guttmacher, the abortionists have dropped several rather explicit hints pointing in this direction. One of these is the argument that abortion should be considered simply as an aspect of the mother's "freedom," with which the state is illicitly interfering. If this is so, then quite clearly abortion should be allowed on demand, since pregnancy termination is a matter entirely within the mother's discretion.

Also indicative is the remark of one authority quoted in a pro-abortion article to the effect that "our responsibility is to guarantee that no child comes into the world unwanted, unloved, uncared for."[6] Since the child-to-be becomes *ipso facto* "unwanted" by the mere desire of the mother to have an abortion, the logic of this position is that every desired abortion should be carried through to completion. Against this backdrop, the arguments about rape, deformity, *etc.* become merely window-dressing helping to sell the real program of abortion-on-demand.

The fact that the chief beneficiaries of the abortion campaign are devotees of impulse-release and not hapless victims of rape or thalidomide is made plain by the Kinsey figures. The researchers found, as noted, that pre-marital and extra-marital relations leading to pregnancy, and abortion to end unwanted pregnancies from whatever cause, are far more frequent among the religiously inactive than among the religiously devout. *Statistically, the Kinsey researchers discovered, the distinguishing factor most common to induced abortion cases is the relative absence of religious-moral conviction.* People who honor religious injunctions about responsible behavior do not find themselves so frequently troubled by unwanted pregnancies and are less likely to have them terminated if they occur. The abortion problem about which we are invited to agonize is characteristically a problem of the "modern" or "emancipated" woman. The devout somehow manage to bear up under the intolerable stress of not being able to kill their babies in embryo.

The abortion campaign for the most part boils down, therefore, to a demand that people who have lost interior restraints on their behavior be exempt from exterior restraints as well; that they be allowed to gratify their impulses without shouldering the economic and moral responsibilities hitherto connected with the sexual act. The campaign is an almost perfect illustration of the current desire to have all the pleasures of this world but none of the obligations, carried to the point where a potential human life is extinguished in order to achieve this *summa* of indulgence.

Abortions from the minority motives—concern about deformity and rape—are more understandable, but still subject to confusions. In the case of possible deformity, the choice is indeed difficult. If we put aside the theological argument that all life is precious *per se*, it can plausibly be argued that a hideously deformed child is better off dead than alive. But, in this event, the abortionist should have the courage of his convictions. Instead of killing the child in embryo before it is known whether it will be deformed, wait until it is born: If it is deformed, kill it then; if it is not deformed, let it live.

Harsh? Cruel? Unthinkable? Yes; but, then, so is the alternative argument of the abortionists. On this premise, non-deformed children would live. On the abortionists' premise, non-deformed children would be killed. The difference is that the child would have to be killed after it has emerged from the womb, rather than before. In the latter event, an unseen child is killed; in the former, the victim can be seen. As to the technical point of whether an actual life is at stake, the arguments applied by the abortionists to the embryo can be applied with equal cogency to the new-born infant: A child just emerged from the womb has no waking consciousness; it is just as much, or as little, a "life" one minute after it emerges from the womb as it is one minute before.

A fully developed fetus is not a blob of protoplasm; it is a miniature human being, with arms, legs, and features. It is of course biologically dependent upon its mother, but the new-born infant, while the umbilical cord is unsevered, is equally so. Indeed, even when the umbilical cord is cut, the infant is still completely dependent on its mother. Is it therefore more of a "life" than the fetus it was shortly before birth? If so, why?

Infanticide is often considered at law to be a lesser crime than murder, and the extenuations advanced in its behalf are markedly similar to those employed in the cause of abortion (mental anxiety, economic circumstance, malformation, etc.). Infanticide is also considered quite respectable in primitive cultures, particularly where a child is deformed. Some modern societies (Greece and Bulgaria) recognize deformity of the child as a mitigating circumstance in such cases. To our taste this seems brutal, but it is in essence the same action we are being asked to sanction in the case of broadened abortion statutes. We want to achieve the identical results, but prefer to screen out that fact by killing the child before it emerges from the womb rather than after.

One additional item: the evidence of Scandinavian experience suggests that broadening the abortion laws actually increases the abortion rate, and does not provably lower the rate of illegal pregnancy terminations. Schur notes that in Sweden this question is much disputed, and that "it is always possible that, when broad indications for abortion are legally sanctioned, the over-all abortion rate will increase and a substantial number of illegal abortions will continue to be performed."

The Kinsey researchers likewise observe: "So far, the [Swedish] results . . . do not show any clear-cut evidence of a 'noteworthy' reduction in illegal abortion, and it has been claimed by some that the number has actually been increasing. The statement was made that the 'termination of pregnancy has become a matter of every-day discussion,' and that this has resulted in the population becoming increasingly 'abortion-minded.' One conjecture is that the legal abortion clientele is a group of women quite separate from those who would resort to illegal abortion. If this were the case, it might well be that total abortions have risen."[7]

What, then, to do about the complex problems of rape, illegitimacy, and the abortion mill? Some possible answers might include: (a) Stop releasing rapists on technicalities. It is an odd fact that the abortion advocates who complain so much about the traumatic experience of pregnancy resulting from rape seldom suggest dealing with the original source of the problem—the rapist. Why not prevent the trauma by cracking down on rape itself? Why not move to counteract the actions of the courts, in *Mallory* and similar decisions, which free rapists to strike repeatedly at society?

(b) Stop subsidizing the birth of illegitimate children through ADC programs. Again, advocates of abortion, sterilization, and birth control programs seldom mention the overriding major cause of the problem: The fact that, under ADC, there is a positive bounty for giving birth to illegitimate children. They prefer to dwell on the symptoms of the problem rather than the cause of it.

(c) Start enforcing the existing and presently non-enforced laws against abortion. Part of the immense difficulty in the field of abortion is that both doctors and police have taken to winking at abortion statutes. Non-enforcement of the laws obviously encourages the abortion mills to function, and leads women with unwanted pregnancies to believe they can have abortions without running excessive risk of legal consequences.

The capital punishment issue is, if anything, even more emotional and bitterly contested than the question of abortion. Among the charges mounted by those who would abolish the death penalty, three in particular shall occupy our attention: That it is *per se* immoral, that it is "irrevocable" and sometimes punishes innocent men, and that it does not deter potential criminals.

On the morality of the question, the essential point is whether the state has the right to take a life in order to protect other lives. By general consent, it does; that awful authority is implicit in the war-making power, and a state without that authority could not in fact exist. The same moral sanction which holds it proper to wage war and to kill people in order to protect the lives of the citizenry from external enemies applies equally to the power of the state to inflict capital punishment to protect the lives of the citizenry from internal enemies. The only philosophical position from which capital punishment can be *a priori* condemned is an anarchist-pacifist stance which in effect holds that the state itself has no right to exist. This is not, needless to remark, the position taken by the majority of those who advocate repeal of the death penalty.

As for the argument that justice is sometimes miscarried, this is true, and tragic. It is not, however, the fault of the death penalty as such, but of the machinery of justice which arrives at the wrong decision. As Jacques Barzun observes: "What is at fault in our present system is not the sentence but the fallible procedure . . . What the miscarriages point to is the need for reforming the jury system, the rules of evidence, the customs of prosecution, the machinery of appeal."[8] Human fallibility is always with us, of course, and should be guarded against in every possible way. But it should be remembered that the human beings who run the judicial system have it as their mission to strike a law-enforcement balance that maximizes lives. And just as a mistake on the side of rigor through the death penalty *can* result in the death of an innocent man, so mistakes on the side of leniency *can* result in the deaths of many innocent men. The present evidence shows the balance has been struck far on the nether side of leniency, and life is not being maximized. To abolish the death penalty under these circumstances would be to throw the system still further out of phase, to minimize life rather than to maximize it.

The chief issue in the capital punishment controversy is whether it deters crimes such as murder, treason, rape, and kidnapping. The record is extraordinarily unclear. Opponents of the penalty point out that some states which do not have capital punishment have murder rates as low as, or lower than, those which do have it. This is true, and as such constitutes an argument against capital punishment; if it does not in fact deter, there is no reason for it. The question is complicated, however, by the fact that the states without the death penalty are, on the whole, small states which are doubtful indicators of national trends. Police Chief Edward Allen of Santa Ana, Calif., comments on this fact as follows:

> Where crime and murder are at a low level and where community life is governed by respect and reverence for law, rather than by its enforcement, then severe punitive measures may be relaxed . . . On the other hand, where crime and murder are a serious problem, then the removal of stringent punitive measures further aggravates it. The eight states which re-enacted the death penalty after a trial period without it discovered this to their dismay.*
> The seven states within the corporate limits of the United States which do not have the death penalty are among the smallest, in territory and/or population: Delaware, Maine, Michigan, Minnesota, North Dakota, Rhode Island, and Wisconsin. There is among them only one really large state, Michigan, whose 1958 population of 7,865,547 exceeds by more than a half-million the six other states. Michigan's 1958 murder rate per 100,000 population was 3.1, not only the highest of these seven states, but higher than both Pennsylvania and New York, two of the three most populous states in the union—with over eleven [and] 16 million respectively . . . New York has a 2.8 rate and Pennsylvania 2.5.[9]

---

* Kansas, Iowa, Colorado, Washington, Oregon, Arizona, Missouri, and Tennessee.

Law enforcement officers believe the penalty is a deterrent in the case of the professional criminal—the burglar, bank robber, or stick-up man who steals for a living. Without the death penalty, police officers say, this kind of criminal has less compunction about shooting down the policeman who attempts to arrest him. With it, he is likely to surrender before incurring a murder rap.

Killings committed during the execution of other crimes—"felony murders"—are of particular concern to the FBI. J. Edgar Hoover states: "It is the law enforcement position that this is generally the type of killing for which the death penalty should be retained as a deterrent."[10] Again the data are inconclusive, with the felony murder rate as a percentage of total population lower in non-capital punishment states, but higher as a percentage of total willful killings. The self-preservation instincts of the police lead them to believe that, on a common sense analysis, the death penalty is in fact a deterrent to this kind of homicide.

Perhaps the most crucial element in the capital punishment controversy is the fact that the repeal effort is occurring precisely at a time when other deterrent factors are being removed—and when many criminals, as we have previously noted, are being released from jail on various technicalities. Under the impact of Supreme Court decisions, expanded use of "insanity" findings to acquit defendants, and relaxation of parole procedures, the number of criminal repeaters is large and constantly growing. The result is that many innocent people are being attacked and murdered by criminals who have been in the clutches of the law and turned loose.

Measured against these facts, the current effort to repeal the death penalty does not make a great deal of sense. To remove one more possibly inhibiting factor will certainly not deter potential killers, and if it emboldens only one that is one too many. To add one more evidence of concern for criminals to an already lenient system can only be interpreted as adding one more token of indifference toward the victims.

This indifference becomes the more obvious when we note the stages by which the capital punishment argument progresses. In urging repeal of the penalty, abolitionists assert that "society is amply protected by a sentence of life imprisonment." Once the murderer is in prison, however, that argument fades from view; the thought of protecting society is replaced with the notion of "rehabilitating" the criminal. He must therefore be eligible for parole (the characteristic stance of the abolitionists is that life imprisonment without parole is unacceptable, hardly better than execution itself). Thus a murderer may not only escape with his life, but in time regain his freedom as well.

It is difficult to believe considerations of this sort do not have some kind of impact on the mind of a potential killer, resulting in homicides that could have been avoided. It is significant that no less than eight states which had at one time abolished the penalty returned to it—almost invariably as a result of garish murders. In Washington state, restoration was spurred by the case of a murderer who "boasted that he would be sent to the pen for life and cared for" by the state. In Michigan, restoration very nearly came about when a convicted murderer escaped, killed two people, was recaptured and killed the prison warden and his deputy.

Thorsten Sellin and others argue that, on the average, murder rates have not gone up when capital punishment has been abolished, and that, on the average, recidivism among murderers is low. But the average is of little comfort to the individual citizen killed by a murderer who is conscious that his own life is not at stake, or who has been imprisoned and escaped, or who has been paroled. In Pennsylvania, between 1946 and 1956, 64 murderers received parole and five of them committed additional murders. In California, between 1945 and 1960, five murderers who had received parole committed additional homicidal offenses. J. Edgar Hoover cites a grisly 1930s case in Florida in which a prisoner "committed two murders, received clemency for each, then committed a double murder to show how much he was reformed."[11]

The satisfaction of the abolitionists on the grounds that recidivism among murderers is not statistically high suggests a peculiar insensitivity to the real nub of the problem. The point is that even one additional murder committed under such entirely avoidable circumstances amounts to innocent blood on the hands of the authorities. While the penologists congratulate themselves on the murderers they have rehabilitated, the unrehabilitated residue find additional victims who would otherwise be spared. The abolitionists who complain of "judicial murder" and express horror at taking the lives of the guilty seem altogether too complacent about the lives of the innocent.

It is an established maxim of legal studies that certainty of punishment is more important than severity of punishment—a point frequently made in opposition to the death penalty. In present circumstances, however, the argument could well be reversed. With the growing lenience of courts and parole boards, it is the rare criminal who cannot calculate that, even if he is caught, he can soon enough regain his freedom. The psychological result is to replace the idea of certain punishment with the contrary idea of certain escape. Capital punishment, whatever else it may or may not do, supplies a needed element of finality.

There is, after all, one absolutely certain deterrent factor in capital punishment which the abolitionists do not mention: The criminal the death penalty infallibly does deter is the one who has already killed and been convicted. Once executed, such mad dogs are incapable of getting out and killing anybody else. In an age of elasticized judicial tolerance freeing killers on any number of pretexts, that is a protection law-abiding citizens can ill afford to be without.

Finally, it should be noted that if the arguments we have reviewed on abortion and capital punishment make little sense when considered separately, they make almost no sense when considered together. They illustrate, indeed, the curiously ambivalent attitude of modern-day crime theoreticians toward human life. On the one hand, the modern-day advocates of greater permissiveness favor snuffing out a human life in embryo if the birth of a child is deemed hazardous to the physical or mental health of its mother.

On the other hand, the permissivists argue strenuously against capital punishment, asking that society spare the lives of twisted human beings who have actually killed or grievously injured other people and may well do so again if given the opportunity.

The contradictory implications of these two views are apparent, but will become more definite if we relate them to a single crime, that of rape. Broadening of abortion laws would, in general, allow the termination of pregnancies resulting from rape on humanitarian grounds, arguing that society owes this much to the mother. But what does society owe the mother with respect to the rape itself? Is it possible rape can better be prevented by making it a capital crime?* Those who favor abolishing capital punishment say it cannot, arguing that such "judicial murder" is barbaric.

Thus according to the two lines of reasoning prevalent in current discourse, it is justifiable to extinguish the life created by the crime of rape, but not justifiable to extinguish the life of the person who committed it. An innocent child-to-be may be killed, but a guilty man may not.

It is argued, of course, that the embryo to be killed in the case of rape or other special factors singled out in the abortion crusade is not really a "life"—merely a potential one. But in the absence of the abortion that potential life would become a living, breathing human being. The murderer or rapist is a human being in whom the potential of true humanity has already gone awry. Why is it justifiable to take a life which could have great potential, but unjustifiable to take a life which has already gone smash and has visited terrible harm on other people?

Reflecting an equally contradictory set of emotions is the subject of firearms regulation. In response to a number of 1966 shooting incidents, strenuous demands were raised for measures controlling gun sales. This was imperative, said numerous editorialists and lawmakers, if episodes like the Charles Whitman tragedy in Texas were not to be repeated.

While this show of energy in seeking an end to crime is commendable, it is curious to observe that most of the anti-gun agitation has proceeded from segments of the community not previously noted for urgent concern on the topic of law enforcement. We are entitled to wonder, in fact, where all these people

---

* Capital punishment is specified for rape in 16 states and the District of Columbia.

have been during the controversy over the Supreme Court decisions, judicial leniency in general, civil disobedience, and capital punishment.

The demand that somebody "do something" about guns has, nonetheless, a certain merit. Easy access to hand-guns and mail-order firearms in general plays a contributory role in the crime wave, and deserves attention. But the evidence suggests that emphasis on firearms as the *cause* of crime repeats the error committed by the poverty theoreticians—it mistakes a material instrument or condition of lawlessness for the impulse behind it.

The most obvious flaw in the guns-cause-crime argument is the fact that so many people are stabbed, beaten, or strangled to death, with firearms in no way involved. Repeated episodes of this sort indicate that, in the absence of guns, a prospective killer would simply resort to something else. The case of the eight nurses in Chicago, murdered by stabbing and by strangulation, suggests clearly that the difficulty rests with the killer and not the weapon. All the firearms laws in the world would not have prevented that mass slaying, and if the present logic were extended to cover such situations it would be necessary to require regulation of knives as well as guns.

Conversely, the Whitman case shows how difficult it would be for registration laws to stop even those killers who do employ guns. Whitman allegedly committed one of his killings, that of his wife, by stabbing. He was, moreover, not a criminal type but a clean-living sportsman and gun fancier who would not have been prevented from owning firearms by proposed registration laws. Whitman could have committed his killings with a registered gun just as well as with an unregistered one.

On the other hand, the increased difficulty of getting hold of guns could have an adverse effect on the people who under present circumstances need them most—private citizens who are not hunters or gun-fanciers but who fear the law cannot or will not protect them. Many of the self-protection efforts referred to in Chapter I involve the attempts of such citizens to arm themselves against criminal attack. In Orlando, Fla., women formed a "pistol packing posse" to protect themselves from rapists. In Detroit, a group of 200 grocers got together to receive training in the use of firearms and subsequently shot down five men attempting robberies. The Dallas man who believes people "have lost confidence in the ability of the government to protect them," says customers are flocking to his store for handguns. "If I could get them, I would sell twice as many now as five years ago," he comments.

If a sharp crackdown on legal ownership of guns is enacted, who will be hurt? The criminal who is committed to illegality anyway, and who will not balk at getting an illegal gun? Or the law-abiding citizen who is already fearful his government is powerless or unwilling to protect him?

Is there, finally, any evidence that the prevalence of firearms actually causes crime? Although various crime theoreticians say there is, the existing figures on the subject are not convincing. FBI statistics show that the South, where killing by firearms is most prevalent, has a high murder rate. But the Midwest, where firearms are also prevalent, has a lower murder rate than does the East, where the majority of murders are not committed by firearms. The preponderant evidence seems to show that murder occurs regardless of the implements available.[12]

Sen. Frank Church, D-Idaho, addressed himself persuasively to this point in testimony before the Senate subcommittee on juvenile delinquency. Advocates of gun-control laws, Church said, had cause and effect relationships turned around, as could be deduced from a comparison of crime rates in control-minded New York City with those in his own state of Idaho. Church told the committee members:

"New York City, with its Sullivan Act, imposes regulations so strict upon the acquisition of firearms that only 17,000 out of a municipal population of 8 million own handguns. Yet, in 1965, the city's rate per 100,000 persons for the crimes of murder, robbery and aggravated assault was 244.2.

"In Idaho, for the same three crimes most generally perpetrated by a gun, the rate was 65.7. If there are statistics to prove that the strict provisions of the Sullivan Act have diminished crime in New York City, I have not seen them . . .

"It simply stands to reason that a man who wants a gun to commit a crime will find a way to get one . . . As for sudden crimes of a passion, they will continue to be committed by whatever weapon is at hand—a club, a gun, a knife, or broken bottle.

"Does it follow that housewives, then, must be licensed to purchase carving knives? Should teen-agers be required to show sandlot permits in order to buy baseball bats? Logic alone would seem to compel the conclusion that the control of crime depends upon how effectively we track down and deal with the offender, not upon futile attempts to foreclose his choice of weapons."[13]

This is also the view of Marvin E. Wolfgang of the University of Pennsylvania in his authoritative *Patterns In Criminal Homicide*. In a meticulous case-by-case analysis of murders committed over a period of years in the city of Philadelphia, Wolfgang sought to establish various causative links for homicide. Examining motives, immediate physical circumstances, emotional relationships between criminal and victim, and the types of weapons employed, Wolfgang concludes that motivation is of the first importance, choice of weapons secondary.

In some cases in which the killer is much smaller and weaker than the victim, he says, the use of firearms may be decisive. But on the whole: "It is probably safe to contend that many homicides occur because there is sufficient motivation or provocation, and that the type of method used to kill is merely an accident of availability; that a gun is used because it is in the killer's possession at the time of incitement, but that if it were not present, he would use a knife to stab, or fists to beat his victim to death."

Wolfgang subsequently adds that "material . . . reported in the present study regarding the place where homicide occurred, relationship between victim and offender, motives, and other variables, suggests that many situations, events and personalities that converge in a particular way and that result in homicide do not depend primarily on the presence or absence of firearms."[14]

Thus it appears this particular effort to place the blame for crime on aspects of the material environment is no more successful than the attempt to trace responsibility to the stress of poverty. It once more appears, in fact, that what a man does in his environment is of considerably more importance than what his environment does to him.

TWELVE

Ideas Have Consequences

Why, then, do we have a crime wave?

The preceding chapters have attempted, so far as is possible, to take up, individually, a number of contributing influences. A more realistic assessment, of course, must consider them all together, since the pressures and tendencies dominant in our society operate simultaneously, interacting upon and reinforcing one another.

If we take such an overview, it hardly seems surprising that we have increasing crime. It would be far more surprising if we did not. Every conceivable incentive, from the exalted regions of philosophy to the materialistic immediacies of getting and spending, has been deployed to encourage rather than to thwart the criminal impulse.

Civilization is at best a compromise with crime—a veneer of order, superimposed upon powerful impulses pressing us toward the jungle. On this point, such disparate authorities as Judaeo-Christian tradition, Freudian psychoanalysis, and modern sociology are agreed. Drives to self-gratification are born inside every child; the value restraints controlling and directing those drives must be slowly and often painfully learned. The prevention of criminals, in the simplest case, depends on this effort to make value superior to impulse.

There are four methods which, taken together, make this problem more or less manageable: (1) an interior limitation of desires through the inculcation of moral and religious value; (2) learning what is proper when one does seek gratification (*e.g.*, that it is correct to gain fulfilment through industry and self-help, but not through taking what belongs to someone else); (3) replacing the childish urge to have one's immediate wants fulfilled with an understanding that certain prospects must be deferred—that long-range interests can often be disserved by heedless indulgence of immediate whims; and (4) grasping the somewhat sterner lesson, through the formal mechanisms of society, that one is subject to penalties at law for criminal behavior.

If these precepts are successfully imparted, young people can be assimilated to the society as law-abiding, functioning citizens, and outbursts of criminal impulse can be held tolerably in check. In our present condition, however, we find the reverse of this process taking place. Instead of combining to limit impulse, major tendencies in our society are combining to secure its release. Instead of taming primitive appetites, we are doing everything to expand them. Instead of directing energies into the channels of labor and diligence, we are teaching people they have an inherent right to take what they want. Instead of teaching the long view, we are urging young people to live for the moment and forget tomorrow. And, instead of teaching the sanctity of the law, we are telling young people they can indulge themselves in illegality and get away with it.

The influences leading to this result cover a broad range of activities—from permissive child-raising and progressive schools to "civil disobedience" and judicial leniency. But if any of these can be singled out as primary, it is the revolution in ideas—the no right, no wrong philosophy that has ushered in the "new morality." As the late Professor Richard Weaver observed, ideas have consequences. If you preach long enough that there is no right and no wrong, you may sooner or later expect people to start behaving as if there were no right and no wrong.

As stated, this may seem obvious enough. But in our day and age, nothing is considered less obvious. No one is more startled by the rise of crime than the academicians who have told us there are no fixed standards of value; no one is more aghast at Smerdyakov's crime than Ivan. The sources of human motivation these days are not sought in ideas. They are sought in economic circumstance, childhood trauma, promptings of the "unconscious mind"—in anything but the conscious, more or less formally maintained value systems of society.

Yet proofs of the efficacy of belief in controlling behavior are impressive. As we have noted, Dr. Kinsey's own researches and other similar data repeatedly confirm the impact of religious conviction on the ways in which people act. Reinhold Niebuhr comments that ". . . the evidence points to the fact that religion has an effect on conduct, particularly sex conduct, beyond and above specific requirements of moral law. The religious heightening of the sense of personal responsibility, for covenants in which one is engaged, of mutual respect and fidelity between persons and the religious accentuation of personal self-respect, must certainly be operative in the lives which yield these impressive statistics."[1]

The same point is demonstrated in the ghetto evidence pertaining to Chinese and Jewish families. In both these cases, the distinctive feature is a strong emphasis on religious and cultural value and on the solidarity of the family. Conversely, the findings at Vassar and other universities show that a student subjected to four years of "relativist" teaching is likely to emerge a good deal more receptive to various kinds of dishonesty or lawbreaking than when he or she entered college.

At a less spectacular level, a graphic illustration of the impact of ideas on action is afforded by the subject of academic cheating. A 1965 study by Columbia University's Bureau of Applied Social Research found a high level of cheating in America's colleges. Several elements produced variations in the level of cheating, including such things as fraternity or sorority membership, grade level, and family income. In most cases, however, these differences resulted in variations of only a few percentage points. The single most important distinction was simply *the attitude of the school and the students toward cheating*. In cases where disapproval of cheating was rated "very strong," the number who cheated came to 23 per cent; in cases where disapproval was rated "very weak," the number who cheated came to 69 per cent. No other single difference produced a variation of this size.[2] Cohen's "normative reference group"—in this case one's fellow students—is obviously quite influential in determining patterns of conduct.

One's personal attitude toward right and wrong is shaped, additionally, by the view of the matter taken by the authorities to whom one is accountable for his actions. In this respect, too, the major influences in American and other Western cultures have been arrayed in opposition to law-abiding behavior. Social and political authority has absolved individuals of responsibility for their conduct, remitted penalties for criminal behavior, and seconded the concept of "civil disobedience." This constant stress on non-accountability for various kinds of malperformance contributes measurably to crime.

Laboratory studies in the prevention of violent action tell us that if aggressive behavior is punished it tends to diminish. If it is rewarded or held up for admiration, it tends to increase. As Dr. Richard H. Walters observes concerning a number of laboratory tests with children: "A model who is rewarded or is not punished for breaking a prohibition is likely to be imitated by children . . . whereas imitative prohibition-breaking is unlikely to occur if the model is punished for his behavior."[3]

The experiments summarized by Walters yield two important conclusions. First, that certainty of punishment will act as a deterrent to lawless behavior—an ancient principle reaffirmed; second, that rewards and approval for violent behavior will induce other people to imitate that behavior.

Most of the things we have reviewed so far in this essay tend toward removing punishment for wayward behavior, be the punishment moral disapproval, social sanctions, or economic loss. "Civil disobedience" both extends and complements these tendencies, since as currently espoused it not only seeks to do away with punishment but actively encourages lawlessness and portrays it as admirable. In Walters' terms, it has provided us with countless "models" who have been praised and rewarded for "prohibition-breaking."

The effect of such "models" on American young people is obviously profound. The young are the inheritors of the whole intellectual, moral and political machinery we have been building—the legatees of "relativism," permissiveness, disobedience and the rest of it. They are the products of progressive homes, progressive schools, and the progressive society at large. And they are the particular beneficiaries of judicial lenience. Above all others, they are held non-accountable for their acts, in need of compassion and understanding when they commit an infraction of the law.

Most important, young people are susceptible to the impact of ideas. Coming fresh into the world, they are more easily impressed by some rather simplistic conception than are adults. We may be certain the influence of such things as increasingly bold pornography, the exploitation of sex and sensationalism, will be most decisive in the minds of the young. Having been told to "express" themselves, and having seen such practice smiled upon in the adult world, they can be counted on to redouble the effect of permissive doctrine. They may even be relied upon to pick up what is relevant to them among the more esoteric matters under discussion. Some young people in trouble with the law, according to former Washington, D.C. Police Chief Robert Murray, have said: "You can't ask me questions. Don't you know about the *Mallory* decision?"[4]

Second only in influence to the no-right, no-wrong philosophy and its derivatives is the day-to-day operation of the welfare state principle that rewards in life are unconnected with effort. This is a major source of "boredom," of the idea that people are entitled to something for nothing, and the notion that the individual should not have to suffer the consequences of improvident behavior. If there is no need to labor to achieve things, the idea of purposeful work—of any work at all—is foreclosed. The amenities of life have no functional connection with employment. The provision of cradle-to-grave security by the state relegates the individual to a kind of vegetable limbo, where he is merely an integer in the calculations of the planners. Eroded value and the transfer of responsibilities from the individual to the state, taken together, effectively preclude the possibility of human dignity.

The combined influence of relativist ethics and welfare economics produces almost perfect conditions for what we have called the "infantilization" of our culture, and for the emergence of crime: We are getting a character type which places no restraints on impulse and wants everything "now," but which is incapable of organizing behavior rationally for the fulfilment of wants. The net result closely resembles Prof. Norman O. Brown's definition of "prolonged infancy," which combines the impulse to "omnipotent indulgence in pleasure" with "powerless dependency on other people."[5] The tension between ravenous desire and indifferent skills militates in favor of psychopathic character disorganization and criminal activity.

As a pre-vision of what can happen under this dual influence, it might be well to take a glance at Sweden—the most celebrated exemplar, outside the Iron Curtain, of "new morality" and welfare economics alike. Since Sweden has proceeded a good deal further than we down the twin paths of permissive morals and collectivist politics, and since its performance has so frequently been commended to America for emulation, a few observations on its track record may provide some insight into what could eventually happen here.

Sweden is noted, to begin with, for the permissiveness of its moral atmosphere. As one commentary has it, "atheism, religious indifference and moral 'nihilism' are found among young and 'radical' intellectuals who are now dominating public discussion in Sweden."[6] The influence of organized religion, despite official recognition given the church, is shaky.

Herbert Hendin records in his study of suicides that while "about one-half of the Swedish suicide patients stressed that they believed in God," only half of these in turn thought there was an afterlife. "Some of the believers in God denied their belief at first, but expressed it later, indicating that they had been ashamed and did not want to be ridiculed. It seemed to be more shameful to believe than not to believe."[7]

The absence of strong discipline in home and school is also a notable feature of Swedish life. "Police officials who have examined thousands of young delinquents," says *U.S. News*, "find that many lacked care and moral guidance in their early childhood because both parents were working, or because the father was an alcoholic." The magazine also notes "Sweden's extremely liberal methods of education, lack of discipline and a high percentage of truancy in schools."[8]

An important factor in this picture, according to Swedish authorities, has been the decline of the father in Swedish life—a suggestive finding which confirms Lord Russell's view of the diminishing role played by the male parent in the welfare state. The "new morality" also contributes to this result, since the whole thrust of the sexual liberation movement and associated developments is to break up the old patterns of normal family life.

Also characteristic of Sweden is a fade-out of historical memory, a reliance on TV, movies and superficial pop culture for knowledge and patterns of emulation. Anders Garai, a public school teacher in Stockholm, conducted a survey of Swedish young people in elementary and secondary schools. "Tests handed in by pupils in the highest secondary school grades," Garai reports, "contained an alarming number of spelling errors. There was considerably less interest manifested toward arts and letters than toward science, technology, and all sorts of specialized detail . . . Ignorance as regards art and music was almost total . . ."

Garai concludes that "while social engineering has improved both living standards and educational facilities, the cultural standards of Sweden's youth are declining . . . Sweden is becoming a culturally impoverished country in which an anti-cultural mentality is almost fashionable."[9]

Erik Anners gives us a similar picture of Swedish education. He notes that Swedish elementary schools, in which free range of subject choice is open to the pupils, are characterized by all the usual problems of crowding, shortage of teachers, and "a disturbingly low level of knowledge." As a result, he writes, "departures from normal standards of behavior and disciplinary difficulties multiply." In mathematics lessons, surveys showed that "only about half the pupils of the higher grades were able to follow the lessons. The intellectual participation of the rest in the lesson amounted to nil." As a result, educational standards have been lowered. "Parliament decided in 1964 to create a new grammar school whose structure permits an easy adaptation to the far lower level of knowledge of the pupils finishing elementary school."[10]

In keeping with the most advanced moral ideas, Swedish young people are instructed minutely in matters of sexual behavior and are more or less expected to sleep together in their teens if they feel like it. *Look* magazine reports that "in some schools, ninth-grade classes visit birth-control centers to learn contraceptive techniques."[11] Contraceptives are sold throughout the nation at special stores; a survey of one test group of young people found 75 per cent of them had slept with members of the opposite sex before they were 21.

Since 1946, Sweden has allowed abortion on the grounds of "anticipated weakness" of the mother in bearing and raising the child. Swedish law also allows "humanitarian" abortion where the expectant mother is under 15 years of age. As Schur observes, these provisions have not done much to prevent illegitimate births in Sweden. He adds that "the more lenient attitude toward unwed motherhood in Sweden partly accounts for this . . ."[12]

Much of this activity has received the approval of religious figures in Sweden—although the matter is still subject to controversy among more conservative clergymen. The editor of a Lutheran magazine speaks favorably of pre-marital intercourse "because, in reality, there are many young couples not yet married who are living together and are not acting immorally . . . We must have respect for all opinions."[13] The chief medical officer of the Swedish Royal Board of Education believes young people should be given even more knowledge about contraception in order "to make people more free—to not be so terribly inhibited."[14]

In the politico-economic realm, Sweden is a welfare state with few peers. Among other welfare provisions, the Swedish state offers government-subsidized care at childbirth and subsidies to mothers; provides subventions of $180 a year for each child; provides free education, textbooks and meals; gives high-school and university students a government-paid allowance of $35 a month; pays hospital, doctor and other medical bills, plus sick pay; offers old age and disability pensions irrespective of need; gives housing and rent subsidies. An additional fillip is the provision of relief funds to "work-shy" citizens who refuse to accept employment.

According to current theory, Sweden should be a sane, healthy, crime-free paradise. The evil "frustrations" and "inhibitions" of an outworn morality have been shattered; people are free to do what they will. A "healthy" wide-open attitude about sex and wide distribution of contraceptives should cut down on such things as illegitimacies and venereal disease. Systematic welfarism at every conceivable level should relieve everyone of economic hardship or anxiety concerning it, so that if "poverty" is an essential cause of crime Sweden should have no crime at all.

The record, however, is otherwise. Sweden is in fact racked by a crime explosion. It is beset by violence, theft, alcoholism, venereal disease, drug addiction, juvenile delinquency, rape and assaults, and the whole gamut of vice. As a result of the "new morality," venereal disease in Sweden is not down, but up. Look reports "the rising incidence of venereal disease in Sweden despite the virtual absence of prostitution, the presence of sex education and the easy availability of contraceptives that would prevent most cases of gonorrhea, baffles the experts."[15]

According to journalist Alfred Zanker, "costly welfare and educational reforms" in Sweden have not forestalled a sizable increase in "such social ills as crime, alcoholism, and drug addiction." Swedish crime, Zanker says, has doubled since 1950, with a particular upsurge notable among young people. He reports that "officials attribute the rise in crime and antisocial behavior among youths to a deterioration of family life. It appears, these officials say, that the welfare state has not strengthened either family ties or moral standards."[16]

So far has the development proceeded that Sweden, by informed estimate, has become a global leader in the field of juvenile delinquency. Roul Tunley says:

> Checking into official figures, I was surprised to find that Sweden probably has the highest juvenile delinquency rate in the world, higher than ours. According to Karl-Erik Granath, direc-

tor of the Child Welfare Council in Stockholm, 3 per cent of Sweden's teen-age youth go through their courts.[17]

The general crime picture is little better. U.S. News discloses that

> Official statistics reveal that crime is booming in Sweden. Known offenses against the penal code have risen from 172,000 in 1950 to 373,000 last year [1965]. The crime rate per 100,000 of population has gone up 97 per cent in 15 years . . . In the last two years, the crime rate has shot up even more [rapidly]. Criminal offenses in that period have gone up 22 per cent. Reported rapes and robberies went up 55 to 60 per cent in the two-year period. Delinquency alone is said to account for the whole increase in offenses since the early 1950s . . .

The magazine adds that Swedish "law enforcement is often slow and inefficient because of a chronic shortage of qualified policemen. Influential newspapers and welfare officials frequently side with the criminal and there is a tendency to excuse the young offender, especially if he has an unhappy family background. Most young offenders, among them many repeaters, get away unpunished or are placed on probatioa or parole."[18]

We do not pretend to have given anything like a complete survey of events in Sweden, or of the causes behind them. We have culled a few journalistic highlights to point up a rather striking parallel to what is going on in America, and to suggest the possible net impact of various influences at work in our country in the years and months ahead. We believe the resemblances are notable. "New morality," ethical relativism, the crusading fervor for sexual liberation, all have their obvious counterparts in the Vassar results, the "new left," the campaign to disseminate the pill, the break-up of the family and so on. The permissiveness of Swedish homes and schools is being duplicated in American homes and schools. Also similar is the tendency among certain elements of the clergy to yield to all this, to go along with the moral "revolution" in order to keep the church "relevant" to secular society. On the economic front, the resemblances are plainer still. We are rapidly enmeshing ourselves in the same system of cradle-to-grave security, government-sponsored medical programs, public housing, and so forth that has been the norm in Sweden for three decades.

Perhaps the most striking point of resemblance is the common life-style emerging from the two societies. The general phrase for the "typical" Swedish personality is "lack of affectivity"—emotional remoteness, a deadening absence of all feeling for others. Hendin offers these comments:

> One of the most common marital complaints in Sweden concerns difficulty in reaching the marital partner emotionally . . . There is an apt Swedish idiom, *tiga ihjäl*, meaning—to kill somebody through silence. . . . The [Swedish] man is . . . likely to keep aloof from close emotional contact with his children . . . [19]

That these allusions reflect an underlying reality in Swedish life is seen in suicidal patients. Consider this emotional portrait of one such patient, described as being thoroughly representative:

> The patient was preoccupied with religious problems. He suspected that his suicide attempt was foolish, since life after death would probably be a continuation of the pleasureless, apathetic deadness that he had always known.
> His feeling of emotional deadness, his view of his life as a pleasureless chore, and his conception of an afterlife as a continuation of that chore were themes that recurred in many Swedish patients and have a uniquely Swedish quality. His idea of an afterlife contained no special punishment; none was needed, since continuation would be punishment enough . . . In varying intensity this syndrome was found to be characteristic of the Swedish patients.[20]

Granted the wide distinctions that exist between almost any two cultures, it is possible to see parallels between the Swedish life-style and the American. There has been, in the first place, a profound change in American psychology toward welfare-style collectivism, and a corresponding loss of "affectivity." We have become, as David Riesman argues, a nation of "other-directed" people, no longer capable of self-reliant behavior.

There has been in America, Riesman says, "an enormous ideological shift favoring submission to the group."[21] He describes one sampling of American youngsters who have come under his analytical microscope as follows: "They want social security, not great achievements. They want approval, not fame. They are not eager to develop talents that might bring them into conflict; whereas the inner-directed young person tended to push himself to the limit of his talents and beyond." Of still another group, he says: "More 'socialized,' more cooperative than their parents, they do not react as individuals to what happens to them."[22]

William H. Whyte similarly observes that the new "social ethic" holds that man, "by sublimating himself in the group . . . helps produce a whole that is greater than the sum of its parts . . . Boiled down, what they ask for is an environment in which everyone is tightly knit into a belongingness with one another; one in which there is no restless wandering but rather the deep emotional security that comes from total integration with the group."[23]

The dialectical relationship between loss of identity and the search for security in the annihilating potencies of the group is also noted by Keniston. Even though his subjects have resisted the urge toward immersion, he finds it a dominant theme of their personalities. Their self-conscious lack of commitment, he says, is intimately related to "a yearning for absolutes." He opines that "lack of commitment to any positive value overlays an unconscious search for absolute, embracing values, causes, and goals":

> In part the latent desires of these youths for a totally comprehensive ideology results from their conscious confusion: total commitment to a positive philosophy of life would indeed give coherence, structure, and meaning to an existence that is now perplexed, confused, and dull . . . A revolutionary cause, a religious conversion, a total immersion in a unitary group would come close to the loss of self and erasure of boundaries which one part of them wants. Here, as in so many other areas, the alienated struggle most intensely against what they covertly desire. Young men with a heightened potential for self-loss, they fight it by repudiating all values and causes in which they might lose themselves.[24]

At the less reflective level of the teeny-bopper and the overt delinquent, the same result appears in more direct and obvious form. The youthful "rebels" intent upon flouting adult society are like automatons where the demands of their own subculture are concerned. In hair styles, clothing, musical tastes, language, and ideas, they seem in many cases to be interchangeable.

The Crime Commission observes: ". . . being inexperienced, unsure of themselves, and, in fact, relatively powerless as individuals, adolescents to a far greater extent than their elders conform to the common standards of dress and hair style and speech, and act jointly, in groups—or gangs."[25] Reacting against the conformity of adult society, adolescents rush headlong into an even more tyrannical conformity of their own.

At first glance, this passion for drowning oneself in the group would seem conducive to law-abiding behavior. But the fact is otherwise. The group submission is a sign of interior emptiness; and that same emptiness can and does lead on to crime. This is one of the reasons modern welfare states feature the seeming paradox of citizenries that are submissive and unimaginative in normal social activity but are increasingly involved in lawless behavior. The "other-directed" citizen drifts into mass activity precisely because he has no certain identity and no mechanism of self-direction. The spiritual void and lack of interior control which mark the mass-man are also the principal characteristics of the psychopath. The most obvious illustration is the juvenile gang, which satisfies the need for group immersion and for psychopathic violence simultaneously.

Lacking interior restraints, the psychopath must have instant gratification; lacking life purpose, he resorts to bizarre and criminal acts; lacking emotional appreciation of the needs of others, he rides roughshod over the rights of his fellow citizens. As John Bartlow Martin puts in in his study of one such criminal who committed a senseless murder: "A psychopath functions well. But his emotions are out of kilter. His moral development, what laymen call his 'character,' is deficient. He lacks ordinary human warmth and sympathy. He is cold, remote. He is indifferent to the plight of others . . ."[26]

A vivid expression of this mentality was the so-called "Moors

Murder Trial" in Great Britain, in which a man and a woman
were found guilty of the sadistic torture-slaying of a teen-age boy
and two children, aged 10 and 12. As reviewed by Pamela Hans-
ford Johnson in her book, On Iniquity, these slayings were
perpetrated for "kicks" by two people emotionally dead to the feelings of others and concerned only for their own pursuit of sensation. The resulting character profile corresponds quite closely to
the strange psychopathic combination of lost "affectivity" with insane surges of impulse. Miss Johnson comments: "We are in
danger of creating an Affectless Society, in which nobody cares
for anyone but himself, or for anything but instant self-gratification. We demand sex without love, violence for 'kicks.' We are
encouraging the blunting of sensibility; and this, let us remember
was not the way to an earthly paradise, but the way to. Ausch-
witz."* [27]

A life oriented to "sensation," devoid of human sentiment and
severed from principle, must descend ultimately to this condition. A personality which knows only the itch of impulse and the
need to make its will supreme all too often seeks its absolutes
with gun or bludgeon. This is at once the psychology of the infant terror who runs berserk in a treatment home and of an Adolf
Hitler—the final victory of impulse, the ultimate denial of civilization.

---

* Compare with Martin's psychopath and Miss Johnson's sadistic killers the
personality style of a bank robber in one of our Federal prisons, who describes his
innermost feelings as follows:

My mania for power, socially, sexually, and otherwise, can feel no degree
of satisfaction until I feel sure I have struck the ultimate of submission and
terror in the minds and bodies of my victims . . . It's very difficult to explain all the queer fascinating sensations pounding and surging through me
while I'm holding a gun on a victim, watching his body tremble and sweat
. . . This is the moment when all the rationalized hypocrisies of civilization
are suddenly swept away and two men are standing there facing each other
morally and ethically naked, and right and wrong are the absolute commands
of the man behind the gun.

Here is the culmination of impulse release and annihilated value. This American psychopath bears close comparison with the personality type described by
Sweden's Nobel Prize winner Par Lagerkvist, who equates "life with death, based
on the inability to love or feel . . . the vicious or antisocial are more alive than
others, and those who see society as the enemy are at least protected from such
feelings of deadness."

Our new-style ethics and new-style practical incentives thus go together very nicely. The old system relied on strong internal discipline at the philosophical level to make people capable of organizing their lives and of acting sanely and purposefully, combining internal discipline and external freedom. The new system reverses the equation. By destroying the internalized system of values it makes people incapable of deciding things for themselves, of selecting a purpose and organizing their behavior according to value guidelines to attain it. The new system combines a lack of discipline internally with an increasing need for discipline externally.

The progress of the modern mass-man thus follows the course charted in Dostoevsky's epigram: "Starting from an unlimited liberty, I reach unlimited despotism." The personality that is without interior limits becomes lost, and must end by burying itself in some larger collectivity in the hope of attaining significance and definition. What is true of youth gangs is true as well of whole blocs of Western society. That the age of maximum "freedom" in the moral sphere is also the age of maximum despotism in the political sphere is no accident. The second is a necessary consequence of the first.

PART TWO

A LOCAL SOLUTION

ONE

Is There a Way Out?

To grasp the full extent of crime in America, and to fathom some of the causes behind it, is a beginning. But it is a beginning which will be wasted unless corrective steps are taken. Knowledge of where we are and how we got there must be intelligently acted upon if we are to redeem our society from its present troubles.

The most deeply rooted causes of crime are, of course, the most difficult to get at. The moral revolution in American life, which undergirds the crime spree and contributes to it daily, is a matter of ideas. And there are no ready-to-order ways of changing things at this level. In particular, there are no patented formulae for reversing a process of moral and intellectual disintegration once it has achieved momentum.

This does not mean the job is incapable of accomplishment. In this sphere, there is nothing quite so helpful as the critique itself—to alert those who still hold by the old values to the nature of the problem. The unhappy effects of "de-moralization," the socially disastrous consequences of irreligion, the intimate connection between "sophisticated" doctrine and savage practice, need to be described in full to an imperiled nation. Telling and re-telling the story is an essential feature of the necessary therapy.

The incursions of the "new morality" need, it is plain, to be countered by the force of more cogent ideas—by an articulate reaffirmation of America's religious and moral heritage. Some hard work is going to be necessary in theoretical terms to break the hold of relativist ideas on American intellectual life—to reverse the commitments of the intelligentsia to impulse release and moral confusion.

At the most fundamental level, these things can be dealt with only in general terms and over the long pull. Certain contributory influences can be handled, however, on a more immediate basis. Parents and alumni should interest themselves more actively in the kind of instruction being purveyed on college campuses, where "breaking the mold of value" is looked upon as a kind of mission. Demands should be made that the religious-moral point of view receive, at a minimum, an *equal* hearing in the college curriculum. Similarly, parents and taxpayers should move to insure that their elementary schools are not in thrall to the dogmas of "progressivism." Most important of all, the home itself must be re-established as a center of moral discipline, "acculturation," and belief in law-abiding behavior.

At the level of public policy, the preceding discussion suggests some necessary corrective steps. Efforts should be made to reverse the effects of a welfare program which makes it more profitable to loaf than to work. So long as practical incentives are deployed in favor of indolence and against initiative, self-reliance will suffer. So long as a placid material "security" is valued more than opportunity and orderly achievement, "boredom" will mark the social landscape. So long as American culture is obsessed with levelling rather than the encouragement of excellence, we are going to produce "other-directed" and "anomic" citizens.

These observations concern the general social-political-cultural context within which the American character is formed. Adequate treatment of the subject, obviously, lies beyond the scope of this book. Suffice it to say a strenuous effort is going to be required, at the theoretical and practical levels alike, to re-establish the necessary pre-conditions of a self-reliant, peaceful society. We shall need both a reaffirmation of value and a rearrangement of practical incentives to get that job accomplished, and the time-span requisite to such an achievement will be measured in decades if not in generations.

We have seen the moorings which hold civilization in place begin to slip; we have seen primeval impulse set free from the restraints and guidelines which make social existence possible. Our task is nothing less, therefore, than to re-impose civilization and bring impulse back into check. It is a formidable assignment, and were these cosmic issues the only materials with which we had to work, we might well despair of success.

There remains, however, one great saving fact. Despite slippage in crucial areas, large numbers of the American people still pay allegiance to the old values and are still capable of functioning in terms of them. Vestiges of "middle-class morality," although condemned in much of the intellectual community, are strong among us, and could, with proper leadership, stage a counteroffensive against the forces of dissolution. We are not, therefore, confronted by the necessity of building everything from the ground up. Given resources of pride, energy, and religious sentiment, there are a number of things which can be done in the immediate neighborhood to stem the advance of crime and moral chaos—things specifically relevant to the problems of here and now.

Foremost among the immediate steps which can and should be taken is a deep-going revaluation of "permissiveness" and leniency in the treatment of criminals. The rehabilitationists and poverty-fighters have had a long time to prove their doctrines will cut down on crime—with the result that crime has been rapidly spiralling upward. We need to take a fresh look at parole practices, "insanity" defenses, juvenile justice, capital punishment, and judicial leniency in general. Such a revaluation should begin, most obviously, with the Supreme Court decisions in *Mallory* and *Gideon* and *Miranda*. That these decrees have contributed to the rise of crime seems, on the record, apparent. Various legislative remedies have been suggested, and while the authors are not experts in legal matters, we believe it is clear that some kind of legislative correction is in order. This is not a call for harshness; it is a call to temper mercy with justice.

Similarly, steps must be taken to quash the notion of "civil disobedience" in protest of any statute one doesn't happen to like. Continued encouragement for this view, and extenuations for those who violate the law in assertedly just causes, can only spread the seeds of chaos more widely. The impact of this doctrine on young people—as demonstrated in the asserted "right to riot" of various university students—has been particularly disastrous.

Also at the immediate level, steps will have to be taken to strengthen America's police forces. With few exceptions, metropolitan police departments today are undermanned and underpaid. In the suburban areas, where population and crime are growing most rapidly, the ratio of police to residents is alarmingly low. Extensive steps are going to be necessary to remedy this failing. Better pay is one obvious answer. Improved techniques—better communications and records, use of computers, and so forth—are another.

Less tangible but equally important is the need to restore police morale. The evidence shows politically motivated cries of "brutality" and the effort to impose "review boards" have had baleful consequences in terms of police service and recruitment. This assault on the police will have to be combatted. Affirmative support for efficient and conscientious police work should be mobilized in every local community. Proper appreciation of the problems confronting police would certainly result, at a minimum, in removing the burden of non-essential matters from the policeman's shoulders. Drudge work, filing of papers in triplicate, and getting cats out of trees now consume an estimated 80 per cent of the average policeman's time. Hours spent doing these things are hours which cannot be devoted to the prevention of crime or apprehension of criminals.

In the realm of citizen support for the police, experience has shown that very effective things can be accomplished. Contrary to some expert anticipations, an aroused citizenry can do a great deal to assist in effective law enforcement. Private citizens can also have an impact on a number of things contributing to crime, in terms of long-range developments and immediate ones alike. Such action has been successfully attempted with respect to the courts, educating young people, material conditions contributing to crime, and reform of existing legal procedures.

That such action is indeed possible—and effective—is a matter known to the authors personally. Various of these techniques have been attempted in the authors' home city of Indianapolis—with salutary results. We believe the things done in Indianapolis, which to date constitute only a beginning, can be duplicated in any other American community. And, given the know-how characteristic of Americans, we have no doubt all these things can be improved upon.

Indianapolis is a fairly typical American city. It has its assets and its liabilities, its problems and its civic triumphs. It is representative of the Midwest, an industrial city set down in the middle of a rich agricultural landscape. Its population of around half-a-million (about a million in the metropolitan area) places it in the middle rank of American cities. In physical characteristics, it could well serve as a prototype for dozens of other U.S. communities.

In keeping with our Chamber of Commerce, we think there are many things about Indianapolis which make it distinctive. Perhaps foremost among these is its reputation as a solid, "conservative" community. As part of the larger American culture, it naturally partakes of many of the influences we have previously described; yet on balance its history has been marked by resistance to many of these tendencies, by a partiality for "unsophisticated" morality, and by opposition to indiscriminate welfarism. It has been known as a self-help city, reluctant to seek Federal "aid," interested in taking care of its own. Its school board, welfare apparatus, local government and business community have been oriented to private initiative. It has been the scene of literally dozens of self-help innovations in the field of housing, employment, and education. It has had, for the past several years, an extremely low unemployment rate, and a crime rate lower than many communities of comparable size.

There has nevertheless been a good deal of crime in Indianapolis—much more than its citizens thought either necessary or desirable. And, in the self-help tradition, a group of these citizens set out to do something to correct things. These people were not, by any means, "experts." Their approach to the problem was not at all theoretical or abstract; it was eminently practical, intended to find solutions to the particular difficulties which presented themselves to the community on a day-to-day basis.

The interests of these citizens comprehended the courts, the police, the schools, the outside activities of young people, the physical environment of the city. They engaged all of the everyday things which could have some direct bearing on the level of crime. And, by the available statistics, they have had a measurable impact in lowering that level.

The chapters which follow tell, in abbreviated form, the story of this community-wide effort. They are not intended as an exhaustive discussion of all phases of anti-crime activity. They are instead meant to show, in a very practical way, some of the things which can be achieved in any American community concerned to halt the mounting tide of crime.

TWO

The Community Gets Going

The Indianapolis counterattack on crime got under way early in 1962. Beginning with a small group of interested citizens, it soon expanded to include a broad cross-section of the community. The city's tradition of self-help and practical initiative stood it in good stead.

Among the groups helping in the law enforcement drive were the Chamber of Commerce, the Rotary Club, Kiwanis, the YWCA, the PAL clubs, the Scouts, Boys Clubs, countless women's service clubs, and so on. A central role was played by a private self-help group called Citizens Forum. One private committee attacked the problem of school dropouts. Others took up such matters as street lighting, better relations with the police, improving court procedure, and education of young people.

The key organization in igniting interest and focusing the disparate efforts of thousands of people has been a group called the Indianapolis Anti-Crime Crusade. This organization began with some 30 interested people as a kind of ad hoc body; today it numbers no less than 50,000 women in its ranks, and enjoys an established and honored place in the community.

Because of the success of the Anti-Crime Crusade's work in crime prevention and law enforcement, and the subsequent work of other cities using the Indianapolis pattern, the National Crime Commission opened the citizens' action section of its official report with the following statement: "The most dramatic example in the country of a citizen's group that has addressed itself forcefully and successfully to the problem of crime and criminal justice is the Anti-Crime Crusade in Indianapolis." The commission listed several examples of successful crime prevention resulting from the work of the Crusade.

Original impetus for the project was the brutal slaying of an elderly school teacher by a 15-year-old purse-snatcher. The horror of this crime convinced local women the time had come for action. Presidents of major women's organizations—civic, church, school, and professional groups—therefore gathered at a luncheon in late March, 1962, to launch a determined war on crime. Committing themselves and their organizations to the fight, they vowed to make the streets "safe for women," and, by extension, for everyone else.

To the ladies who founded the group, it seemed quite logical that the anti-crime campaign should originate on the distaff side of the community. Women, after all, are physically more vulnerable to criminal depredations than are men; as the life-givers of this world they have always been particularly concerned about the preservation of life; and as homemakers responsible for the rearing of children, they believe it imperative that their youngsters be brought up in a city where crime is despised, not tolerated. In addition, they have the time to devote themselves wholeheartedly to the task.

The original members of the Crusade decided they would attack the roots of crime—ignorance, pridelessness, indifference—wherever they saw them, immediately and personally, in a practical manner. Instead of looking at the citywide, nationwide problem as a gigantic aggregate, they agreed to curb one crime at a time—get one dropout back in school, provide a job for one youth, get one bright light on a dark street, help one boy or girl released from a correctional institution. They knew that it takes just two items to make a crime—a criminal and a victim. Eliminate one of these and a crime is also eliminated.

The Crusaders, headed by Mrs. C. B. LaDine, wife of a local physician, invited the officials of almost every key city agency, administrative unit and service organization to speak on his or her work at a series of weekly meetings. As these talks progressed, the volunteers quickly discovered the most important question they could ask was, "How can we help?" Accustomed to criticism when things went wrong, the administrators were stunned by the offer of private citizens to combat lawlessness. As they came to grasp the ways in which such private assistance could be of use, they were more than happy to accept.

The volunteers listened to the administrative assistant to the mayor, the chief of police, the executive secretary of the Board of Works, the president of the Board of Safety, the prosecuting attorney, various judges, school officials, the director of state police, the special agent to the Federal Bureau of Investigation.

They heard the head of the vice squad, the officers in charge of narcotics, the head of the detective division of the police department. They took notes on talks by the commissioner of corrections and the heads of various penal institutions including the Indiana Girls School and the Indiana Boys School. And, in cooperation with social workers and administrators assigned to juvenile work, the women spent six evenings looking at films on juvenile delinquency.

As their knowledge of the crime picture grew, they set up a functioning organization. They listed areas of work and named chairmen to begin practical projects on lighting, dropouts, court watching, juveniles, rehabilitation, employment, legislation, churches, police, public officials. In all, 14 separate chairmen were named to head divisions within the Crusade. Each group is an autonomous body, specializing in a particular area of concern. Every six to eight weeks, the various chairmen meet together to discuss problems, plans, accomplishments. The meetings also include presidents of major sponsoring organizations and public officials invited on a rotating basis.

Making their daily rounds of the city, all heads of committees and hundreds of volunteers carry with them giant maps of Indianapolis on which they have marked: 1) high crime areas and the directions in which these are moving; 2) street lighting projects needed, those in process, and those completed; 3) parks and playgrounds—and the lights within and around them; 4) public buildings where people gather in large crowds; 5) theaters, hospitals, and other places where crimes might occur at night; 6) shopping centers; 7) wooded areas which might be unsafe for children; 8) slum areas which needed rehabilitation; and dozens of other areas in which there was work to be done. With maps in hand, the women explain the work of the Crusade—at hundreds of club meetings, at luncheons, even at small gatherings in their homes.

In like fashion, large charts showing the work of court watchers are in great demand by clubs, sororities, and other organizations. As will be discussed in the succeeding chapter, these charts show what is happening in the courts—how many cases the women have observed, delays and continuances, guilty and innocent, age levels of defendants, numbers of pro-tem and special judges, etc.

The sincerity and dedication of the Crusade volunteers have proved contagious. As the program gathered momentum, various civic-action, fraternal, and service organizations came forward to lend a helping hand. The Seventh District Federation of Clubs, made up of nearly 3,000 women, solicited the aid of its 75 clubs and sororities. The Indianapolis Council of Women, representing nearly 40,000 women, sent a delegation to see the mayor. Four major women's service clubs offered their help in 1963, and have been hard at work ever since.

Men's service clubs pitched in with equal enthusiasm. Rotarians asked how they could cooperate with the Crusade, and a list of club and individual items was distributed at a Rotary meeting at which Crusade leaders spoke. A cooperative program was launched with the local Optimists clubs, and Kiwanis. The Exchange Clubs joined with the Crusade in sponsoring awards to policemen, quarterly and annually, for "work beyond the ordinary."

The list of cooperative groups grew even more rapidly as soon as the Crusade publicized a few of its results. The Indianapolis Women's Personnel Association offered to help with jobs, the Indiana Psychology Association asked for help in legislation, the Junior League of Indianapolis asked for cooperation with a two-day conference on "Solving Social Problems," and the Indianapolis Chamber of Commerce asked for help with a series of "Stop Shoplifting" clinics.

For a time this outpouring of volunteer energy was a source

of bafflement to professional social workers. Many full-time guidance and counseling people were doubtful that amateurs, however enthusiastic, could do much to correct social ills in our community. If the volunteers were dealing with dropouts, for instance, could they successfully cope with problems in the home? What if psychological difficulties were involved? Could they handle these? Many professionals were skeptical, hesitant to accept offers of assistance.

The volunteers, however, were not entirely greenhorns. Although unfamiliar with some aspects of the crime problem, they numbered countless people in their ranks with impressive academic and professional credentials, including hundreds of former teachers, social workers, and guidance directors—even a former president of the Indiana State Teachers' Association. As these people handled first one problem and then another successfully, the skepticism began to dissipate. By degrees, the professionals came to see that this volunteer effort would indeed be a help and not a hindrance. Close co-operation between volunteers and social workers was the result.

Relations with public office-holders have followed a parallel course of development. In dealing with officials, the Crusade has followed two precepts: Take the time to listen to their problems, and be sure that projected action urged upon them is authentically helpful, not busy-work. The volunteers operate on the assumption that public officials have the authority and the resources to do the job, and that private citizens should not attempt to duplicate official efforts. The Crusade prefers to support official budgets where they are justified, then demand that government perform the tasks for which the taxpayers have provided salaries and equipment.

In the matter of elections, the Crusade has taken a lively interest from a non-partisan position. Each election year the Crusade sponsors public meetings featuring candidates for offices involving law enforcement. Statements are tape-recorded and used from time to time to remind the candidates of their promises. The Crusade backs no party or candidate, but takes advantage of the election season to press for better law enforcement.

Additionally, volunteers regularly attend meetings of the City Council, the School Board, the Board of Safety, the Board of

Public Works and similar governmental units. Some are in fact members of these bodies. A volunteer who served as chairman of one Crusade subdivision subsequently became a member of the School Board.

In relatively short order, the Crusade was working in tandem with the Indiana University Department of Police Administration, the Central Indiana Literacy Council, settlement houses, the Young Women's Christian Association, the Catholic Deanery, the National Council of Jewish Women, the National Council of Negro Women, the Council of United Church Women, and the Indianapolis Community Service Council. Crusaders were also invited to the annual state conference of judges sponsored by the National Council on Crime and Delinquency and Criminal and Juvenile Court Judges. Municipal Court judges asked for help in establishing a driver improvement school.

Like the professional social workers, public officials at first seemed uncertain whether private citizen-action could have an effect on the crime rate. Then the results started to come in. Five years after its inception, the Anti-Crime Crusade had achieved full recognition among case-hardened professionals.

Indicative of this fact was the comment of New York youth counselor Vince Riccio. A former professional boxer, Riccio is no dreamy idealist. He prowled the asphalt jungles of New York from 1950 to 1955 as a "detached worker" for the New York City Youth Board. In the language of his book, *All the Way Down,* Riccio's job was to help kids in a world "where sexual deviation was normal, where 15-year-old boys were hopeless narcotic addicts, where murder was familiar and robbery a way of life among the better element."

Commenting on the Crusade's stay-in-school program, Riccio said: "It's tremendous. I'm delighted that in Indiana people are taking the initiative, that laymen are getting involved in this way. I know of nothing like it anywhere else in the United States." As more and more results became apparent, Riccio's verdict was increasingly accepted. Self-help was getting the job done. The following chapters discuss the way in which it was accomplished.

THREE

Citizens and the Law

In a campaign against crime, the obvious place to begin is with the agencies of law enforcement. That is what the Crusaders, early in their career, set out to do. In order to learn more about the law and those who administer it, they turned their attention to local courts and the police department. They found that, in comparatively short order, they were able to learn a great deal. And, as time went on, they found they were able to make some valuable contributions in turn.

The Court-Watchers

The volunteers' experience in the courts was both dramatic and effective. Stepping into an area where they had little knowledge, members of the Anti-Crime Crusade were able to help law enforcement officers and conscientious judges establish a better program for the protection of the citizens of Indianapolis. As a result of this effort, similar projects have been launched in Buffalo, Cleveland, Tampa, Minneapolis, and other cities as far away as Christchurch, New Zealand.

The program is called "court-watching"—and it consists of exactly what the name implies: Members of the Crusade sitting in the courts, day in and day out, keeping track of the proceedings and taking notes on what they see and hear.

When the program began in the Indiana capital in 1962, Judge Charles Daugherty urged increased citizens' participation. "Few people pay attention to the courts," he said. "They are familiar with the legislative and executive branches of our government, but they seldom look in on the courts unless they are there as defendants or witnesses." Daugherty, former Indiana Supreme Court Judge Arch N. Bobbitt, Police Chief Daniel T. Veza, lawyers, members of the prosecuting attorney's staff, correction department officials, probation officers and judges helped the watchers begin the court program.

Working with the municipal and criminal courts and the Marion County juvenile court, the watchers systematically record on report sheets the following information: date, judge or referee, kind of case (juvenile, paternity, child neglect, etc.), sex, race, age, whether the youth is a dropout, defense attorney, witnesses, prosecutor or plaintiff and attorney, witnesses, intake worker's report, disposition of case, remarks or questions. These findings are tabulated every three months—showing both patterns and variations in the conduct of the courts.

Few citizens who are not professionally involved with the law are aware of the large number of abuses which can occur in a court of law and hinder effective law enforcement. Anti-Crime Crusade members learned of them piecemeal as they became familiar with the operations of local courts, and mounted pressures to have some of them corrected.

More than 70,000 case reports have been filed by Indianapolis court-watchers. The results have been aggregated and transferred to large multi-colored charts which show at a glance what the various courts are doing. An excess of findings in which judgment is withheld, compared to other courts of the same caliber, shows up vividly in the charts and prompts appropriate questions. Likewise a too-heavy reliance on pro tem, or substitute, judges. The charts additionally raise questions about crime trends generally—say, the fact that the median age of defendants is rapidly declining.

Some of the most obvious failings which struck the court-watchers were repeated continuances granted defendants, loose bail bond practices, use of pro tem judges, and failure of arresting officers to appear in court.

Since court-watchers began their program several changes in courts and court procedures have taken place in Indianapolis:

1) Arresting officers are absent less often.
2) Most judges appear in court on time.
3) There are fewer pro tem judges.
4) A hallway bailiff has been appointed to keep court corridors clear.
5) There are fewer delays.
6) Appearance of police witnesses has improved.
7) There is improvement in serving of re-arrest warrants.
8) A permanent Driver Improvement School has been established under the direction of four Municipal Courts.
9) Cases are more thoroughly prepared by the prosecutors.

In order to make sure that the County Council would allow funds in the budget for the Driver Improvement School, court-watchers attended meetings of the Council and spoke in favor of the program. Of 7,728 people assigned to the school in two years, only 97 have received a second violation ticket. The school also set up a literacy clinic with the help of court-watchers, since it developed that five per cent of the drivers haled into court could not read.

Court watcher comments are returned regularly to the judges. Frequently the comments are as pointed as "I think that judge put a pro tem so the defendant could get off." One judge made the mistake of remarking too loudly, "I'll try those shoplifting cases as soon as I get rid of the court-watchers." The court-watchers continued to sit in his court. Policemen, prosecutors, and judges began to view the watchers as a major force for better law enforcement. The police saw the volunteers as allies. The prosecuting attorney said that, with the watchers present, his deputies did a better job. Judges called their reports "the only honest evaluation we get."

Project chairmen wrote a Court-Watcher's Guide which judges, police, prosecuting attorney, and others directly involved in law enforcement and crime prevention reviewed for accuracy. Court-watcher identification cards were printed, so participants could be scheduled, two by two, into the various courts.

In May, 1963, an attorney filed a motion to have court-watchers removed from court during a murder trial. Judge Saul I. Rabb ruled that the court-watchers could remain. "The court-watchers have as much right to be here," Rabb commented, "as members of Murder, Inc., or the gambling syndicate. It's within their right to see that the judge is not fixed."

The judge's denial of the motion was no more than should be expected, but it served to remind defense attorneys and the public at large that in open court spectators have a right to observe, listen and take notes, so long as they create no disturbance. The Indiana Supreme Court upheld Rabb's decision.

The presence of the court-watchers also had a deterrent effect on a practice which was for a time fashionable in Indianapolis—filing injunctions against the police department. In one such case involving the vice branch, several watchers decided to attend the hearing. Questioning revealed the suit had been brought by a known prostitute, living with her procurer, mother of his child; the procurer was at that time training a 15-year-old in the arts of sodomy. The suit asked that the police be enjoined from arresting her as a lewd woman under the provisions of a city ordinance.

The judge of the quiet civil court was unaccustomed to an audience, let alone 15 neatly dressed women conspicuous in their flowered hats and white gloves. As the first women arrived, the judge sent his clerk out to learn who these people might be. The women sat quietly and observed the proceedings.

The case began. After the city's attorney pointed out that some papers were improperly drawn, the judge shook his head, waved a hand violently at the plaintiff's attorney, and said, "You just go home. You just go home and fix up those papers. You fix up those papers and you come back here in two weeks." Two weeks later, the judge, the attorneys, the plaintiff, the defendants, and the women returned. The injunction was granted. But when a similar case came up several weeks later, the injunction granted at first thought was rescinded in three days.

Many of the things the volunteers observed in court pointed the way toward other activities outside it. Examples of the many episodes which prompted remedial measures beyond the halls of justice are the following case histories from juvenile court records:

A 15-year old boy, head in bandages, left arm in sling, right foot in cast, is asked by the judge:

"Why did you steal the car?"

"Well, sir, the keys were in it, and I always wanted a Thunderbird."

"But the car didn't belong to you or to your family."

"No, sir, but we won't ever have a Thunderbird."

Such was the justification for taking a car, speeding through the city streets, trying to outrace a police car, and ramming into a stone building.

A 16-year old blonde high school sophomore came into the courtroom crying. With her were her grandmother and mother, also crying. The family waived the right to attorney and said they wished trial at once.

"Did you take a pair of shoes from the store?" the judge asked the girl.

"She's a good girl," the grandmother sobbed.

"She's making better grades," said the mother.

"Please," the judge said, "I must talk with the girl now. There will be time for both of you."

The girl admitted taking the shoes without paying for them, even though she had sufficient money. In fact, she admitted she really didn't need or want the shoes. She just had an urge to exercise her "five finger discount," a local euphemism for shoplifting.

What had led this girl to do such a thing? In subsequent questioning, her mother and grandmother both said they didn't think it was wrong to take a little thing like a pair of gloves. The mother herself had a record of shoplifting.

Three high school seniors, all from families at the high or middle-class level, told their story to the juvenile judge.

They didn't know why they did it. They were driving down a city boulevard after school when the driver said to the other two: "Looks like those people aren't home. Let's go in."

The other boys objected.

"It might be fun," persisted the driver.

So they broke in.

A Persian cat ran across the room. They killed the cat. Next they threw a few china cups at mirrors, and then mirrors at tables. Then they slashed rugs and broke up chairs. The house was a shambles when they left.

They didn't know why they did it. They just didn't have "anything to do."

In the first case, the court-watchers found two ways to improve law enforcement—urging people throughout the community to remove keys from cars, to reduce temptation. Also, they learned the need for classes in "laws for juveniles" in elementary and high schools.

In the second case, the watchers learned much about home environment—and the importance of removing some young people from a corrupting atmosphere. Since this was one of hundreds of cases where neither return to the home nor commitment to an institution would solve the problem, the volunteers decided to establish a home for problem girls.

In the third case, court observers saw the necessity of showing young people the many important things they can do with their time. They were also made acutely aware of the fact that parents must teach children the importance of discipline, responsibility, respect for their own homes and for the rights and property of others.

Various results of these and other insights are discussed in succeeding chapters.

Observations in court constantly yielded guidelines to better understanding of the causes of crime. Truancy, incorrigibility, runaway, dropout, curfew violation, second offense, parents not in court: These notations, charting incipient careers in lawlessness, run like a red thread through the reports of juvenile court observers. They highlight the stress points of necessary action— and they often lead to such action in a very direct way.

A representative case of volunteer assistance proceeding from the court-watchers' efforts involved a 16-year-old girl brought to book for the second time. She had run away from home and was gone for five days. Although she had made good grades in elementary school, she had been failing during one year in high school. In another year her record showed Ds. She had been called "incorrigible."

An aunt and uncle appeared with her, and with their promise to "look after her and take care of her," her face brightened. "If somebody cares," she said, "I'll try to do better."

The girl was placed on probation in the custody of her aunt and uncle. A woman volunteer was asked to serve as assistant to the probation worker—making sure the girl got along better in school, had a tutor if she needed one, and had someone to express interest in her work.

The beneficial results of this activity have been acknowledged by leading jurists in Marion County. In a "meet-the-judge" symposium, in April, 1964, judges strongly urged court-watchers to continue visiting the various courts and asked for their constructive criticism.

"Tell people in the community what you see and hear in court," said the late Judge Eugene Fife, Jr. of Criminal Court I. "You see people in court you never thought really existed—some who couldn't care less about law and order, property or even lives. There are, of course, some people who have strayed from the straight path one time, only," he said, "but there is too much thought today that we can rehabilitate almost everyone."

Judge Rabb commented: "There are fewer continuances when court-watchers sit in our courts. When you are there taking a look at procedures, the prosecuting attorneys prepare cases a little more carefully. Of course, a citizen has a right to a continuance—but we have far too many filed by the state of Indiana."

Encouraged by that sort of response, Indianapolis volunteers continue to check the dockets and take their by-now accustomed places to make sure that everything is in order in the courts.

Supporting the Police

It is easier to scold the chief of police for failure to catch criminals than to take the responsibility for setting the moral climate of the community high enough to discourage lawless activity.

Obviously, no organization is more clearly involved in fighting crime than the police department. But the Anti-Crime Crusade at first postponed the police question because its members quickly learned it was too easy to blame police for a high crime rate when their job was to enforce the law, not to eliminate the causes of crime.

When contact between volunteers and police was established, cooperation was immediate and effective. The police provided cars and escorts for light-checking tours of the city, particularly in high crime areas where women would be ill-advised to move alone at night. They helped volunteers to write a booklet on self-protection for women.

The police also allowed volunteers to ride in patrol cars and motorcycles to learn what policemen do, go on tours with the vice squad to see, first hand, the dozens of girls who roam the streets, night after night, and witness the great mass of people who sit impassively on crumbling steps, watching rats run through trash and debris, never once lifting a finger to clean up the mess. Police pointed out areas a few blocks distant where ambitious people cleaned an area once a slum, and built homes, garages, and beautiful yards. They did a lighting survey on their own throughout the city, based on their knowledge of each district's needs.

They allowed volunteers to speak to the more than 900 men in the department to explain the Crusade and its bearing on law enforcement. Inviting the volunteer leaders to speak at roll calls, the police chief threw the whole official and moral weight of his office behind the program. He also permitted volunteers to attend police administration classes and address new recruits on what the community expects of its policemen. The department also provided speakers for parent programs, club meetings, and church organizations.

Members of the Juvenile Branch of the Police Department have also been helpful. Officers working in this field made available to Crusade members statistics concerning the number of boys and girls brought into custody; how many were released to parents or turned over to the juvenile court (and why); the nature of the offense, including breakdowns among burglary, robbery, vehicle theft, sex charges, larcencies; the percentage of repeaters; and areas from which the defendants come.

Similar cooperation has been offered the Crusade by other law-enforcement agencies. In a project aimed at teaching the law to young people, the volunteers received help not only from city police but from the Superintendent of the Indiana State Police, who offered to assist the program throughout the state. And the Sheriff of Marion County has named the Youth Division of the Anti-Crime Crusade as his youth council on law enforcement.

Crusade members have reciprocated by giving strong support to better law enforcement. When the police needed recruits, volunteers went to bat by talking to their organizations about careers in the police department. Mothers, grandmothers, and aunts took the message back to their neighborhoods and young men appeared at the police department to apply for positions as cadets or policemen.

Crusaders have attended classes, panel discussions, seminars, Board of Safety meetings, City Council budget hearings, every function that would provide a forum for learning about police activity. They held a tea in honor of policemen's wives for their years of uncomplaining service. It was the first time wives of policemen had been thus recognized—and the first time many of them had met the wife of the police chief.

A quarterly award program for policemen in cooperation with the Exchange Clubs was instituted, with award winners being eligible for annual awards given during Crime Prevention week in February. So appreciative were policemen of these honors that one patrolman drove 125 miles on his first free day to show his citation to his aging parents.

Consistently, volunteers maintain a hands-off policy on daily operation of the department, insisting instead that those charged with this responsibility do their jobs well. They urged people of the community to quit calling the overburdened police to take care of such matters as lost Mynah birds, getting a 300-pound woman out of a cab, rescuing cats and helping a woman get her finger out of a computer. Police in every city badly need extra manpower to deal with crimes of violence, and that need would obviously be alleviated somewhat if they were not required to spend 80 per cent of their time on such problems as family fights and lost car keys. Saving of lives is, of course, a different story. The rescue squad is always available when lives are in danger.

The volunteers got out a simple one-page directory, available to all families, setting out telephone numbers of non-police agencies to call for such emergencies as finding a raccoon in the basement, what to do with a dead animal, where to call when a child has taken poison. Policemen still are willing to offer services wherever needed, but more calls in Indianapolis now go to the correct emergency agency, thus leaving more time for police to take care of crime.

Visiting police departments in various cities has become a habit for many of the volunteers. Chicago, Dallas, Washington, New York City, Cleveland, Buffalo—these and others have offered much information on how citizen groups can help. Outstanding, of course, is former Superintendent O. W. Wilson of the Chicago Police Department. Indianapolis volunteers helped to set up an interview for 12 Illinois women who wanted to talk with Wilson. He told them about the "Operation Crime-Stop" program which has been so effective in Chicago.

"The object of this project is two-fold," Wilson said. "We want to enlist the 'eyes and ears' of all Chicagoans to report possible crimes, suspicious persons, incidents or circumstances before crimes are committed; and we also want them to call us when they see a crime being committed." Police agencies have too long assumed the entire burden and responsibility for all that is criminal. Crime is a community problem as well as a social problem; and it is important that we alert our citizens to their responsibility in the prevention and suppression of criminal activities.

A similar citizen program, "Crime Alert," was started in Indianapolis in February, 1967. Thousands of billfold-size cards containing instructions on how to relay information to the police were made available to men and women throughout the city. A simple brochure described "earmarks" of suspects, identifying characteristics such as "high forehead," "wide-set eyes," "a limp," etc. Already a number of arrests have been made through citizen tipoffs.

Local citizens also backed stronger law-enforcement measures in the Indiana General Assembly, including efforts to allow police recruitment outside the confines of Marion County, more money for better police uniforms, a crackdown on local vice, and a special bill concerning shoplifting. They endorsed police raises before the Indianapolis Safety Board and City Council.

It costs each Indianapolis taxpayer less than a penny and a half per year to pay a policeman's salary. This is derived from the 1966 Indianapolis Police Department budget of $7,189,132 for a department serving an estimated population of 530,000. This would mean an expenditure of $13.57 per person for 917 policemen. For this the taxpayers get law enforcement in over 83 square miles of the city—with a population growing at two and one-half per cent annually. This is why Indianapolis volunteers do not hesitate to stand up at City Council meetings and say: "We are in favor of increased salaries for policemen."

In addition, the Crusade works with newsstands, drugstores, merchants, and supermarkets to make sure that prurient literature is not sold heedlessly to young people. This is done, not through the compulsions of the law, but through face to face cooperation with the dealers. Most of them are anxious to avoid having salacious material sold to youngsters.

One of the Crusade's most effective efforts in aiding the police has been a campaign to curtail shoplifting in Indianapolis stores. The volunteers offered to work with the police department and the Marion County prosecutor in preparation of a booklet for merchants and their employees on the prevention of this all-too-lucrative crime. Equipped with the booklet, "Stop Shoplifting," policemen and Crusade volunteers have presented anti-shoplifting clinics in 50 different areas of the state, and shoplifting arrests and convictions have gone up sharply. One store reported a 49 per cent decrease in thefts in a relatively short period.

A frequently discussed factor in the shoplifting binge was the merchant's fear of a false-arrest suit filed by someone wrongly accused of theft—although at a shoplifting clinic staged by the

Indianapolis Chamber of Commerce it was discovered that not one of 250 merchants in attendance from across the state had ever been faced by such a suit. To help ease the psychological problem, however, volunteers supported passage of an anti-shoplifting bill which allows merchants to detain suspected shoplifters without incurring this danger.

FOUR

Combatting Delinquency

"Something to Do"

Juvenile delinquency is the ultimate key to America's crime problem. The breakdown of the value circuits between the old morality and the new is most apparent with teenagers and others under 25. If delinquency can be curtailed, then in the final analysis adult crime will be curtailed as well.

There is a potential delinquent in every home where parents are not teaching children the importance of discipline and responsibility. There is a potential delinquent in almost every home where parents give a child everything money can buy without asking the child to do his share of the work, without teaching him the value of what he is receiving, without showing him how to be of service in his home, neighborhood, church, community.

The task of preventing the continued growth of delinquency may seem impossible—but it isn't. There are enough energetic people in every city to work on a personal basis with young people in behalf of law-abiding behavior. Some adults, of course, will not do the job. Some are lazy, uninformed, apathetic. But eliminate all of these and there are still enough adults to combat delinquency successfully.

In Indianapolis, a broad-gauge program has been undertaken

to do this job—to get at as many of the root causes of delinquency as can be handled in one city amid the general confusion of the times. The key to the program is to establish *responsibility* —to transmit to young people precisely those qualities which our preceding survey shows are getting to be in such short supply. The reaction has been surprisingly good.

There are four principal areas of concern in the Indianapolis anti-delinquency program—all revolving about the concept of responsible, mature action by young people. The first concerns youth action to help others in distress. The second concerns schooling—combatting dropouts and habitual truancy. The third concerns better understanding of the law and of the young person's obligation to obey it—even if he doesn't agree with it. And the fourth concerns re-instilling a sense of responsibility in youngsters who have got in trouble and have been placed in correctional institutions.

No Federal funds are needed for this program. In fact, no funds at all are needed to get it launched and fully operating. It is not necessary to wait for national or state legislation. As few as three people can begin the work—or 30, or 300.

We have noted that one of the chief complaints of trouble-prone youngsters is that they have "nothing to do." Indianapolis crime-fighters gave them something to do—in a big way. The keynote of the program was sounded in a 1963 statement to Anti-Crime Crusaders, including high school students, by Inspector Edward L. Kemper of the FBI. Asked by an Indianapolis teen-ager, "What can we do to help?" in the cause of law enforcement, Kemper gave this reply:

"The answer is . . . Go home!

"Hang the storm windows. Paint the woodwork. Rake the leaves. Mow the lawn. Shovel the walk. Wash the car. Learn to cook. Scrub the floors. Repair the sink. Build a boat. Get a job.

"Help your church, the Red Cross, the Salvation Army. Visit the sick. Assist the poor. Study your lessons. And then, when you are through—and not too tired—read a book.

"Your parents do not owe you entertainment. Your village

does not owe you recreation facilities. The world does not owe you a living. You owe the world something. You owe it your time, and energy, and your talents so that no one will be at war or in poverty, or sick or lonely again.

"In plain, simple words, grow up. Quit being a crybaby. Get out of your dream world. Develop a backbone, not a wishbone. Start acting like a man or a lady.

"I'm a parent. I'm tired of nursing, protecting, helping, appealing, begging, excusing, tolerating, denying myself needed comforts for every whim and fancy, just because your selfish ego instead of common sense dominates your personality . . ."

As a direct result of Inspector Kemper's speech, concerned teenagers in Indianapolis, working with the Anti-Crime Crusade, decided to find a way to get more juveniles involved in volunteer work. They interviewed judges, policemen, city officials, representatives of the National Council on Crime and Delinquency, and staff members of the state Department of Corrections. They asked these local experts about the value of volunteer service for teenagers.

Guided by the director of personnel training at the American Fletcher National Bank, high school pupils from metropolitan Indianapolis attended the first youth division meeting early in 1963—and came up with the following affirmations:

"1) We want discipline and law enforcement. We respect parents who have rules and we respect officials who enforce the law.

"2) We need to stand up for decisions of judges. We can't have order in our city if we gripe, 'The judge shouldn't have sentenced that poor guy who broke the law.'

"3) We've got to get word to all young people about the importance of high school graduation. That message is, 'I want to make something of myself and this is the way to start.' As leaders we can help young people who aren't sure of themselves, invite every young person to participate in some school activity, and talk with 'loners.'

"4) If anybody destroys property, he should be assigned work like washing or painting the walls he has marred or rebuilding what he has destroyed.

"5) We need more vocational training and more direct leads to employment for many young people. We can help by conferring with adults we know.

"6) Even though young people may have many problems at home, there are ways for them to rise above these situations. They need not get into trouble.

"7) We would like to serve as a youth council for the Sheriff and Police Department—to point out the problems we see and possible solutions."

Since that first meeting, Indianapolis young people have helped with all the points suggested and dozens of others. They now serve as a youth council for law-enforcement officials. On a volunteer basis, they study government on the scene—interviewing the police chief in the police department, the FBI agent at the FBI, the mayor in his office, the sheriff, the legislators, the governor. Junior and senior student leaders in the Youth Division also introduce policemen who speak in their schools on law enforcement. They encourage other students to visit public officials.

Following Inspector Kemper's lead, the young people named committees to gather information from clinics, hospitals, day nurseries, settlement houses, agencies, nursing homes, museums, the YWCA, United Fund agencies and dozens of other institutions and organizations. They found out how many teenagers were needed for various kinds of work. Then they edited a booklet called, "Directory for Teen-Age Volunteers."

Requests came quickly for copies of the book. Teenagers who had never before served as volunteers offered to help. Cities across the nation asked for hundreds of copies. A new edition has been published—an edition twice as large as the first. As a direct result of this effort, new service groups have been organized. For instance, the James Whitcomb Riley hospital in Indianapolis —known nationally for its work with children—employs a force of volunteers known as the Riley Cheer Guild, made up of women who devote long hours to service in hospitals. Through the work of the young people who edited the teen-service booklet, the women of Riley Cheer Guild were prompted to organize a teen-age branch which will provide volunteer service for more than 1,000 young people.

In a similar endeavor, one group of teenagers who worked as tutors for second, third, and fourth grade pupils at Christamore House in Indianapolis received a $300 award from *Parents* magazine for volunteer work. Howe High School students in Indianapolis served as volunteer "big brothers and sisters" to 12 seventh grade pupils who had after-school help at study tables sponsored by the Irvington Methodist Church. Former teachers assisted with the study program, and the high school students made sure the seventh graders were invited to ball games, parties and other recreational activities. Eleven of the 12 improved their grades so much that they moved with ease into the eighth grade, where they are making good records.

All in all more than 3,000 youngsters who had never before volunteered for service now assist in hospitals, clinics, day nurseries, nursing homes, and community centers. They are learning first-hand about community service and the importance of taking part in civic affairs. And they are seldom plagued by the complaint that they have "nothing to do."

Staying in School

One of the principal problems uncovered by these young people and by workers for the Anti-Crime Crusade was that juvenile delinquents usually have a bad, or non-existent, relationship with their schools. The "typical" delinquent is a dropout or truant. Indeed, an estimated 98 per cent of the youngsters who show up in court have at one time or another been truant. The Anti-Crime Crusade dug in on this problem.

There have been countless "studies" of dropouts, commissions appointed, funds appropriated. But not much has been done about getting pupils back in the classroom. The Crusade members hit upon the apparently novel approach of contacting the youngsters themselves to discover why they had dropped out, and trying to remedy the causes on an immediate, face-to-face basis. The idea was greeted skeptically at first, but when it achieved impressive results was embraced by school officials and others.

The project is simplicity itself. Names are obtained from school administrators, letters are sent to the young people asking them to return to school, a stamped, addressed card is enclosed on which problems may be checked, and return of the card is the invitation for a capable volunteer to come calling. From then on the program is a one child, one volunteer program in which the volunteer takes the responsibility of helping solve the youth's problems.

When the program was launched, Crusade members were given the names of 28 dropouts to see if they could do anything about getting them back in school. Individual contacts were made, and it was found the youngsters had dropped out because they had "lost interest" in school, did not have a pair of shoes, needed a part-time job, etc. Crusaders talked with these young people, supplied some of the things that stood in the way of class attendance, and, above all, let them know that they were not merely ciphers in the system, but individual human beings with lives and careers and responsibilities. Twenty-six of the original dropouts, within a few weeks' time, returned to school.

Viewing these results, school officials turned over hundreds of names to the Crusade. Similar one-to-one contacts were made for all of them, and within a short time—using no tax money of any sort—more than 2,000 teen-agers had returned to school or been persuaded not to leave in the first place. Self-help had achieved what months and years of commissions and Federal appropriations had not.

The key to the program's success—and the missing ingredient in many grandiose efforts to "deal with" dropouts or other social difficulties—is the volunteers' direct, personal interest in the problems of the troubled youngsters with whom they are working. Volunteers familiarize themselves with the many factors which characterize the dropout. By obtaining a student's complete record from the school principal, the volunteer can achieve a preliminary understanding of the student's capabilities. Thus armed, the volunteer then writes a personal letter to the youngster, suggesting he or she think about returning to school, pointing out that more education means greater opportunity and a fuller, more enjoyable life. The letter further pledges the volunteer to "help solve problems which may have caused you to drop out . . ."

On an enclosed self-addressed card the youngster can check the principal items he feels kept him out of school. These may include lunch money, bus fare, books, school fees, remedial reading, advice on careers, part-time employment, etc.

The card is assigned to a counselor who telephones (if a number is listed) and gives the youth the opportunity to invite the volunteer to his home, but affords an "out" if the youth is hesitant. The volunteer often suggests a meeting at the "Y," at a community center, or lunch at a restaurant. From this point on the volunteer assumes responsibility for getting him to return to school, counseling him and following his progress to make sure his problems do not recur, being sure his grades continue to be satisfactory, and letting him know that someone is interested in what he is doing. The help may include rehabilitation of the entire family—a job for the father, medical help for the mother, clothing for brothers and sisters as well as returning the youth to school. In each instance the volunteers work in cooperation with a guidance director at the high school in question, assigned to the case by the Indianapolis School Board.

Funds for the needed items—books, shoes, lunch, bus fares— are provided by clubs, sororities, auxiliaries, service groups, and church circles to which volunteers belong. The organization "adopts" the youth. Bazaars, suppers, benefits, and individual contributions help pay the bills. The "adoption" continues through graduation and beyond, until the youth gets a job, goes into service, marries and has children.

The Stay-in-School effort costs on the average $7 to $12 per returning pupil for a semester, although in some instances the cost is as much as $100. Sometimes no money at all is needed. One girl simply couldn't find Room 374 in a metropolitan high school with enrollment of more than 4,000. The volunteer offered to drive to her home and go with her to meet the school principal.

Another girl needed an alarm clock and a dictionary. She said there was so much noise and confusion at her house with many people in a small space that when finally everyone got to sleep, no one awakened in time to get to school on time. She was always late. The needed items were quickly supplied.

Indianapolis experience shows that 75 per cent of all dropouts read below their grade level. Tests reveal that some high school juniors read at third grade level. Reading difficulties originally encountered in the first, second, and third grades are never overcome. Sometimes the difficulties are physical, such as poor vision, sometimes educational, such as failure to grasp the idea that symbols on paper mean actions or objects or ideas.

An index to the help the Crusade has been able to provide can be obtained by listing the items or special services offered the youngsters. Among other things, the Crusade has:

Purchased 703 pairs of new shoes for returning dropouts.

Found and provided tutors (free) for returned dropouts.

Trained volunteer reading teachers.

Provided remedial reading teachers for children who would have dropped out without help.

Arranged for high school pupils to serve as "listeners" for children who have no one at home to listen to them read.

Set up study tables in settlement houses, churches, YMCAs, and other places for pupils and returning dropouts who have no place to do homework.

Found homes for 27 returning dropouts.

Got jobs for returning dropouts. In one six-week period, the Crusade found 32 jobs with no expenditure except a few 5¢ stamps.

Provided glasses for 78 returning dropouts.

Provided a Voice-Writer for a returning dropout.

Provided clothing for 1,600 youths and 460 families. Got jobs for fathers and mothers so children could go to school.

Got the invalid baby of one returning dropout (a married evening student) into James Whitcomb Riley Hospital.

Paid for lunches, bus fare, fees for returning dropouts.

Obtained baby-sitters so that teen-age girls with babies could return to evening school.

In some instances, it develops, the youngsters do not require material assistance of this sort. Often the youth merely needs advice. Sometimes he needs someone to accompany him to the school office; once a dropout, he is shy about returning to meet the dean, the guidance director, or the principal.

In one prosaic instance, the purchase of a new broom actually made the return of one dropout possible. A high school girl's mother had been sick in bed for months, and the girl had to stay at home to take care of younger children. A physician verified the fact that the mother had long ago recovered from a cold, but conveniently developed hypochondria. The volunteer tried old-fashioned remedies. One day she took homemade soup which she heated and served. The mother sat up in bed and said she felt better; she allowed as how she should help with the housework, but that she hadn't had a new broom in years. The volunteer arrived with a broom, cleaning supplies, and a mop. The mother got out of bed and began working. The girl returned to high school and was graduated in the top 10 per cent of her class. On the commencement invitation to the volunteer, the girl wrote: "Without you, this would not have been possible."

Each dropout has an individual problem. One girl had three successive stepfathers and she said no one cared about her problems. One boy, with help from a volunteer counselor, went back to high school despite the advice of his engineer father: "Forget school; join the Navy." A 16-year-old amateur thespian who thought high school pupils were "immature" enrolled in a school for young actors in New York. Legislation and money would not have solved the problems of these dropouts. The personal touch did.

The Indianapolis plan has also helped hundred of young adults to return to school. In order for one mother—a young widow—to attend evening classes, her teenagers served as baby-sitters for younger children of another evening school student who provided transportation for both women. The first woman held down a daytime job while going to school. When she graduated she was so grateful for her high school diploma that she placed it under her pillow at night. She also took it with her to apply for a job, and when the personnel director of a large company asked, "Are you a high school graduate?" she showed him the diploma. She got the job.

Another young woman who returned to class with Stay-in-School assistance now helps other dropouts go back to school. Recently she appeared on two television programs urging young people to complete their high school education and take advantage of all educational opportunities. She is now attending evening classes at the Indiana University extension department in Indianapolis.

The late Miss Sara C. Ewing, former president of the Indiana State Teachers Association, worked with the Stay-in-School committee from its beginning. She helped nearly 50 youths return to school. Once when she visited a dropout at his home, she met his brother, also a dropout, and the brother's wife, who had left school when she married at the age of 14. Miss Ewing helped all three of them to return to school and graduate. Another brother was in the U. S. Army in Germany. He, too, was a dropout. Miss Ewing wrote to the chaplain in Germany, who helped the young soldier take courses offered through armed service programs.

One of the young women whom Miss Ewing helped said: "Sometimes it was difficult to find enough time to study, what with our baby, but Miss Ewing always had an encouraging word, and we just couldn't give up." This young woman, on graduation, obtained a position in the accounting department of the Wabash Life Insurance Co.

A youngster graduated from evening classes at George Washington High School, Indianapolis, through help from the Stay-in-School committee, also got his job through the volunteers. He is now with the U.S. Army in Vietnam, and his job at Allison Division of General Motors is awaiting his return. Before this young man left for Vietnam he said: "I just didn't think it would be possible for me to get such a good job—one in which I could work up in promotions. But Mrs. Edgar Archer of the

Anti-Crime Crusade helped to make contacts for me, and recommended me. It was personal interest that helped me to have confidence in myself."

In 1966, Mrs. J. C. Fix, who was honored the same year by Depauw University as a distinguished alumna, was responsible for getting nearly 50 youths back in Arsenal Technical High School. She worked directly with the guidance director assigned to the Stay-in-School program.

In cities across the nation there are millions of private citizens who could serve successfully in programs similar to the Indianapolis Stay-in-School approach. Countless youngsters who actually want to get an education have dropped out of school for one reason or another, and will go back if someone helps open the door for their return.

FIVE

Citizens of Tomorrow

Learning the Law

As a result of dropouts, augmented truancy, and absence of parental training, many young people are profoundly ignorant of the law—even when they have no intention of breaking it. They simply have never been informed of what their legal responsibilities are, or of the fact that they have any such responsibilities at all.

Hoosier court-watchers discovered that literally hundreds of juveniles did not know about the law. Again and again, youths face to face with the judge would say: "But I didn't know that I was breaking the law." For years adults have had meetings on leadership, safety, character, and problem children. They have called in panels of experts to expound the causes of juvenile delinquency. They have attended national conferences. But they have forgotten to get the message to the children.

In cooperation with the Anti-Crime Crusade, Indianapolis teenagers decided something should be done about this problem. Student council members, Eagle Scouts, Horizon Club members and other young people from 30 high schools named their own committees to look up Indiana statutes—18 in number—affecting juveniles. They also appointed high school students to talk with judges, the prosecuting attorney, the mayor, the chief of police, the sheriff—everyone involved directly with law enforcement. The result was a booklet called, "Teen-agers Want to Know: What Is the Law?" Requests for more than 50,000 copies of this pamphlet came less than two weeks after publication. Now it is in its fourth printing, 125,000 copies have been presented to young people by policemen, and more than 2,000 classroom talks have been made by policemen on "Laws for Juveniles."*

Direct involvement of the police in the "learning the law" project has proved to be its greatest asset. This phase of the campaign began with a pilot program reaching some 3,000 or so youngsters in sixth, seventh, and eighth grade classes in Indianapolis public and parochial schools. In a series of talks arranged by the Crusade, six officers especially trained to lecture before young people distributed booklets, discussed laws, showed their equipment, explained what happens to a juvenile who is stopped by police, and answered hundreds of questions.

The youngsters thus had a chance to meet policemen face-to-face and hear directly from them about laws affecting juveniles. They learned, among other things, that there are not "good" and "bad" laws—there are laws. And that, as long as there are laws, children and adults alike are obliged to obey them. They learned as well that the proper way to change or modify a law is through the legislature or the courts—not through the willful disobedience of a single person who decides he is a law unto himself.

When the success of the pilot project became apparent, the program was extended to cover all the schools in the city—so that, ultimately, some 100,000 pupils heard the talks. This figure included 28,000 seventh and eighth graders and some 32,000 fifth and sixth graders at local schools. The rest were high school students. The result has been apparent in the reactions of the youngsters and in law enforcement. The juvenile branch of the police department now keeps records which include not only name, age, address, parents' names, and so forth, but also grade in school and the school attended. Previously the records merely

---

* Judge William Sharp of Municipal Court 4, Marion County, Indiana, has commented that if juveniles throughout the nation could be informed about laws which affect them, and have an opportunity to ask any questions they want about laws, delinquency could be cut by at least one-fourth in one year.

showed whether the youth was in school or a dropout. One school conducted a seventh grade debate on capital punishment. Another invited a municipal court judge to visit one afternoon to explain the operation of the courts. Pupils went to the City-County Building the next day to see the courts, tour police headquarters, interview a civil court judge, and fill the jury and attorney chairs in a criminal court while a bondsman spoke to them. In still another school, eighth grade student council members rewrote "What Is the Law?" in simple language for first, second, and third graders. Thousands of pupils have visited the courts, the police department, and municipal offices.

As these results suggest, the talks by the police officers proved both informative and stimulating. Countless questions were asked, covering almost every conceivable aspect of law enforcement as it relates to juveniles. Following is a cross-section of some of these exchanges, with the policemen's answers condensed:

Q. "Can we play in a vacant house if we don't do any damage?"

A. "No, you are trespassing."

Q. "Is it against the law to throw snowballs?"

A. "It is unlawful to throw anything which might injure a person; playing ball according to accepted rules provides occasion for exercise and good fun."

Q. "Martin Luther King says that if you don't like a law you don't have to go by it. Is this true?"

A. "We do not choose good or bad laws from our statutes,.our constitution, our ordinances. Laws are made by law-making bodies in our nation, our states, our counties, our cities—and we abide by them. If adults believe that some laws should be changed, then they should contact our lawmakers in whatever area the law falls."

Q. "What can I do with a B-B gun I got for Christmas if I can't shoot it in Indianapolis?"

A. "Put it away, unless your father or another adult builds a safe range in your basement, or unless your father gets permission in a safe place in the country where it is lawful to shoot a B-B gun."

Q. "Should my mother carry a tear gas gun?"

A. "No, unless she knows how to test the wind and has time to test the wind before using it. She may get tear gas in her own face, and make her doubly vulnerable to attack."

Q. "What do I do if the people for whom I am baby-sitting come home 'looped' and I am afraid to get in a car with them to go home?"

A. "Quietly call your parents and ask them to come for you. Do not baby-sit for these people again."

Q. "How old do we have to be to ride motorcycles?"

A. "You apply for a beginner's license at 15 and a half years, and if you pass the tests, you can get a license at 16. But be careful; cycles are involved in accidents almost every day."

Q. "Could I get in trouble with the curfew law if I have to go to the all-night drug store to get medicine for my sick little sister?"

A. "If this is an emergency, you have valid reason, and, if we stop to question you, we will find out the circumstances. But without valid reason, the curfew law says that you must be home between the hours of 11 p.m. and 5 a.m. Newspaper carriers are exceptions."

Q. "Can we visit the police headquarters or courts?"

A. "Yes, you certainly can visit both, as classes or as individuals."

Q. "Is it against the law for a 10-year-old girl to be baby-sitter all day for four little brothers and sisters?"

A. "Children should not be left in the care of a 10-year-old."

Q. "Do you get in trouble if a buddy sells you something that is stolen?"

A. "Yes, you are in real trouble, and the boy certainly isn't a buddy. You are free to choose the people with whom you spend your time. Choose carefully; they may change your life."

Q. "If a boy throws a brick at me and misses, is it against the law for me to pick up the brick and throw it at him?"

A. "It is against the law for anyone to throw a brick. Bricks are to be used to build houses and schools. If you hit someone with a brick or anything else you can be charged with assault and battery."

Q. "Is it against the law to commit adultery?"

A. "Yes. This is answered, too, in the Ten Commandments."

Q. "Can I carry an ammonia bottle?"

A. "What is that?"

Q. "A bottle with ammonia that you can clean floors with and on the end is a squirt cap so I can squirt it."

A. "Good heavens, no, you can't carry such a thing with intent to squirt it at someone. If you buy a bottle of cleanser to take home to help your mother scrub the floor, fine, but don't use it for anything else."

Q. "If my father owns a liquor store, can I work there?"

A. "No, it is against the law. You can call your father to lunch or take a message from your mother to the door, but you cannot be in the store."

Q. "Can we ride two on a bike?"

A. "No, it is unsafe."

Q. "What about a bicycle built for two?"

A. "That is made for two—for two people to pedal. Be sure the one at the lead handle-bars is capable."

Q. "Why is it against the law to walk on railroad tracks?"

A. "Railroads are private property. Also, and very serious, a train is bigger than a boy, and faster. Children are killed almost every day on railroad tracks."

Q. "Is it against the law to commit suicide?"

A. "Yes, and very sad."

Q. "What if a fellow has stolen a car and is out on probation and takes another car?"

A. "Probation ends there and confinement in an institution begins."

Q. "Why can a policeman come into a dive and arrest somebody when all he is doing is gambling?"

A. "You are young to know about dives and gambling, but frequenting dives is against the law and so is gambling."

Q. "If I got a record, could I get a job?"

A. "Certainly not a very good one, and there are many other

things you can't do—like get a commission in the Armed Services, vote if convicted of a felony, be a doctor, lawyer . . . the list is long."

Q. "If you are caught fighting in the street, what will happen?"

A. "You are not allowed to fight. If someone is injured, you can be charged with assault and battery. Don't fight, and don't get in the street except to walk across it according to safety rules."

Q. "If somebody says I did something and I didn't will I get into trouble?"

A. "If you did not do it, and your answers satisfactorily reflect this, you will not get into trouble. But choose your friends carefully. If you are with people who get into trouble, you will be in trouble, too, just by associating with them."

Correcting Corrections

Correcting or rehabilitating those who have engaged in criminal activities, juvenile or adult, is perhaps the most difficult problem in the field of law enforcement. Undoing the mental and moral makeup which leads to crime is somewhat like unscrambling an omelette. The arduous task of preventing criminals is simplicity itself compared to the effort of retrieving them once they are launched into a career of lawlessness.

As previously noted, unsuccessful efforts have been made to deal with this problem at the youth level. Extreme permissiveness in the handling of juvenile delinquents seems, over the years, to have made the problem worse. On the other hand, indifference to the fact that a wayward youngster (or adult) is still salvageable has also had calamitous results. Mere institutionalization often serves to harden criminal attitudes.

In Indianapolis, the search for an appropriate answer to this problem has once more depended upon the personal touch—dealing with each case as an individual matter with its own peculiar assets and liabilities. The Anti-Crime Crusade has vigorously opposed indiscriminate leniency in the corrections system, along with other abuses; but it has also tried to work with and rehabilitate those youngsters who have stepped into lawlessness only tentatively and can still be won back to civilization.

The corrections problem, in Indiana as elsewhere, has long been a serious one. In recent years citizens have watched in dismay as turnover in personnel, retention of unqualified people, riots, extreme permissiveness, ineffective counseling, little or no vocational guidance and other disorders have racked the system.

In years past, for example, there have been superintendents of the Indiana Boys School whose previous training was (1) ownership of a milk plant, (2) the profession of dentistry, (3) coaching a football team. The Indiana Girls School had 19 superintendents in 10 years.

A study of Indiana corrections by the National Council on Crime and Delinquency listed many of the things Hoosier citizens already knew—including poorly trained personnel, overcrowding of institutions, substandard methods of operation, lack of a sound classification and treatment program. And vivid headlines in 1965 and 1966 drove the lesson home more deeply still. A long series of escapes from detention centers for adults and juveniles, capped by riots at the Girls School, put Hoosier citizens on notice that things were not well in their corrections system.

The state commissioner of corrections, since replaced, tried to deal with this situation by promising the rioters augmented benefits. The results were disastrous. Granted the privilege of writing totally uncensored letters, the inmates quickly abused it —one of them firing off an obscene letter to President Johnson. When the corrections commissioner went to the Girls School and told the inmates they would get more benefits—he actually allowed them to rifle his pockets in search of cigarettes—the result was to spur the defiant youngsters on to new acts of disobedience. Lee Eads, now Marion County sheriff, commented that the girls needed "more discipline and less coddling." He added that "the girls, not the officials, are running the school," and that officials were "begging" the girls rather than telling them what to do. Some months later the rioting broke out again, prompting one Hoosier corrections official to comment: "We do not at this point have control. The girls have control."

Hoosier citizens protested these disorderly conditions, and the Anti-Crime Crusade set out to support a constructive program in the corrections field. Early in 1967, a new corrections commissioner, Anthony Kuharich, moved to crack down on some of the hyper-permissiveness and to reorganize the department. He is training untrained personnel, providing a consistent communications system for staff members, establishing new, practical vocational programs within institutions, and setting out better parole systems which will fit released prisoners for life as useful citizens. He seems to be moving toward a balanced position which seeks to rehabilitate without letting the inmates take over the institutions. Volunteers of the Anti-Crime Crusade have been working in the same direction.

In 1966, Indiana courts sent over 250 girls to the Indiana Girls School at Clermont. Of that number, Marion County (Indianapolis) alone contributed one out of every four girls. Women of Marion County decided it was important for the county to provide for its own. Many of the girls sent to such institutions simply need a break from their present associates or a better home life. Some girls need desperately to know that living can be pleasant and gracious. The volunteers realize it is time to care about girls—that there is need for more places to send girls who need a change, but not necessarily confinement in a penal institution.

Indianapolis volunteers are therefore establishing a home for Marion County girls who would be assigned by the judge of the Juvenile Court. Because this is to be a home, the girls would go to local schools, attend the church of their choice, and do home chores many of them haven't yet learned. Major maintenance would be provided, as would be meal preparation, to allow the girls full time to devote to school work, to keeping their own rooms clean and to taking turns at chores. But there would also be time for recreation, for getting to know other people, for learning better manners, for discovering libraries and museums, and for participation in youth activities. The professional staff would be patterned after the highly successful Youth Service, Inc., in Philadelphia, and other similar homes.*

While this program is being organized, volunteer citizens

---

* Youth Service, Inc., in Philadelphia, has been in existence for 14 years. The program offers placement for adolescent girls between the ages of 12 and 18.

are already assisting in a self-help rehabilitation program aimed at breaking patterns of delinquent behavior. The rehabilitation chairman of the Crusade, working with the parole department, gets the name of young people released from the Girls School and Boys School. She finds a woman or a man in the home town of the youth who is released, and makes sure that he will get back in school, get a job, have good clothes, and become adjusted as a useful, worthwhile citizen. For too long, released youths, and adults, have been lost in the shuffle of the city or the everyday routine of the town. Nobody cared. The parolee committed another crime. He returned to the institution.

To counteract such tendencies, the Anti-Crime Crusade has a rehabilitation chairman, Mrs. Floyd Hughett, who now works on a full-time basis through the Indiana Federation of Clubs.

Volunteers are, in addition, supporting legislation which would establish regional detention centers for juveniles. A year or so ago, a teen-age boy, detained in an Indiana jail overnight awaiting a hearing, was isolated to protect him from adults charged with crimes. During the night the youth became so depressed that he hanged himself. Group homes for girls—and boys—are also being established by Indiana volunteers. In Kokomo, for example, Friendship Home will house 12 to 15 problem girls. Crusade members work weekly with 225 girls at the Indiana Girls School, locating job opportunities for them, counseling them on careers, assisting them with projects which help them to adjust to good citizenship when they are released.

On the negative side, the volunteers prompted the resignation of one Indiana Boys School counselor and unmasked a local colleague who was getting case referrals on the grounds that he was a "practicing psychologist," which he was not. Following the episode, arrangements were made to get authentic psychological counseling, including such simple steps as arranging for a Yellow Page listing to make it easier to find a qualified psychologist.

Finally, in an effort to prevent the development of antisocial attitudes, the Crusade has encouraged the work of youth organizations like the Police Athletic League. Members met with the police director of the PAL clubs and asked how they could help in its activities. They were put to work on such projects as raising funds for summer camps, gymnasium work, building cars for the Soap Box Derby. The Crusade has similarly worked with groups like the Boy Scouts and the Girl Scouts, the Camp Fire Girls, and the 4-H Clubs. In addition to trying to assist them in advancing their programs, the Crusade set up contacts between these organizations and the police and probation officers.

SIX

Those Who Help Themselves

Good Housekeeping

If indiscriminate welfarism contributes to the crime problem, rather than relieving it, how does one go about dealing with bad living conditions, illiteracy, and deprivation? The answer favored in Indianapolis is self-help. In this sphere as in others, Crusade members have stressed the need for individual responsibility. Help there has been in plenty for those who need it—but help aimed at generating activity among people willing to help themselves.

We have referred to the Indianapolis tradition of local and personal initiative. The entire Anti-Crime Crusade embodies this tradition, and many of its subdivisions are vivid examples of it in particular areas of community concern. One of the most impressive of these is a group called Citizens Forum, an organization led by Mrs. Mattie Coney, former school teacher and "Spruce-Up" chairman of the Anti-Crime Crusade. Mrs. Coney's work in the downtown areas of Indianapolis has won nationwide recognition.

As a school teacher, Mrs. Coney has worked for 30 years in areas where many parents took little care of their children, often sending them to school unfed and badly clothed. "I worked and struggled with these families for years," she says, "and I finally decided that I would try to develop a plan to show these families how to live. But I was so busy teaching school and taking care of responsibilities for dozens of children that I had little time to get out into the neighborhood."

Mrs. Coney approached the Lilly Endowment of Indianapolis and received a grant of $9,000 which made it possible for her to take a leave of absence from teaching and devote all her time to her block-by-block work. "Things aren't nearly as futile as they are pictured," she says. "So many people have just got into the habit of sitting day after day and letting things go to pot. We hope to instill in these people the need to expend a little energy, at least enough to clean up their houses, wash the children's faces, take care of the garbage, and get out and work."

Citizens Forum work encompasses both white and Negro citizens in greater Indianapolis. But much of its emphasis has been on self-help programs in the Negro community. This means, says Mrs. Coney, improving the care of property, upgrading manners, speech, dress, and social customs, "so Negroes can fully accept and exercise both the rights and the responsibilities given to them."

Mrs. Coney has recruited an organization of teachers; clergy, businessmen, policemen, church leaders, city officials, and attorneys to plan, organize, and assist neighborhood self-improvement programs. Education, employment, and delinquency are among priority areas in which the committee works. One of the Forum's programs has been the organization of more than 600 block clubs. The purpose of these clubs is to arrange for clean-up, fix-up campaigns, to provide guidance and recreation for children, and to help newcomers to the city become useful residents of the neighborhood.* Another effort, in the same connection, is to demand full enforcement of local health, safety, and building codes.

"So many parents can't read well enough to know which bus

---

* Sample Citizen Forum programs: A straight-from-the-shoulder talk by Dr. Henry Nester, director of public health of Marion County (metropolitan Indianapolis) on "The Growing Problem of Illegitimate Births in Center Township." Another talk by a committee chairman of the Anti-Crime Crusade on "Whose Child Is This?" Also, a lecture by a school official on "Whatever Became of the Hickory Stick?"

to take," Mrs. Coney says. "They see a big 'C' heading up a word on the front of the bus, but they don't know whether the word is 'Central' or 'Crosstown.' We just have to get these people to learn to read." Mrs. Coney printed signs to put in buses which transport high school pupils from their homes daily. "It would be useless in some areas to put up a sign which says, 'Please talk in a well-modulated voice,'" she comments. "That's why our signs say, 'Don't Be a Loud-Mouth.'"

Then there is the matter of obeying the law. If children are not good citizens in their homes and neighborhoods, how can we expect them to be good citizens of the community or nation at large? Discipline, in Mrs. Coney's view, begins at home. "We certainly don't need marches to get our city in better shape," says this Negro leader. "The only way we might march is with a broom in one hand and a rake in the other."

Through diligent effort, Mrs. Coney has been able to help a number of people get jobs; and while the men are working, she helps the women learn how to do housework more efficiently. The Forum also urges women to visit school and attend parent meetings. A few "look-see" school visits by parents may result in questions about "Where can I learn to read?" Pictures and writing by the children may be hung on the wall at home instead of being trampled and torn to bits. One mother in Indianapolis found some old bricks in an alley and made the first bookcase her family had ever seen to shelter her children's school books.

Volunteers from the Anti-Crime Crusade met with welfare officials and home economists, and arranged a cooking school for volunteers. Casseroles, bread, meat pies, soups, cookies and dozens of other dishes were prepared. On the day arranged, volunteer women took along extra cooking utensils, salt, baking powder and soda, milk, and flavoring. Often they included a casserole baking dish or a large kettle or pan, and a cookie sheet. Just for good measure, in an unrelated area, they carried needle and thread—items which often turn up missing in many homes. Frequently, neighbors would gather to observe and they too learned about new ways to cook.

In a downtown church, a home economist helped volunteer women and church leaders to set up a continuing program of "learning how to live." The women came from fourth-floor flats, from two-room homes which housed families of seven and eight. A seminar in human relations developed without a textbook. When asked their problems, the women just shook their heads. But answers came when they were asked, "What happened at your house this morning?"

"My kids wouldn't eat anything I cooked."

"My in-laws are a pain in the neck."

"Everything is in a mess because the kids throw stuff on the floor; they won't pick up things."

"I can't keep food; the kids steal everything I have to eat."

"They won't wash; they run out dirty to school."

From these comments, cooking, sewing, washing, ironing, family relations, marriage problems, and some dozen other subjects were taken up, one by one, and related to the home life of the women in the neighborhood. As a result, the church set up a workshop where these women could come regularly for help. A washer and dryer were installed, and cooking lessons were offered regularly.

Meanwhile, the owner of many of the flats and apartments in the neighborhood became so interested in the program that he gave a small lot—which he had utilized for used cars—for a playground for children. He installed swings, see-saws, and other playground equipment. Boy Scouts helped to clear the lot. In the summer an ice cream social was sponsored there by the neighborhood.

In one Indianapolis area, a call to a veteran principal verified the fact that a "Spruce-Up" day would be welcomed. A teacher suggested that three or four women volunteers meet with as many women from the school neighborhood. The Anti-Crime Crusade furnished rakes and brooms—two station wagons-full. Volunteers arranged for motorcycle police to rope off three blocks of the street one autumn Saturday. Arrangements were made for a city truck to pick up the trash. Within 15 minutes after the station wagons arrived with rakes and brooms, 63 children and teenagers set to work. The school principal and other adults helped out. At a nearby settlement house, volunteers cooked a meal for the workers. The children, for the first time in many of their lives, established friendships with the police. They had previously encountered law-enforcement officials only when there was trouble in their neighborhood or at their homes. When the work was done, 15 truck loads of debris had been hauled away in three hours.

The spirit of this first undertaking caught on rapidly elsewhere. In two separate clean-up drives sponsored by Citizens Forum in 1966 and 1967, some 175,000 tons of trash were picked up and hauled away. As a result of these efforts, yards and neighborhoods were neater. Houses were cleaner, with more room for orderly living. Families quit yelling at one another, children made better grades, fathers stayed home, police were seldom needed. Good housekeeping (and good neighborhood-keeping) had joined the list of crime deterrents.

In 1966, Mrs. Coney's efforts won a major national award from Freedoms Foundation in Valley Forge, Penna. The citation singled her out for her special contribution to the American way of life, and for her commitment to the values of personal dignity and individual freedom. In 1967, further recognition was accorded her work by *U.S. News and World Report*, which offered this statement of her philosophy: "Slums are made by people, not by plaster or bricks. Bad neighborhoods develop because individuals who live in them fail to do what they can . . . If I am a sloppy, dirty, noisy, rowdy neighbor in one part of town, I will be the same in another neighborhood. You don't get culture on a moving van . . .

"With every opportunity and privilege comes responsibility. Freedom is not free to anybody. You work at it all the time from the day you are born to the day you die. You have to pay your bills; you have to keep up your property; you have to train your children to be good citizens."

In fulfillment of this philosophy, the Citizens Forum "Good Neighbor" plan includes the following 15 points:

1. Help keep premises clean; tie waste paper in bundles so that it will not litter streets and alleys.
2. Place garbage in cans; keep cans covered.
3. Urge children not to break bottles in streets and alleys.

4. Have children clean and tidy before letting them go out to play.

5. Renters, as well as owners, should protect property. (Destructive tenants pay higher rents.)

6. Lower musical instruments at 11. Loud talking and unnecessary noises reflect on any neighborhood.

7. Ring bells, do not toot horns, when calling for friends. Ask friends and cab drivers to cooperate. Ask paper boys to ring bells and not yell their wares from the sidewalks.

8. Guard lawns and parkways. Short-cuts destroy their beauty.

9. Do not buy from front-door fruit, vegetable, ice or coal dealers. Their place is in the alley. They do not call their wares on the front streets of a well-kept neighborhood. We should go to them and not yell our orders from doors and windows. People cannot sell on front streets if you do not buy. Observe these rules and improve the character of your neighborhood.

10. The beautiful appearance of streets, sidewalks, alleys and yards, and the neatness of doors and windows tell who you are.

11. Washing and repairing cars on front streets show disregard for the appearance of the block.

12. Deliveries of milk, laundry, groceries and furniture should be made from rear entrances. Try to have drivers use alleys; if not, have them bring packages to the rear. Owners of business trucks should not park them on residential streets.

13. Let us try to keep uniformity in outside painting by using neutral colors.

14. Let us keep our windows clean; fresh curtains.

15. Obscene and vile language reflects character; respect the ladies and children.

Lamp Lighters

Although physical conditions are not the ultimate cause of crime, they can contribute to it greatly. They can provide the occasion and context for it. A hoodlum is more likely to attack under certain circumstances than under others. A wise anti-crime program should concentrate, therefore, on avoiding development of conditions which favor the criminal element.

Studies by Indianapolis volunteers suggested that one of the central factors in many crimes of violence—and in other law violations as well—is the presence or absence of light. Criminals do not like the light; they prefer, for a number of obvious reasons, to strike where they cannot be seen. Lighting discourages night crime in several ways: The intended victim has a better opportunity to see and evade the attacker; criminals are more apt to be seen by passers-by; police patrols can more readily spot a crime in the making; more people will be on the street which is lighted; and so forth.

One step toward reducing the crime rate, therefore, is to improve street lighting—a step which has such other fringe benefits as cutting down on traffic accidents. Indianapolis has made a concerted effort on this score, and has come up with a street-lighting program which may be valuable to many cities whose councilmen have not realized that crime is expensive, or that most modern street-lighting systems now run so economically it's expensive *not* to have them.

Obviously, surveying for needed street lights can't be done in daylight. In fact, the dark of the moon is the best time to see the full effect of darkness and light. Riding in police cars to insure their safety in high crime areas, Indianapolis volunteers went forth on the darkest nights of the year to see what their city looks like. They traveled with police escorts, power light experts and engineers—and made notes of needs. Then they presented reports to an advisory committee consisting of volunteers and experts in various areas related to lighting.

The plan used in Indianapolis to improve street lighting and lower the crime rate is simple but effective. It consists, first of all, in finding out certain things about street lighting in the community, such as: Who is responsible for it? Who decides where it will be put? What kinds are available? How much does it cost? What's the simplest way to get money into the city budget? Once the lights are in, who owns them and who is responsible for their maintenance?

The Crusaders started with the local electric utility, which provided a specialist in street lighting to explain the technical aspects of lighting as well as how to get more lights. He referred inquiries to officials who control the budget and placement of lights, and who were astonished to know people were willing to support a budget for adequate lighting and had ideas on the location of street lamps.

Indianapolis volunteers formed a committee to help in the selection of locations for new lighting and to support adequate financing for it. The committee is composed of representatives of the Chamber of Commerce, the Metropolitan Plan Commission, the police department, the traffic engineer, the city engineer responsible for lighting, club women, and the executive secretary of the Board of Works (the government unit in Indianapolis responsible for lighting).

Maps of the Hoosier capital were drawn and colored to show various factors such as present lighting, high crime areas, density of population, night-time accident rates, heavy-traffic streets, location of community centers, night schools, hospitals, theaters, auditoriums, and other centers of nocturnal activity. It was necessary to learn how many streets were lighted up to the code set by the Illuminating Engineers Society. Also how many lights were mercury vapor, how many fluorescent, how many incandescent, and which areas have only intersection lighting.

In Indianapolis' high crime areas, checks were made of zones that have a heavy incidence of street crime (assaults, purse-grabbings, muggings, car theft, etc.) or where the incidence of police coverage and service was above average. Census figures indicated the density of population by census tracts. Such maps are usually available from the United Fund, Chamber of Commerce, utility companies, and the United States Department of Commerce.

In checking night-time traffic accident rates, the volunteers avoided getting trapped in high-flown figures such as "accidents per vehicle-mile" and the like. What was needed, they found, were the locations of vehicle and/or pedestrian accidents for the preceding year and indications of how many accidents at each location took place in the day-time and how many at night. Any site where nighttime accidents outnumber daytime accidents was regarded as a candidate for a light; other accident locations were checked for other causes.

The traffic engineer, state highway department, and police departments supplied records of the density of traffic on streets. There was no need to break down the study of density of traffic into nighttime and daytime because in many cases they were the same and because there are many hours of the year—overcast, stormy days, or shorter winter days—when the lights are on during the hours of heaviest traffic movement. Location of community centers (with attention to the residential streets children cross to get to them), of night schools, of theaters and auditoriums (with attention to streets on which the audience must park) were fully noted. These showed where people were apt to congregate after dark.

The police department was then asked to have its men report the areas in which street lights were needed. The man patrolling a district knows a great deal about purely local needs that doesn't turn up on charts and graphs. Indianapolis residents were also asked to look at lighting from the air whenever they flew over the city. It's amazing what you can see flying over a lighted community—Indianapolis, Los Angeles, Washington, D.C., Cleveland, Chicago, Seattle.

Crusaders cooperated with the Power & Light company in distributing a pamphlet on protective lighting, as well as in other projects. As a result, homeowners immediately began lighting up their own yards, bordering alleys and other dark spots. Other corrective measures in the private sector included action by the Apartment House Owners' Association to improve lighting and related protective measures for their tenants.

As a result of these actions, more than 9,000 new street lights have been installed in five years' time, and 6,000 "dusk to dawn" lamps have brightened alleys and residential neighborhoods.

Hoosiers found it wise not to set out a 10-year or even one-year plan for lighting. Indianapolis, like many other communities, changes rapidly: Crime rates alter, shopping centers are built, a new theater goes in, new highways transform traffic patterns, a community center is abandoned. All of these things need to be taken into account as each year's purchase of new lights is made. Each year Indianapolis volunteers simply ask for an increased appropriation to use where additional lighting is most needed.

SEVEN

Toward Responsibility

The examples cited in the preceding chapters are only two among numerous instances of private and local action in Indianapolis to eliminate the sources and conditions of crime.

Anti-Crime Crusaders have addressed themselves to all zones of influence in the battle against lawlessness—and since the Crusade approach is highly particular and individualized, the result is a variegated picture. Crusade work in almost every conceivable sphere of Indianapolis community life can be observed every day of the week.

The Crusade has established a clothing center for children and adults reluctant to attend school or apply for a job in their tattered clothes. This was accomplished without use of public funds. The downtown YWCA donated a room for the project, and since a cafeteria, swimming pool, and ping pong table are located on the same premises, there is no stigma attached to going to the room for clothing.

Other such activities include work to improve the condition of playgrounds and parks to insure that young people have proper recreation areas; establishment of study tables in churches and settlement houses to make facilities available to young people in need of help; making sure that youngsters have an opportunity to go to musical and dramatic entertainments; insuring that all grade schools have good libraries and adequate supplies of books; insuring, once the libraries are stocked, that children are introduced to them, acquainted with procedures for getting books, and offered library programs.

In areas where youngsters did not have enough to eat, Crusaders attempted to supply the deficiency. Some schools, it developed, had cupboards in need of replenishing. In cooperation with the Power & Light Company and the Gas Company, Crusaders held programs in downtown areas showing women how to plan and manage family budgets. Volunteers also demonstrated new ways of utilizing food.

A particular problem in any large city is the takeover of city parks by derelicts, winos, aggressive panhandlers, and worse. A self-help innovation of the Anti-Crime Crusade to deal with this headache was a "park-sitters" program—in which a large number of women would simply go into a park, pre-empt the benches, and knit. In conjunction with stepped-up police surveillance of the parks, this exercise in audacity worked wonders.

The matter of literacy, stressed by Mrs. Coney, is another area in which the Crusade has interested itself with beneficial effect. A case in point was the widowed mother of ten children who learned through a basic literacy program to read the sentence "Complete your education." She had never attended a public school. She wanted to read and write because she felt helpless when her first and second grade children asked her to read to them or check their papers. "I still can't help much," she said, "but I tell them how important school is, and I see to it that they do everything their teacher tells them to. I plan to enroll in another course this winter."

The Anti-Crime Crusade has helped this woman and countless others like her. It has worked with the Board for Fundamental Education, the Indiana Literacy Council, teachers using the "Direct Approach to Reading and Spelling," and Indianapolis Public Schools in providing volunteer teachers and transporting people who want to learn to the place where they can do so.

Of equal moment is the matter of gainful employment. The employment committee of the Anti-Crime Crusade got 32 jobs for Indianapolis youngsters in six weeks' time—again without using public money. Letters were sent to personnel directors asking: "Is it possible that you have one job for one returning dropout?" They did. When other jobs were needed, an appeal went out to service clubs. One community center now has a staff man assigned to job-searching. A high school principal says publicity given the need for jobs brought many offers. Personnel men and women from major retailing businesses sat down at lunch and offered to help back-to-school youths so that each youngster has someone standing behind him. Systematizing the idea, quarterly job clinics sponsored by the Anti-Crime Crusade and the Mayor's Manpower Committee helped several hundred youngsters find jobs. A job fair sponsored by the Chamber of Commerce and local businesses attracted more than 15,000 people to the Indiana State Fairgrounds in 1966—and brought jobs and in-training help for some 1,600 young people and adults. The Crusade's "Spruce-Up" committee has set up a "Helping Hands" clearing house where citizens can call for help, and youths can provide services.

Heading the Crusade's employment committee are two civic leaders: a former state president of the American Association of University Women and an officer of the women's division of the Chamber of Commerce.

Housing is still another area of concern. Homes unfit for habitation or which need repairs and cleaning are inspected by Crusade volunteers. Representatives of Zonta, Altrusa, Soroptimist and Pilot Clubs—all working in the Crusade—toured areas in which volunteers could help in clean-up projects. They assisted in slum clearance and better housing plans, helping upgrade neighborhoods and preventing children from getting into trouble through trespass on condemned sites or other mishaps which might occur in dilapidated structures. One Crusader, Miss Phoebe Jane Huey of Pilot Club, has also served as secretary of the mayor's slum clearance committee.

In one instance when these four service clubs united to sponsor a clean-up campaign in a three-block area, they found the owners of a house "unfit for habitation" lived in a distant city. A local bank managed the affairs of the elderly landlords. The bank was contacted, and trucks were sent at once to clean out a basement full of wet ashes and debris.

In one housing area, Lockfield Gardens, built in the '30s with Federal backing, the clean-up campaign was not so easily started. The length of residence in the apartments is short, and there has been little civic pride on the part of some of the residents. Children helped the women, however, with clean-up drives.

Although pursuing such projects energetically, the volunteers have not deluded themselves into believing these activities by themselves can put a halt to crime. An occasional outside boost is helpful, in some cases critically important; but the ultimate objective is and must be to get people to do things for themselves. The volunteers have tried to stress this concept throughout. Just as the Crusade points out to young people that they have a responsibility to obey the law, so does it point out that, in all departments of life, they have duties that correspond to their rights.

Repeatedly, emphasis is placed on the fact that the basic duty of young people is, in Inspector Kemper's phrase, to "grow up," to do useful and honest work; to abide by the law and to help out around the house; when employed, to give a day's work for a day's wage. One of the chief efforts of the Crusade, in fact, has been to reactivate the concept of daily "chores" for children— a 19th century concept which some modern-day reformers apparently find repugnant.

The Crusaders have also attempted to rejuvenate the seemingly outmoded concept of simple morality. Their researches showed that slightly over half the young people in trouble with the police (51.6 per cent) had formal religious affiliations, and they worked with the Church Federation, the Catholic deanery, and the heads of parochial schools to see what could be done about these youngsters. In the majority of cases, a good response was offered. But in others the signs suggested that the "new" way of looking at things had gone too far: When one minister asked how he could help combat delinquency, and was told that a few sermons on morality might be beneficial, he was incredulous. "In *church?*" he said. It evidently struck him as a revolutionary notion.

Moral conduct and obedience to the law are, as noted, the principal theme of learning-the-law sessions, of the multi-sided work of the Crusade's youth division, and of the Citizens Forum campaign for better living conditions. All aspects of the Crusade place equal emphasis on opportunity and responsibilities. Neither, the volunteers believe, is possible without the other.

What the Crusaders advance by precept they also try to support by practice. Believing that the ultimate keys to law-abiding behavior are self-reliance and responsibility, the volunteers try to exemplify these virtues as well as talk about them. That is one reason they have conducted their anti-crime campaign so strenuously on the basis of personal effort, without running to Washington or some other branch of government for money.

The controlling premise of the Crusade is that Indianapolis citizens should care for their own problems. The volunteers believe this approach gets the job done better, and they believe it is morally sound as well. How, they reason, can they urge someone else to take care of his own needs and develop a sense of responsibility if they in turn are consigning their own responsibilities to distant planners in Washington, D.C.? The idea of asking the Federal government to step in as a means of curing the default of responsibility strikes the Crusaders as neither logical nor effective.

This outlook has on occasion proved confusing to Federal and other officials eager to press government funds on the Crusaders or to lay plans for Indianapolis in Washington. In more than one instance Federal representatives have called in Indianapolis to "help" local citizens combat crime, only to find the local citizens already hard at work on the problem being "studied" in the nation's capital.

One notable example of this was the receipt of a letter from Vice President Hubert Humphrey, offering the services of the Federal government in "studying" the dropout problem. The Vice President was informed that Indianapolis was already returning dropouts to school in record numbers, without Federal or other public money.

In another memorable episode, an official came before a Citizens Forum meeting and told those in attendance how they could get Federal dollars. They replied that theirs was a self-help project aimed at building personal character, and that acceptance of

Federal money was not compatible with this objective. The official was extremely puzzled.

After several encounters of this sort, Federal officials began to understand that Indianapolis was actually *doing* something about crime on its own. They began coming around to get advice rather than to give it. Thus the Johnson administration put in a hurry-up call to Indianapolis to get information on the Crusade for inclusion in the President's national crime report. Crusade representatives traveled to Washington to give testimony before the House Education and Labor Committee. And the Department of Labor requested a complete rundown on the methods employed in Indianapolis to get jobs for young people.

In keeping with its local autonomy theme, the Anti-Crime Crusade has maintained steady contact with other self-help agencies in Indianapolis. The splendid work of these groups has done much over the years to keep spirit and initiative alive in our city—and to create an intellectual and moral atmosphere in which an operation like the Crime Crusade can attain success.

Foremost among the agencies which have worked in this direction is the Indianapolis Chamber of Commerce, under the leadership of the late William H. Book and now under Book's able successor, Carl Dortch. The Chamber attitude down through the years has been that local problems are best handled on the local level. It has generally opposed the deadening hand of Federal welfare intervention, and has conducted numerous drives to raise funds and promote programs contributing to augmented rather than diminished personal responsibility. We have previously detailed the Chamber's cooperation with the Crusade in staging anti-shoplifting clinics and its work in securing jobs for those who want them. In addition, this energetic agency maintains its own full-time law-enforcement committee to cooperate with the police department and others combatting crime.

Individual business firms have also pulled a sturdy oar in the anti-crime campaign. The Indianapolis Power and Light Company, Indiana Bell Telephone, and a local cleaning establishment, Tuchman Cleaners, have cooperated in lighting crusades, anti-dropout campaigns, cleaning wearing apparel for needy youngsters. Women of the Anti-Crime Crusade whose husbands are employed by the Indiana Bell Telephone company did such a good job that their husbands decided to help. The men found jobs for the youths—and offered valuable counsel, too. The *Bell Telephone News* featured a page-one story about the men who helped as job-finders and counselors for returning dropouts. The Indianapolis Exchange Clubs have, as noted, co-sponsored the Crusade's effort to honor policemen. These are typical examples of the help given the Crusade by an enterprising business community.*

Other agencies have set a similar good example. Flanner House, a leading self-help agency both in Indianapolis and in the nation (its national affiliate is the Board for Fundamental Education), has promoted a unique home-building effort called the "sweat equity" program, in which people who want new housing are supplied materials and build their own homes. Under the leadership of Dr. Cleo Blackburn, Flanner House has also launched a nationwide project to upgrade job skills, to supply instruction in such things as typing, and to obtain employment opportunities for those who want advancement. Teachers from the Board for Fundamental Education have provided life-saving literacy lessons at Indianapolis Driver Improvement Schools for the approximately five per cent of local drivers who cannot read or write. As noted, BFE has cooperated with the Crusade in other ways as well.

The Indianapolis Board of School Commissioners has displayed a consistently helpful attitude. Superintendent George F. Ostheimer and School Board leaders Mrs. Ralph Coble, Col. L. Robert Mottern, Mrs. John A. Alexander and others have conducted a school program that stresses moral values, self-reliance, and sound instruction. Former Board Member Ortho L. Scales repeatedly emphasized these principles on the board and in his work with the YMCA. The board and the school community as a whole extend every cooperation to the Anti-Crime Crusade, from the anti-dropout program to learning-the-law sessions.

---

* Working with the Chamber is the Committee for Employment Opportunity, which maintains Indianapolis headquarters and has undertaken surveys in downtown neighborhoods to get jobs and job-seekers together. This is the agency formerly headed by Richard C. Cornuelle, author of *Reclaiming The American Dream.*

Also a major factor in keeping Indianapolis on an even keel is Marion County welfare director Wayne Stanton. Stanton tries to make sure that all who need assistance receive it, but also insists that chiselers and those who seek to make relief a way of life do not wax fat at the expense of the taxpayer. This attitude has led him into frequent conflict with Federal welfare officials, who have tried to impose controls on his operations and to forestall his inspection efforts to make sure relief goes to the deserving and not to free-loaders.

Other Indianapolis citizens who have promoted the self-help idea are State Sens. W. W. Hill, Jr. and Leslie Duvall and State Reps. Robert L. Jones, Jr. and Danny L. Burton. Hill is a former director of United Student Aid Funds, a private group which makes loan money available to needy youngsters who want to go on to receive a college education. USAF guarantees bank loans to the students which they repay after graduation. Jones and Duvall sponsored a bill which passed the 1967 session of the Indiana legislature, allowing a $50 tax credit for private contributions to colleges and universities. Jones also sponsored a tax-credit bill which allows businesses to deduct funds used for training young people in job skills. Burton and Duvall led the way in obtaining passage of a resolution asking a constitutional amendment restoring prayer in the classrooms. These legislators and others cooperated in such projects as passing a law allowing the Indianapolis Police Department to recruit new members outside Marion County and another permitting merchants to detain suspected shoplifters up to an hour or until a policeman arrives.

It is against the background of this continuing and energetic effort toward self-help that the Anti-Crime Crusade is able to do its work in Indianapolis. A self-reliant spirit in the people is the key to success in combatting lawlessness and moral breakdown. If Indianapolis people were resigned to becoming mere ciphers in a collectivist system, there would be no hope for the Crusade. But because a strong individualism and a keen spirit of local pride prevail, the Crusade has found literally thousands of citizens who are ready, willing, and able to pitch in.

CONCLUSION

What Has Been Achieved?

Has the Indianapolis Anti-Crime Crusade been effective? Does it point the way for responsible private action, in cooperation with law-enforcement agencies, to achieve a reduction in crime? Or is it, like so many other crime-fighting efforts, simply another indeterminate factor which might or might not be making a contribution?

Such questions are hard to answer with full precision. Because so many variables are involved, it is difficult to gauge the total impact of the Crusade. Suffice it to say every kind of available evidence shows this volunteer effort has helped cut the crime rate in the Indianapolis community. Statistical data, visible reforms, the testimony of officials and the emulation of other cities all suggest the program has been a success.

When the Crusade set out "to make the streets safe for women," its leaders realized that while crime can be reduced to some extent over the short run, it will not be eliminated for a long time to come. They began both immediate and long-range projects, some of which produced tangible results at an early date, others of which will take months or even decades to achieve a measurable effect.

The most crucial indicators of progress, of course, are the crime statistics themselves. When the Crusade began, Indianapolis had 300 more crimes per 100,000 of population than the national FBI average. This crime rate continued to rise, in accordance with the upward movement of the national figures, until 1965. In that year, things took a dramatic turn for the better. Indianapolis crime suddenly dipped by 2.2 per cent, while the national average rose by 6 per cent. That was, to the Crusaders' way of thinking, tangible evidence of progress. They were pleased but not complacent. They recognized that some categories of crime were up, and that further effort would be necessary.

In 1966, the Indianapolis figures rose once more—by 5.2 per cent. But this was less than the 11 per cent recorded by the FBI for the nation as a whole, and well below the general increase in most major cities. And, in both '65 and '66, there was a decline in the number of forcible rapes, aggravated assaults, and other crimes against the person. The first half of 1967, five years after the Crusade was launched, saw a still further decrease in these crimes compared to the same period of the preceding year. Homicides dropped from 18 to 11; rapes from 51 to 48; robberies from 473 to 403; and aggravated assaults from 206 to 176.

These are the front-line statistics on which crime-fighting efforts must be judged, and unless they reflect some kind of improvement other supposed evidence of progress means little. Right behind them, however, are figures of the second rank, tokens of success which help explain why the crime figures have been kept under reasonable control in Indianapolis. Among these latter are the facts that:

More than 2,000 dropouts have returned to school, or been persuaded not to leave in the first place.

Arrest and prosecutions for shoplifting, with follow-through by merchants, are up sharply, and shoplifting incidents have in turn gone down. One store reports a 49 per cent decrease in shoplifting.

A total of 125,000 Indianapolis residents—most of them high school and junior high students—have heard class lectures by police officers on "Laws for Juveniles."

Nine key reforms, previously enumerated, have been enacted to insure good order and even-handed justice in Indianapolis courts.

More than 600 block clubs with 4,000 members have been organized to clean up downtown neighborhoods. A clean-up drive by the city, spurred by Mattie Coney, picked up 175,000 tons of trash in one three-week period. Follow-ups are made by block clubs.

More than 150,000 copies of a leaflet entitled "How Women Can Protect Themselves," have been distributed to individuals, clubs, and business firms.

Some 3,000 young people who had never before participated in volunteer efforts have been given "something to do" in civic programs cooperating with the Crusade.

Unqualified personnel in the corrections system have been given improved training, a top-down shake-up has been executed in the department, new non-permissive regulations have been handed down, and a new look is being taken at all corrections programs.

Legislation has been passed to improve police recruitment policies, tighten and codify laws governing shoplifting, crack down on prostitution and pandering, and broaden the dangerous weapons law to include switch-blades.

A two-year, 62-credit-hour academic program, which may be applied in entirety to a baccalaureate degree, has been established by Indiana University in Indianapolis for advanced police education. Classes are held in the police wing of the City-County Building—so that policemen can work toward college degrees without leaving the building. Legislation has been passed to provide for a police academy.

Women's clubs and other organizations have launched a scholarship program for policemen who want to enroll in the university courses, established an award program for police, and helped bring police-community relations to an all-time high.

Approximately 9,000 new street lights have been installed in high-crime, high-accident areas.

Viewing these data, Indianapolis officials have given their evaluation on the Crusade in unqualified terms. Typical of their comments are the following:

Mayor John J. Barton: "Women of the Anti-Crime Crusade have been a driving force in keeping the crime rate down, and in helping to establish a sense of responsibility among citizens throughout the city of Indianapolis. Public officials welcome their help, their cooperation in programs of crime prevention and law enforcement, and their consistent effort to make our city a better place in which to live."

Judge William T. Sharp, Municipal Court No. 4: "Work of the court watchers has provided the only evaluation a judge gets. Their reports shake everybody up and make us analyze our decisions. As for women, court watching makes them better citizens. They know better how to deal with community problems."

Judge Saul I. Rabb, Criminal Court II: "If the women of the Anti-Crime Crusade had done nothing more than sit in court day after day for five years, their work would have been invaluable. To have that many women informed about the courts, to take an interest in what is going on in the judicial system, is an asset which few areas of the United States can claim. But their work has gone much further. The women have accomplished wonders in our city, and the best part of this is that they continue to work in more than a dozen areas of crime prevention and law enforcement."

Judge Harold N. Fields, Marion County Juvenile Court: "Teaching laws for juveniles in the classroom is an excellent idea, and no doubt one that will be copied across the nation. There is such great need to teach children the importance of responsibility. I see them day after day—very young boys and girls and teenagers—in trouble because they have not had home training in how to live. Some parents let children learn law on the street, and trouble begins right there. The Anti-Crime Crusade can, within reasonable time, prevent many juveniles from getting into trouble."

Judge John Christ, Municipal Court 5: "Municipal judges of Indianapolis will be ever grateful to women of the Anti-Crime Crusade for supporting our program of getting a permanent Driver Improvement School for Marion County. Until the women got behind the project, we had a school so infrequently that there was no consistency to the program. They not only helped us to formulate the details and write the proposals, but assisted in preparing information for the county council. Better still, they went before the council to support the needed budget."

Police Chief Daniel T. Veza: "I don't know how any police department can be successful in fighting crime without the help of such citizens as the women of the Anti-Crime Crusade. Now that they have worked with us so long, I don't know what we did without them. The women believe that—'A community gets precisely the amount and kind of law enforcement that it is willing to support; crime will decrease when a community acts . . . crime will continue as long as a community condones it.' With support like that—citizens who cooperate with us day after day—police certainly do a better job."

Anthony Kuharich, State Commissioner of corrections: "The great understanding of corrections and rehabilitation shown by women of the Anti-Crime Crusade is amazing. Only with such interest and continuous dedication on the part of the public can we get support to provide the type of institutions we need. Only with this interest can we hope to cut down on recidivism—to re-establish youths and adults released from institutions . . . so that they will adjust well to their communities in the role of good and useful citizens."

As the influence of the Crusade has spread by capillary action throughout the country, the volunteers have received an increasing play in the national and international press. One laudatory United Press International dispatch popped up in the Sydney, Australia *News-Herald*. Long stories about the Crusade's achievements and associated activities have appeared in *Time* magazine, *U.S. News and World Report, Christian Science Monitor, National Observer, New York Daily News, Nation's Business,* countless newspapers across America, and specialized publications such as *National Business Woman, Guideposts, Street and Highway Lighting,* the General Federation of Women's Clubs *Clubwoman,* and many others.

Additionally, the Indianapolis project has drawn the notice of television newsmen—including the American Broadcasting Company and David Wolper Productions, both of whom have compiled film documentaries about the Crusade.

Typical of much of this comment is the statement of the *New York Daily News*, leading off an in-depth survey of the Crusade's achievements: "When it comes to fighting crime, the club women of Indianapolis—all 50,000 of them—are now acknowledged to be the nation's top civilian experts."

One of the developments most encouraging to the Indianapolis group has been the interest expressed by other communities. Inquiries, requests for documents, invitations to address civic organizations, and other such communications are directed to the Hoosier volunteers from all parts of the country—as many as from 50 to 100 per week. Spokesmen for the group are kept busy answering a heavy out-of-town correspondence, talking to visiting reporters, and transmitting information via the spoken and written word.

Volunteer groups in no less than 400 American cities and towns are now using parts of the Crusade's program. Representatives of the Indianapolis project have made more than 400 speeches to interested civic organizations in Indiana and around the country. Cleveland, Dallas, Ft. Lauderdale, Long Beach, Buffalo, and the Borough of Queens are among the larger areas which have duplicated part of the Indianapolis blueprint. Crusade representatives also have counseled with police and prosecutors in Washington, D.C. and New York City.

In 1964, spokesmen for the Crusade were invited to testify before the House Committee on Education and Labor on ways and means of preventing and salvaging dropouts. Crusaders also spoke before the National Conference on Crime Control sponsored by President Johnson in March of 1967. The Crusade was the only private crime-fighting group singled out, in a comment previously quoted, in the Commission's report, "The Challenge of Crime in a Free Society."

In addition, various national groups have taken up projects initiated by the Indianapolis volunteers and promoted them on a country-wide basis. The General Federation of Women's Clubs has adopted the Crusade for Light program and recommended that project to its 11 million members. The National Association of Manufacturers has published three case studies of work done by the Crusade—the Stay-in-School program, work with the police, and court-watching. The first was presented at a convention of the General Federation of Women's Clubs in Chicago in June, 1966, and has since been distributed through clubs, chambers of commerce, schools, churches, and industries throughout the nation. The latter two were first presented at the 1967 convention of the lieutenant governors of the United States meeting in Los Angeles. Other spinoffs from the work of the Hoosier volunteers include the action of the Indiana Federation of Clubs in adopting the Crusade's law-enforcement program and the initiation of a delinquency-prevention campaign by the Junior Federated Clubs.

Earl F. Morris, president of the American Bar Association, praised the work of the Anti-Crime Crusade at the annual Tennessee Bar Association convention in June, 1967, and later wrote: "Your Anti-Crime Crusade seems to me to be an excellent type of public involvement in the prevention of crime, and I am referring to it on every appropriate occasion." United Press International comments: "Today the women's crusade is sweeping the country."

Edward Lindsey, president of Lion's International, has similarly remarked: "In Indianapolis some determined ladies have reduced the number of school dropouts . . . [they have proved] it is not money that is needed: it is human help."

Finally, the Crusade has been the recipient of numerous awards and citations from national groups concerned with civic progress and American ideals. In 1965 and 1966, it received Freedoms Foundation awards in recognition of its effort to advance American principle through practical action; and, as noted, Mrs. Mattie Coney, head of the Citizens Forum and division chairman of the Crusade, received one of Freedoms Foundation's four major national awards for her work in 1966.

Projects of the Crusade won third place in the 1965 General Federation of Clubs-Sears-Roebuck Foundation community improvement contest in which more than 9,000 clubs competed. Prizes for Indianapolis Seventh District Federation of Clubs in this competition totaled $4,300 with the money committed to further community improvement. Indianapolis won first place in

1964, and various other awards in succeeding years, in the National Street and Highway Safety Lighting Bureau contest, in company with the GFWC and *Reader's Digest*. The program won third place nationally in the Catherine O'Brien contest in the field of social work, a citation from the Lane Bryant foundation, and a citation from the Pulitzer prize judges for the "campaign against school dropouts that achieved substantial results without any increase in funds in education."

In the last analysis, however, the Anti-Crime Crusade's real achievement may be none of these things—not even the reduction in the crime rate. Perhaps the most impressive part of the whole undertaking has been the mobilization of local sentiment and private willingness to accept responsibility. To stand up for "old-fashioned" ideals and to take energetic action in one's own behalf is nowadays a major story in and of itself. This seems to be an age in which the individual is helpless and responsibilities are consigned to distant power-brokers. In Indianapolis, private citizens have done what the power-brokers could not. A psychologist in the Indiana Department of Corrections put it this way: "The women accomplished many things because they didn't know that they couldn't."

The Indianapolis crime-fighters realized that, if lack of responsibility was a key element in the advance of crime, then an attack on crime would have to begin with the acceptance of responsibility. The volunteers did not simply preach the theme to others; they acted on it themselves. And what began with a group of 30 women in March of 1962 has now expanded to include more than 50,000 volunteers, and has reached out to touch communities in the far corners of the nation.

It is this surge of energy on the part of private citizens which is the most significant part of the Anti-Crime Crusade. If private citizens don't care enough about law enforcement to work for it, there is little, in the long run, that the police can do. When society stops caring, when the consensus deteriorates, the positive law is at best a kind of rear-guard defense for a retreating civilization. In Indianapolis, private citizens care. The results, in terms of law enforcement, prove it.

NOTES

Notes

PART ONE

One: We Never Had It So Scared

1. Dissenting opinion in *Miranda v. Arizona*, October term, 1965 (June 13, 1966), p. 14.
2. *The Challenge Of Crime In A Free Society*, a report by the President's Commission on Law Enforcement and Administration of Justice (Washington, February 1967), pp. 1, 24.
3. *Ibid.*, p. 4.
4. Message to Congress on Crime and Law Enforcement, March 9, 1966; text in *Congressional Quarterly*, March 11, 1966.
5. *Washington Evening Star*, April 4, 1965.
6. Gladys Denny Shultz, *How Many More Victims?* (New York, 1966), p. 71.
7. *The Challenge Of Crime In A Free Society*, p. v.
8. *Ibid.*
9. *Crime in America*, by Robert Osterman (Silver Spring, Md., 1966), p. 8.
10. *Newsweek*, August 16, 1965.
11. *The Saturday Evening Post*, June 27–July 4, 1964.
12. *Wall Street Journal*, March 23, 1967.
13. *Life*, December 3, 1965.
14. *U.S. News and World Report*, August 1, 1966.
15. *Look*, May 31, 1966.
16. *Crime in the United States* (1964), a report issued by J. Edgar Hoover, Washington, July 26, 1965; p. 6.
17. *Ibid.*, pp. 14–15.

18. *Ibid.*, pp. 7–9.
19. *Ibid.*, p. 16.
20. *The New Leader*, July 18, 1966.
21. *Ibid.*
22. Daniel Bell, *The End of Ideology* (New York, 1962), p. 151.
23. *Washington Evening Star*, April 4, 1965.
24. *The Challenge Of Crime In A Free Society*, p. 26.
25. *Crime in the United States* (1965), a report issued by J. Edgar Hoover, Washington, July 28, 1966, p. 3. See also, for detailed discussion of FBI efforts to verify statistics, pp. 41–47.
26. *Congressional Record*, January 25, 1967.
27. Roul Tunley, *Kids, Crime and Chaos* (New York, 1964), pp. 53–54.

Two: The "New Morality"

1. Joseph Fletcher, *Situation Ethics* (Philadelphia, 1966), p. 26.
2. *Esquire*, December 1966.
3. *Look*, January 10, 1967.
4. *U.S. News and World Report*, July 18, 1966.
5. Leontine Young, *Out of Wedlock* (New York, 1954), p. 1.
6. *Washington Evening Star*, April 4, 1965.
7. Alfred C. Kinsey, et al., *Sexual Behavior in the Human Female* (New York, 1965), pp. 169–171 and *passim*.
8. These quotations are carried on the Bantam paperback edition of Genet's *Our Lady of the Flowers* (New York, 1964) and the cover of the Mentor edition of Jean-Paul Sartre's *Saint Genet* (New York, 1964).
9. Lawrence Lipton, *The Erotic Revolution* (Los Angeles, 1965), pp. 25, 11.
10. Norman O. Brown, *Life Against Death* (Middletown, Conn., 1959), pp. 307–308.
11. *The Nation: 100th Anniversary Issue* (New York, 1965), p. 119.
12. John A. T. Robinson, *Honest To God* (Philadelphia, 1963), p. 117.
13. Thomas J. J. Altizer, *The Gospel of Christian Atheism* (Philadelphia, 1966), pp. 150–157.
14. Malcolm Boyd, *Are You Running With Me, Jesus?* (New York, 1967), pp. 106, 109.
15. *Wall Street Journal*, March 13, 1967.
16. *Ibid.*
17. *Newsweek*, March 22, 1965.
18. Philip Jacob, *Changing Values in College* (New York, 1957), pp. 39–40.
19. Jackson, Miss., *Clarion-Ledger*, March 24, 1966.

20. Paul Goodman, *Utopian Essays and Practical Proposals* (New York, 1964).
21. *Newsweek*, March 21, 1966.
22. Nicholas Von Hoffman, "The Drug Revolution at Berkeley," reprinted in *The Indianapolis News*, August 24, 1966.
23. *New York Times*, March 31, 1965.
24. *The Challenge Of Crime In A Free Society*, p. 17.

Three: What Doesn't Cause Crime
1. *The Challenge Of Crime In A Free Society*, p. 6.
2. Message to Congress on Crime And Law Enforcement, *loc. cit.*
3. Testimony given August 17, 1966; quoted by Paul Harvey, *Human Events*, September 17, 1966.
4. Report of the President's Commission on Crime in the District of Columbia (Washington, 1966), minority report of David A. Pine, p. 870.
5. Andrew F. Henry and James F. Short Jr., *Suicide and Homicide* (New York, 1964), p. 45.
6. Tunley, *op. cit.*, p. 50.
7. Lowell J. Carr, *Delinquency Control* (New York, 1950), p. 73; Marvin E. Wolfgang, *et al.*, eds., *The Sociology of Crime and Delinquency* (New York, 1962), pp. 189, 111.
8. Oscar Handlin, *The Uprooted* (New York, 1951), p. 162; Ernest van den Haag, *Passion and Social Constraint* (New York, 1965), p. 183.
9. *Crime In America*, p. 43.
10. Emile Durkheim, *Suicide* (New York, 1966), pp. 253, 254.
11. Herbert Hendin, *Suicide and Scandinavia* (New York, 1965), p. 5.
12. Erich Fromm, *The Sane Society* (New York, 1965), p. 19.
13. Van den Haag, *op. cit.*, p. 187.
14. Tunley, *op. cit.*, p. 81.
15. *Ibid.*, pp. 81–82.
16. *Ibid.*, p. 83.
17. William S. Schlamm, *Germany and the East-West Crisis* (New York, 1959), p. 129.
18. *Ibid.*
19. Quoted in Tunley, *op. cit.*, p. 85.
20. *Ibid.*, p. 86.
21. *Ibid.*, p. 102.
22. *U.S. News and World Report*, April 26, 1965.
23. Harrison Salisbury, *The Shook-Up Generation* (New York, 1965), p. 94.

24. *The Young Americans*, a *Time-Life* Special Report (New York, 1966), p. 80.
25. *The Indianapolis News*, February 7, 1966.
26. Pitirim Sorokin, *Contemporary Sociological Theories* (New York, 1964), pp. 560–561.

Four: The "Now" People
1. Durkheim, *op. cit.*, pp. 253, 256.
2. Sigmund Freud, *A General Introduction to Psychoanalysis* (Garden City, N.Y., 1956), p. 27.
3. *The Indianapolis Star*, December 8, 1966.
4. *Newsweek*, November 28, 1966.
5. Frederic M. Thrasher, *The Gang* (Chicago, 1963), p. 68.
6. Paul Goodman, *Growing Up Absurd* (New York, 1960), p. 195.
7. John Bartlow Martin, *Why Did They Kill?* (New York, 1956), pp. 119–120.
8. Charles Hamblett and Jane Deverson, *Generation X* (Greenwich, Conn., 1964), p. 9.
9. *Ibid.*, p. 7.
10. Gisela Konopka, *The Adolescent Girl in Conflict* (Englewood Cliffs, N.J., 1966), pp. 92, 93.
11. Maurice Stern, *et al.*, eds., *Identity and Anxiety* (New York, 1960), p. 62; see also Erik H. Erikson, ed., *The Challenge of Youth* (Garden City, N.Y., 1965), pp. 1–27.
12. Salisbury, *op. cit.*, p. 103.
13. *The Atlantic*, November, 1965.
14. Durkheim, *op. cit.*, p. 256.
15. *Look*, February 21, 1967.
16. Hamblett and Deverson, *op. cit.*, p. 34.
17. *The Young Americans*, p. 15.
18. *Newsweek*, March 21, 1966.
19. *Midwest*, magazine of the *Chicago Sun-Times*, September 25, 1966.
20. *Ibid.*
21. Ralph J. Gleason in *Ramparts*, March 1966, quoted by David Greenwald in *The Intercollegiate Review*, September–October 1966.
22. *The Atlantic*, November, 1965.
23. *Esquire*, February, 1967.
24. *The Nation: 100th Anniversary Issue*, p. 169.
25. *Time*, January 6, 1967.
26. *Look*, February 21, 1967.
27. Kenneth Keniston, *The Uncommitted* (New York, 1967), pp. 181–182.

28. Robert Lindner, *Rebel Without a Cause* (New York, 1944), p. 2.
29. *Newsweek*, March 21, 1966.
30. Hamblett and Deverson, *op. cit.*, p. 34.
31. *Newsweek*, March 21, 1966.
32. *Crime In America*, p. 95.
33. Marguerite and Willard Beecher, *Parents on the Run* (New York, 1966), p. 6; Keniston, *op. cit.*, pp. 196 *et seq*.
34. *The New Republic*, January 28, 1967.
35. Barrington Moore Jr., *Political Power and Social Theory* (New York, 1965), p. 166; Richard Hoggart, *The Uses of Literacy* (London, 1957), p. 159; Phoenix, Ariz., *Gazette*, April 5, 1967.
36. Fritz Redl and David Wineman, *Controls From Within* (New York, 1966), p. 17.
37. Marvin E. Wolfgang, *Patterns in Criminal Homicide* (New York, 1966), p. 329.
38. Lindner, *op. cit.*, p. 3.

Five: No Right, No Wrong

1. Talcott Parsons, "Youth in the Context of American Society," in Erikson, *op. cit.*, p. 120.
2. Walter P. Metzger, *Academic Freedom in the Age of the University* (New York, 1961), p. 43; Committee on the College Student, Group for the Advancement of Psychiatry, *Sex and the College Student* (New York, 1966), p. 39.
3. Kinsey, *op. cit.*, pp. 304, 686–87.
4. Bertrand Russell, *Marriage and Morals* (New York, 1966), pp. 208–09.
5. Edwin M. Schur, *Crimes Without Victims* (Englewood Cliffs, N.J., 1965), p. 54.
6. Erwin Stengel, *Suicide and Attempted Suicide* (Baltimore, 1964), p. 22.
7. Hendin, *op. cit.*, p. 7.
8. Seymour M. Lipset, *Political Man* (New York, 1960), pp. 147, 289–290.
9. *Crime In America*, p. 44.
10. Carr, *op. cit.*, p. 73.
11. Robert K. Merton *et al.*, eds., *Sociology Today* (New York, 1965), p. 469; *The Sociology of Crime and Delinquency*, pp. 170, 177.
12. Jacob, *op. cit.*, pp. 7, 9, and *passim*.
13. Metzger, *op. cit.*, p. 43; Paul F. Lazarsfeld and Wagner Thielens, *The Academic Mind* (Glencoe, Ill., 1958), pp. 150–151; William F. Buckley Jr., *God and Man at Yale* (Chicago, 1951), p. 178.

14. Quoted in Russell Kirk, *Academic Freedom* (Chicago, 1955), p. 34.
15. John L. Childs, *Education and Morals* (New York, 1967), pp. 43, 50.
16. Buckley, *op. cit.*, pp. 202–203.
17. *Ibid.*, pp. 24, 38.
18. Lipset, *op. cit.*, p. 314.
19. Lazarsfeld and Thielens, *op. cit.*, p. 149.
20. *Newsweek*, March 22, 1965.
21. *Yale Alumni Magazine*, April 1966.
22. Otto Butz, ed., *The Unsilent Generation* (New York, 1958), pp. 66, 71, 75, pp. 26–27, pp. 41–42, p. 54, p. 75, p. 107, p. 121.
23. *The Indianapolis News*, April 7, 1967.
24. Jacob, *op. cit.*, pp. 39–40, 52.
25. *op. cit.*, pp. 5, 42.
26. *Newsweek*, March 22, 1965.
27. *Harper's*, May 1966; Allan C. Brownfeld, "An Honor Code On Trial," *Christian Economics*, January 25, 1966.
28. *The Atlantic*, November 1965.
29. *The Saturday Evening Post*, May 8, 1965.
30. Phillip Abbott Luce, *The New Left* (New York, 1966), pp. 14–15, 148, 158.
31. Fyodor Dostoevsky, *The Brothers Karamazov* (New York, 1950), pp. 758, 768.

Six: *Permissives and Progressives*

1. *The Challenge Of Crime In A Free Society*, p. vi.
2. *Crime in the United States* (1964), pp. 1, 24.
3. Salisbury, *op. cit.*, p. 94.
4. *The Challenge Of Crime In A Free Society*, pp. 63–64.
5. Jules Henry, *Culture Against Man* (New York, 1963), pp. 112–113.
6. *Chicago Sun-Times*, February 10, 1967.
7. Elizabeth Hardwick, "The Chessman Case," *Partisan Review*, Summer 1960.
8. *U.S. News and World Report*, April 26, 1965.
9. *Ibid.*
10. Marguerite and Willard Beecher, *op. cit.*, p. 35.
11. Redl and Wineman, *op. cit.*, p. 58.
12. Martin, *op. cit.*, p. 118.
13. *U.S. News and World Report*, August 1, 1966.
14. Richard LaPiere, *The Freudian Ethic* (New York, 1959), pp. 103–104.

15. Richard Hofstadter, *Anti-Intellectualism in American Life* (New York, 1966), p. 328.
16. Joan Dunn, *Retreat From Learning* (New York, 1955), p. 71.
17. *Ibid.*
18. *Ibid.*, pp. 168, 172.
19. *Ibid.*, pp. 199, 205.
20. *U.S. News and World Report*, October 21, 1963.
21. *The Challenge Of Crime In A Free Society*, pp. 79–80.
22. *U.S. News and World Report*, August 9, 1965.
23. Howard S. Becker, *Outsiders* (New York, 1966), p. 27.

Seven: The Unethical Ethic

1. Lewis Yablonsky, *The Violent Gang* (Baltimore, Md., 1966), p. 127.
2. *Readers Digest*, May 1966.
3. *Readers Digest*, April 1965.
4. *Ibid.*
5. *Readers Digest*, May 1966.
6. *New York Times Magazine*, November 7, 1965.
7. Quoted in *Esquire*, December 1966.
8. *The Indianapolis News*, September 26, 1966.
9. *Louisville Courier-Journal*, June 3, 1966.
10. *The Indianapolis News*, July 12, 1966.
11. Richard M. Elman, *The Poorhouse State* (New York, 1966), p. 4.
12. *Modern Age*, Fall 1966.
13. *U.S. News and World Report*, July 18, 1966.
14. *Readers Digest*, May 1966.
15. *U.S. News and World Report*, March 8, 1965.
16. Russell, *op. cit.*, pp. 206–207.
17. Marguerite and Willard Beecher, *op. cit.*, p. 20.
18. Quoted in *Counterattack*, December 31, 1965.
19. *New York Times*, December 12, 1964.
20. Reprint of interview with Dick Schaap of *New York Herald-Tribune*, n.d.
21. *Readers Digest*, May 1966.
22. *Time*, August 4, 1967.
23. *New York Times*, June 12, 1963.
24. Salisbury, *op. cit.*, pp. 63–66.
25. *Washington Evening Star*, January 16, 1967.
26. Jane Jacobs, *The Death and Life of Great American Cities* (New York, 1961), p. 76.
27. *St. Louis Globe-Democrat*, February 8, 1965; *The Public Interest*, Summer 1967.
28. *Wall Street Journal*, September 26, 1966.

29. *The Public Interest*, Spring 1967.
30. *The Indianapolis News*, July 28, August 23, 1966.
31. *Congressional Record*, February 7, 1967.
32. *New York Times*, December 30, 1964; *Houston Chronicle*, August 24, 1964.
33. *Wall Street Journal*, August 29, 1966.
34. *U.S. News and World Report*, May 16, 1966.
35. *The Indianapolis News*, October 14, 1966.

Eight: The Courts and the Criminals

  1. *Miranda v. Arizona*, majority opinion, pp. 6–7.
  2. *Ibid.*, dissent of Justice Harlan, p. 14.
  3. *Indianapolis Times*, February 13, 1965.
  4. *Miranda v. Arizona*, dissent of Justice White, pp. 17–18.
  5. *Readers Digest*, December 1966.
  6. Press release of July 12, 1959.
  7. *The New Leader*, July 18, 1966.
  8. *U.S. News and World Report*, October 21, 1963.
  9. *Indianapolis Times*, February 13, 1965.
10. *Washington Post*, October 20, 1966.
11. *Readers Digest*, December 1966.
12. *Washington Post*, October 30, 1966.
13. *Washington Evening Star*, January 21, 1967.
14. *Washington Evening Star*, September 29, 1966; *National Review Bulletin*, October 11, 1966.
15. *New York Times*, September 5, 1966.
16. *Readers Digest*, December 1966.
17. *Congressional Record*, January 25, 1967.
18. *This Week*, February 16, 1964.
19. *Readers Digest*, December 1966.
20. "Crime and Criminal Procedure In the District of Columbia," report of the Senate Committee on the District of Columbia, August 13, 1965.
21. *Washington Evening Star*, April 4, 1965.
22. Report of the President's Commission on Crime in the District of Columbia, pp. 442–444.
23. *Crime in the United States* (1964), p. 36.
24. *U.S. News and World Report*, August 9, 1965.
25. *The Indianapolis News*, January 28, 1967.
26. Shultz, *op. cit.*, pp. 127–128.
27. Report of the President's Commission on Crime in the District of Columbia, p. 893.
28. Wolfgang, *op. cit.*, pp. 323, 336.

29. *Crime in the United States* (1964), p. 27.
30. *U.S. News and World Report,* August 26, 1963.
31. *Crime in the United States* (1964), pp. 28–29.

Nine: Civil Disobedience

1. "Meet The Press," March 28, 1965.
2. Hillman M. Bishop and Samuel Hendel, eds., *Basic Issues of American Democracy* (New York, 1965), p. 291.
3. "Meet The Press," March 28, 1965.
4. *Time,* March 19, 1965.
5. *Chicago Tribune,* July 16, 1966.
6. *New York Times,* September 23, 1963.
7. *New York Times,* August 29, 1963.
8. *Time,* August 20, 1965.
9. *Ibid.*
10. Quoted in Luce, *op. cit.,* p. 105.
11. Allan Nevins, ed., *The Burden and the Glory,* speeches of John F. Kennedy (New York, 1964), p. 183.
12. *Life,* August 27, 1965.
13. *The Indianapolis Star,* September 20, 1964.
14. Hubert H. Humphrey, *The Cause Is Mankind* (New York, 1964), p. 16.
15. *U.S. News and World Report,* August 1, 1966.
16. *New York Times,* July 26, 1966.
17. *The Indianapolis Star,* December 7, 1966.
18. Quoted in David Lawrence column, *New York Herald-Tribune* syndicate, May 6, 1964.
19. *Time,* March 19, 1965.
20. News release from Center for the Study of Democratic Institutions, Santa Barbara, Calif., April 14, 1966.
21. *Life,* August 27, 1965.
22. Interview with Dick Schaap in *New York Herald-Tribune.*
23. *Time,* August 4, 1967.
24. Luce, *op. cit.,* pp. 177, 106.
25. *Life,* December 10, 1965.
26. *FBI Law Enforcement Bulletin,* November 1965.
27. *FBI Law Enforcement Bulletin,* December 1966.
28. *U.S. News and World Report,* September 6, 1965.
29. *Ibid.*
30. *National Review,* October 19, 1965.
31. *Ibid.*
32. Michael V. Miller and Susan Gilmore, eds., *Revolution at Berkeley* (New York, 1965), p. 145.

33. Fredric Wertham, *The Show Of Violence* (New York, 1967), p. 200.
34. *National Review*, September 7, 1965.

Ten: People Brutality

1. *Fact* magazine, November–December 1965.
2. *U.S. News and World Report*, March 22, 1965.
3. *Ibid.*
4. *Life*, December 3, 1965.
5. *Ibid.*
6. *Ibid.*
7. William F. Buckley Jr., ed., *The Committee and Its Critics* (New York, 1962), p. 179.
8. *Ibid.*, p. 199.
9. *Saturday Evening Post*, May 8, 1965.
10. *Ibid.*
11. *U.S. News and World Report*, September 6, 1965.
12. *Ibid.*
13. *Ibid.*
14. *Ibid.*
15. These replies are taken from a questionnaire mailed to police officials by the authors in August, 1965.
16. *U.S. News and World Report*, September 28, 1964.
17. *Life*, December 3, 1965.
18. *Ibid.*
19. *Crime in the United States* (1964), pp. 33–34.
20. FBI *Law Enforcement Bulletin*, January 1965.
21. *U.S. News and World Report*, August 10, 1964.
22. *U.S. News and World Report*, August 1, 1966.
23. *Police*, November–December 1965.
24. *The Indianapolis News*, July 20, 1966.
25. *Saturday Evening Post*, July 9, 1960.
26. *U.S. News and World Report*, August 9, 1965

Eleven: Matters of Life and Death

1. Schur, *op. cit.*, pp. 28–29.
2. Lawrence Lader, "Let's Speak Out On Abortion," *Readers Digest*, May 1966.
3. David Lowe, *Abortion and the Law* (New York, 1966), pp. 22, 12.
4. *Ibid.*, pp. 7–9.
5. *Ibid.*, pp. 95, 60–61.
6. Lader, *loc. cit.*
7. Schur, *op. cit.*, p. 58; Paul Gebhard, *et al.*, *Pregnancy, Birth, and Abortion* (New York, 1966), p. 224.

8. Hugo Adam Bedau, ed., *The Death Penalty in America* (Garden City, N.Y., 1964), p. 163.
9. *Ibid.*, p. 144.
10. *Crime in the United States* (1964), p. 7.
11. Bedau, *op. cit.*, pp. 362, 395–405.
12. *Crime in the United States* (1965), pp. 52–55.
13. *The Indianapolis News*, August 9, 1967.
14. Wolfgang, *op. cit.*, pp. 79, 81–82.

Twelve: Ideas Have Consequences

1. Donald Porter Geddes, ed., *An Analysis of the Kinsey Reports* (New York, 1954), p. 67.
2. *U.S. News and World Report*, February 8, 1965.
3. *The Annals* of the American Academy of Political and Social Sciences, March 1966.
4. *U.S. News and World Report*, October 21, 1963.
5. Brown, *op. cit.*, p. 25.
6. *U.S. News and World Report*, February 7, 1966.
7. Hendin, *op. cit.*, p. 79.
8. *loc. cit.*
9. *The University Bookman*, Fall 1963.
10. Erik Anners, *Socialism vs. Progress: The Swedish Case* (Vienna, 1966), pp. 23–24.
11. *Look*, November 15, 1966.
12. Schur, *op. cit.*, p. 59.
13. *Look*, November 15, 1966.
14. *Ibid.*
15. *Ibid.*
16. *U.S. News and World Report*, April 24, 1967.
17. Tunley, *op. cit.*, pp. 38–39.
18. *U.S. News and World Report*, February 7, 1966.
19. Hendin, *op. cit.*, pp. 75, 81.
20. *Ibid.*, pp. 78–79.
21. David Riesman, *The Lonely Crowd* (New York, 1956), p. 103
22. *Ibid.*, pp. 270, 198.
23. William H. Whyte Jr., *The Organization Man* (New York, 1956), pp. 7, 32.
24. Keniston, *op. cit.*, pp. 193–194.
25. *The Challenge Of Crime In A Free Society*, p. 58.
26. Martin, *op. cit.*, p. 121.
27. *The Wall Street Journal*, March 6, 1967.

Index